Lost & Found

True Tales of Love and Rescue from
Battersea Dogs & Cats Home

BATTERSEA DOGS & CATS
HOME *with* JO WHEELER

PENGUIN BOOKS

PENGUIN BOOKS

Published by the Penguin Group

Penguin Books Ltd, 80 Strand, London WC2R 0RL, England

Penguin Group (USA) Inc., 375 Hudson Street, New York, New York 10014, USA

Penguin Group (Canada), 90 Eglinton Avenue East, Suite 700, Toronto, Ontario, Canada M4P 2Y3
(a division of Pearson Penguin Canada Inc.)

Penguin Ireland, 25 St Stephen's Green, Dublin 2, Ireland
(a division of Penguin Books Ltd)

Penguin Group (Australia), 707 Collins Street, Melbourne, Victoria 3008, Australia
(a division of Pearson Australia Group Pty Ltd)

Penguin Books India Pvt Ltd, 11 Community Centre,
Panchsheel Park, New Delhi – 110 017, India

Penguin Group (NZ), 67 Apollo Drive, Rosedale, Auckland 0632, New Zealand
(a division of Pearson New Zealand Ltd)

Penguin Books (South Africa) (Pty) Ltd, Block D, Rosebank Office Park, 181 Jan Smuts Avenue,
Parktown North, Gauteng 2193, South Africa

Penguin Books Ltd, Registered Offices: 80 Strand, London WC2R 0RL, England

www.penguin.com

First published 2013

002

Produced under licence from Battersea Dogs Home Ltd ® Battersea Dogs & Cats Home

*Royalties from the sale of this book go towards supporting the work of Battersea Dogs & Cats Home
(Registered charity no 206394)*

*Battersea Dogs & Cats Home has been caring for and rehoming abandoned, stray and neglected animals since 1860.
We have looked after over 3 million dogs and cats since then, and we aim never to turn away an animal
in need of our help. To find out more about our charity visit **battersea.org.uk***

Typeset in 12.5/14.75 Garamond MT Std by Palimpsest Book Production Ltd, Falkirk, Stirlingshire
Printed in Great Britain by Clays Ltd, St Ives plc

ISBN: 978-1-405-91272-3

www.greenpenguin.co.uk

Contents

Foreword by Paul O'Grady

I've known about Battersea Dogs & Cats Home ever since I was a kid, but it was only when I got a chance to see the work they do up close that I came to realize quite how amazing a place it is.

I've always been an animal lover and share my home with almost too many four-legged and two-legged friends to count. Each one of them is special in their own way, but my four dogs – Bullseye, Olga, Louis and Eddie (an ex-Battersea dog himself) – are true companions and, like all good dogs, they are always there for me. I can't imagine how hard it would be to have to give one of them up.

People bring dogs and cats to Battersea for hundreds of different reasons and Battersea takes them in, along with others that are lost or have been abandoned, and cares for them until new homes can be found, no matter how long that takes. Last year alone, Battersea took in a staggering 7,808 dogs and cats. That is an awfully large number of animals to house, feed, clean, exercise, care for and love, but every animal gets the best possible care from Battersea's amazing staff and an army of volunteers.

Anyone who knows me at all knows that I am a lifelong animal nut and because of that I find cruelty towards any animal extremely hard to deal with. It makes me sad and angry in equal measure. Seeing some of the cases of abuse towards animals that Battersea deals with first hand has helped me to have a greater understanding of just how badly our society sometimes treats our animals. Some of the stories I encountered will stay with me for ever, but so will the care and compassion I witnessed in each case. I'll also never forget the sense of hope and the happiness felt every time a down-on-its-luck animal eventually finds a new home.

Each story in this book is about how providing a good home for an animal in need is not only life-changing for the animal but can also transform the lives of those who take on a new pet in this way. Emotions can run high in a place like Battersea and these stories also tell of some of the highs and lows that rescuing our most needy animals can bring. Each dog and cat coming to Battersea has a unique story and here you will come across some of those amazing animal tales and discover how their re-homing changed in turn the lives of their new owners.

That we still need places like Battersea Dogs & Cats Home to help the thousands of abandoned and unwanted dogs and cats which find themselves homeless every year is a terrible shame, but we are incredibly lucky to have it. Battersea has been around for over 150 years now and as long as there are animals in need of help it will always be there to help those creatures who cannot help themselves.

When Battersea asked me to become one of their official Ambassadors I just couldn't say no. It's a great honour to be able to help them spread the word about looking after your animals and the importance of being a responsible owner, as well as helping to find unwanted dogs and cats new and loving homes.

As an Ambassador I wouldn't be doing my job properly if I didn't also take this opportunity to mention that Battersea is a charity which does not receive any government funding and which relies on support from the public. By buying this book you will be helping to raise vital funds needed to look after the animals in their care and, if you would like to further support the work they do or are interested in rehoming a dog or cat from them, please visit their website at www.battersea.org.uk.

I hope you enjoy this book. I'm sure you will find the stories as uplifting and moving as I did.

All the best,

Paul O'Grady

Harper: A Boy's Best Friend

Around half the dogs who come to Battersea Dogs & Cats Home are strays. Abandoned and lost dogs found wandering alone get picked up by local authority wardens; if they remain unclaimed, they are brought to a rescue centre such as Battersea for rehoming.

If no owner claims a dog within seven days it becomes the property of Battersea, and can be considered for rehoming. Battersea aims never to turn away a dog in need regardless of breed, medical condition or temperament, and nearly 6,000 dogs come through the home's doors every year. For the staff in our intake department, who first meet the dogs when they arrive, one of the most rewarding things is seeing a nervous or neglected dog regain its confidence over the following weeks and trot off through the gates with its new owners.

For those dogs who may have suffered in their past life, it can take the love of a new owner to make it through. But it's worth remembering that it's a two-way process, and the love of a good dog can also help a person to get through the toughest of times, as Ben Harrison found out.

When I was nine I was pretty much like any other kid my age. I loved football and wanted nothing more than to be a professional footballer. I had great friends at school. I was confident and energetic and didn't have a care in the world. But before I turned ten all that was to change, and it would take a miracle to get me through it.

During the summer holidays, Mum, Dad, my older sister Sophie and I used to go to a caravan park with close family friends who had kids my age. It was a very active holiday. There were swimming pools and we would all cycle around together and generally have the run of the campsite. That summer, though, I suddenly found I couldn't keep up with the others like I usually did. Everyone was wheeling about on their bikes and yelling to each other, but I felt so tired that in the end I had to get off and walk.

Then I got this mosquito bite. I didn't think anything of it at first. Normally they would just last a few days then go away. But this one grew really massive. I kept looking at it, and in the end it looked almost like a gunshot wound that had become infected. My friends marvelled at it, but I just felt sick and uncomfortable. I knew it wasn't right.

When we got home, I tried to forget about it and carry on as normal, making out to everyone that I was OK. But after a few days I realized I wasn't.

They don't normally do blood tests for children at the GP but they made an exception in my case. The first blood tests came back OK, but they said they had to do more, so it became a waiting game. And while we waited, I began to feel worse. I couldn't walk up the stairs any more. In the end, I couldn't even lift my head off the pillow in the morning.

'I'm really worried about him,' I heard my mum say. 'It's like his body is just giving up.'

Eventually the test results came back.

'Dermatomyositis,' said the consultant.

'Wow, what's that?' asked Mum.

'It means his immune system has come on and hasn't switched itself off. About a year ago or so, he probably had a cough or a cold which turned his immune system on and it hasn't turned off like it normally would.'

'So what do we do?' she asked nervously. 'Will it sort itself out?'

'Well, that's the tricky part. There's no cure exactly. It's a one in a million illness, so he's very unlucky to get it. We just have to deal with the symptoms.'

In the end, this disease, which we didn't have a clue about, started to attack my skin and muscles. My neck, legs, everything got weaker and weaker as my immune system attacked my body. I started getting rashes all over my arms and body too.

'His eyes are bright red,' said my mum when we went back to the consultant for more tests. 'What does that mean?'

'If you cut yourself,' he told us, 'the skin around the wound will go red; that's your immune system sending antibodies there to heal it. In your case, it's started attacking the corners of your eyes because it thinks it has to heal them.'

By this time, I looked really strange. As well as the redness, the drugs they put me on had changed the way I looked too. The steroids were the worst. They made my face puff up and completely changed my appearance. Even in the hospital, people would stare at me because I looked so odd. I felt very uncomfortable and began to lose my confidence.

In just a few weeks, my life had suddenly become a round of hospital trips and overnight stays. My old, carefree life seemed a million miles away. Now all I saw were drips and needles, and all I heard was the bleep of machinery and the *clip clop* of doctors' and nurses' shoes coming back and forth across the ward.

One night in the hospital, Mum was trying desperately to get me to sleep. I just couldn't switch my mind off from worrying: *Will I ever be able to play football again? Will I be able to run about like I used to?*

'What can I do? Just tell me,' she said, as I moved around restlessly from side to side trying to sleep, to push the pain away. I could tell by now that she was exhausted too, from all the worry and the hospital trips. 'What can I do to help you get to sleep happily?' she asked, and stroked my forehead.

'Promise to let me get a dog when I'm better,' I said quietly.

'All right, love. If that's what you want,' she replied.

I slept well in the end that night.

I've always liked dogs. My grandma had a dog called Jake, a Labrador, who I grew up with. To this day she's still known as Grandma Jake, because we loved that dog so much. And across the road from where we lived our neighbours had a dog I would always play with, a Golden Retriever called Ginny.

That night in the hospital I dreamt about dogs, of playing with and cuddling up to my own dog. But when I woke up in the morning, I was still in the hospital ward. My heart sank.

'Morning, Ben!' said a particularly chirpy nurse. I did not feel chirpy.

'Hold out your arm for me, would you?' she said and started looking for a vein from which to extract some more blood. 'Can't seem to find it!' she said, and started scrabbling about with the needle.

Mum and Dad were both there by now, at my bedside. They were trying to distract me as the nurse jabbed the needle all over the place, looking for a vein.

'What would take your mind off it?' asked Dad. 'Let's talk about something you're looking forward to, when you get back home.'

'How about the dog you're getting me!' I said, and looked over at Mum, who tensed up slightly.

'Dog?' asked Dad, and he looked at over at Mum too.

'Well. We can talk about it. You know, as a family. Once you're out,' she said.

'But you told me . . .' I began.

'There we go!' said the nurse, triumphantly, as she finally found the vein.

And my parents were off the hook, for the moment.

Once Mum had said I could have a dog, though, I would not let the matter drop. And as soon as I was out of hospital I made it my life's mission to convince my parents as soon as possible that a dog was the answer.

Both my mum and dad worked full-time, so when I was younger we couldn't have a dog. But when I got ill, Mum realized she would have to give up her work as a child-minder in order to look after me, because the doctors couldn't stabilize the illness. They told us that there was a possibility it could take up to five years to return to a normal lifestyle. The other thing they had told us was that part of recovery from dermatomyositis is keeping fit. So having a dog suddenly didn't seem so out of the question.

But it was far from a done deal yet. There were still hospital trips and tests going on, and Mum and Dad had to think about it carefully before taking on another big responsibility.

For the time being, my life was just a constant round of hospital visits.

When Grandma found out I was sick, she bought me a PlayStation 3. They were brand new then, and I absolutely loved it. When the doctors came in to see me, I put it down at first, thinking they had come in to do tests. But there was one who used to come to see me just so he could play on my PlayStation! One day I said to this doctor, who was spending a lot of time on my ward, 'Are you ever going to look at me?' and he said: 'When I've finished this game, when I've finished this game,' his head down in my PS3. I was one of the most 'tended to' patients on the ward, because all the doctors wanted to play on my new machine.

I remember there was also a cleaner who used to come in every day and say exactly the same thing, like Groundhog Day. I'd be lying there, all swollen and red, and she'd come to clean around my bed. She'd kick open the door every day, like clockwork, and every day, as I was lying there with tubes everywhere, she'd say: 'Is he better yet? Is he better yet?' Every single day, when it was pretty clear I was nowhere near better! She was lovely, though, and it was comforting to see her every morning.

Another time, a consultant from another hospital came in, because the disease is so rare that they needed a second opinion. I was sitting in bed, with all my Chelsea FC football kit on. And the consultant walked in and the first thing he said was: 'I'm not sure I can treat you if you're a Chelsea fan, when I support Arsenal.' So I said, quick as a flash, 'I'm not sure I'm gonna let you treat me if you support Arsenal!'

It might seem like it would all be serious, being so ill in hospital, but it was the funny moments like these that got me through it in the end.

At other times, though, when reality kicked in, it was hard to laugh. I wanted to know what was going wrong with my body. I remember really hating all the tubes and injections. And I was confused a lot of the time because of the drugs. I also began to realize I wouldn't be able to do everything I loved when I got out, like playing football.

One day I asked Mum: 'Does this mean I won't be a professional footballer, like Frank Lampard?' That had really been my dream for years. And maybe some people wouldn't tell the truth, to try to protect someone so young. But my mum decided to be honest with me.

'Most little boys think they're going to be a professional footballer,' she said gently, 'and in the end, most of them aren't. Like that chef, on the telly, Gordon Ramsay, he wanted to be a footballer, and an injury stopped him. And now look at how successful he is.'

I'm glad Mum was honest. It helped me to deal with things, knowing she wasn't hiding anything from me. But I also had to grow up quickly. When I went in to hospital I had been just a little kid in a football kit. By the time I came out, I was face to face with reality. This was life, I could no longer do the things I wanted to, and I had to deal with it.

With my football dream off the cards, I developed a new obsession. Dogs.

Ever since I had asked Mum for a dog, that night when I couldn't sleep, I had thought about little other than how to bring my parents round to the idea. Our neighbours, the owners of Ginny the Retriever, heard about my new obsession and brought round a big book all about dogs for me. It listed all the different breeds and had loads of colourful pictures. I studied it nightly, and knew almost every breed in a matter of weeks.

Mum and Dad were cautious at first, though. They didn't want to get a dog on a whim, and then realize they'd made a huge mistake. 'It's a big thing in the animal's life as well, to be in a new home,' Mum told me.

I heard them talking about it when they thought I was asleep one night.

'Perhaps if we get a dog, it will help him get out more, though?' said Dad.

'I suppose it might be a distraction from all this illness. Something happy and fun for him, and for us.'

When she came up later to check on me, I showed Mum my research. I had been on the web for hours looking up dogs.

'I've found these. On the Battersea site,' I croaked.

'What's all this? You should be asleep by now,' she said, tucking me in.

But I had laid out dozens of emails and pictures of all the dogs from Battersea Dogs & Cats Home on my bed.

'Well, you certainly are persistent!' she laughed.

I think she must have spoken to my dad again that night, because the next day she said we were going to Battersea, just to have a look.

I was so excited. All the way there in the car I talked about nothing else. What all the breeds were like, their histories, their characteristics. When we arrived I was even more excited about the shop. They gave me a sticker with a dog on it, and there were all kinds of stuffed toys and books about dogs and cats.

'Let's go and see some real animals, shall we?' said Mum, dragging me away. 'So what kind of dog did you have in mind, anyway?'

'I'd like a Labrador, or actually maybe a German Shepherd. Or a Husky.' I chattered all the way up in the lift.

'Oh, they're all way too big, though, aren't they?' she said. 'We want something small, don't we, so it's not too much for you?'

I was still really weak at this point. Some days I couldn't get out of bed at all, and even when I did, going out on a trip like this would take it out of me for days afterwards.

We walked towards a door that led to a long corridor with rows of dogs in their kennels; I could hear some of them barking and scratching. Because the door to the corridor opened somewhat across the first kennel, it was easy to miss that one. My mum had walked off to look for smaller dogs. But for some reason I stopped there, at the first kennel. Inside was a beautiful – and not particularly small – Lurcher, lying calmly on the floor, his head in his paws.

'Hello, there. What's your name?' I asked, and he came over and leant by the side of the kennel. I stood there for ages, stroking his nose.

'Come on, Ben!' Mum was still peering in at all the little dogs further along.

'This one's sweet,' she called out.

But I couldn't stop looking at this lovely Lurcher.

His name on the kennel said 'Harper'. I hadn't come across him on my web searches.

'How long have you been here, then?' I asked and he nuzzled up against the bars.

'What are you doing?' asked Mum, coming back down the corridor. 'What have you found?'

'It's a Lurcher. He's nice.'

'That's a quite big breed, isn't it?'

When she saw him, her face fell.

'Oh, Ben. He is big. Look at him. He's nearly as tall as you. Come on, let's keep looking.'

I looked back at his little nose poking out as we walked away down the corridor.

There were lovely dogs there, and it was fun to look around, but I didn't see anyone who compared to Harper that day. He was so gentle, and I couldn't get the image of him out of my mind. The way he just leant against the door to be stroked. Even though I had thought I wanted a Husky, or something like that, I couldn't really have coped with a big animal sprinting and leaping around.

From the moment we left Battersea that day, I could think of nothing but Harper, and making him part of our family.

*

All my classmates had gone back to school in September, but we knew by now that I wouldn't be going back for a while. Even so, Mum thought it would be a good idea if I went into school one day, just to see all my school friends and let them know what was going on. We hadn't realized quite how much my appearance had changed at that point. I was quite a skinny blond-haired boy with freckles before I got ill. But I'd swollen up so much since, I now had what they call a 'moon-face', and rashes everywhere. I really looked completely different and it would be quite a shock for all my friends. I was really nervous and scared of what they would think.

In the end, when we went on to the playground, they were all really nice, and rushed up and started asking all these questions. I had scars around my ears, and someone even asked me if I had had my ears pierced, which was quite funny. After that, my classmates sent me a huge Get Well card with comments like:

'I'm most interested to hear what is wrong with you, if you could send me a letter back so I could look up what is wrong with you'.

Another one wrote about the school playground as if it had become some kind of war zone since I had left. Because I was so sporty I was quite good at keeping people motivated and playing together. 'The groups are separated because you're not here,' the card read. 'Some of the gang now hang out near the tree, the rest of us are by the shelter. It's terrible.'

My mum found the card funny and sad at the same time. Their comments were all so kind, and so earnest. In the end she couldn't look at the card any more because it kept making her cry.

As soon as I was well enough I was home tutored, and in my spare time it became my mission to go and see Harper the Lurcher at Battersea as often as I could. My sister Sophie had a friend who lived near the Battersea Old Windsor site, so whenever she went to see her, we'd always go to visit Harper on the way back. In the end we were going about two or three times a week, because I really didn't have much else to do at that point. All the way there in the car I would talk about nothing but Harper. What will he be doing, what would we do when we got him? I must have driven Mum up the wall.

'He might be gone, you know,' she said as we drove up there one day. She didn't want me to get my hopes up. There was every chance a family could have come and taken him. 'You can't set your sights on one dog,' she said. 'And Dad hasn't even seen him yet.'

But every time we went Harper was still there, looking at me with those eyes.

There were all these new and different dogs. Lots of the animals I had seen would come and go, rehomed to different owners. But Harper was the one constant. It was terrible to leave him there every time.

After our visits, I would spend a lot of time on the internet, searching for information about Lurchers: what they eat, what their natures are. I even made a folder with all the information I had found catalogued in it. I drew a picture of a dog on the front cover, with a question mark under it. Harper? I came downstairs with the booklet and showed it to Mum and Dad. They laughed.

'You really are taking this seriously, aren't you?' said Dad, flicking through all my notes.

When I had gone to bed, I heard them talking about it together in serious tones.

'Maybe we should reserve him. Harper. Just in case.' Mum sounded like she was starting to panic a bit. 'You know, just in case he is the right dog for Ben. If we miss out on him, it could be a disaster, couldn't it?'

'Isn't he too big, though? You said he would be too much.' Dad still hadn't seen Harper yet.

'Well. I thought he was. But Ben seems to think he's so gentle it'll be all right. I've never seen him like this. So sure about something.'

'You might be right,' said Dad after a while. 'I should come and see him. When I can get a chance with work. Before we decide. But if you can put a hold on him or something maybe that's the thing to do.'

I was so excited I could hardly contain myself. We were one step closer.

When Battersea knew we were serious about getting a dog, they did a quick test to see what would be suitable for me. They asked questions about what we wanted, our home situation and so on. Then the woman who was interviewing us fed the information into their database. After a while she said, 'We've found a match,' and swung her computer round. There on the screen was a picture of Harper.

I couldn't believe it, and neither could Mum. It was obviously meant to be.

Next we got to take Harper for a walk, to see how he reacted to us. It was hard at first, because he was quite reserved. I was really worried about whether he would accept us or not.

'Look, he's got scars on his legs. He looks like the walking wounded,' said Mum as we took him around the Battersea grounds. 'Like your bullet wounds.'

I had several scars since my illness where insect bites and other injuries hadn't healed properly – we jokingly called them 'bullet wounds'. And it was true, Harper had his scars too.

'He was found on the golf course, just roaming, by a family out walking with their dogs,' said the woman showing us around. 'They had him for two days, to settle him down, and then they brought him in to us. He's got what we think is at least one dog bite, at the front of his leg. It's still a bit sore.'

I felt very sad, but even closer to Harper that day. We had both been through the wars. I was more sure than ever that he was the one. But we still had to get Dad down to Battersea, to make the final decision.

Not long after that, we were in Norfolk visiting our grandparents, and I found a toy model of a curled up Lurcher in a gift shop. I bought it and gave it to Dad.

'It's Harper,' I said quietly and walked away. I think this was the final reminder to him of just how much I wanted this dog, and the next day he made an announcement:

'I've been hearing so much about this Harper, I was thinking, why don't we all go up and see him this weekend?'

'Really?' I asked.

'Well, you haven't stopped talking about him for weeks. So it's the least we can do, isn't it?'

So the following weekend we all went to Battersea as a family. I was clutching my Lurcher folder, as always, and I was really nervous about what my dad would think. What if he didn't like him? That would be too much to bear.

'Hello again, Ben,' said the woman at the desk. I had been there so often everyone at Battersea knew me now. 'Come to see Harper again, have you?'

'Yes, my dad's here this time,' I told her, collecting yet another dog sticker for my fast-growing collection.

When they brought Harper out again, he was on his best behaviour. Almost as if he knew it was decision time.

'He's handsome, isn't he?' said Dad, and stroked his back. 'Is he fully grown?' he asked the woman from Battersea.

'We're not sure,' she said. 'He's a bit big for a puppy. He's not very toy-oriented. But I'm sure he'll be a good learner.'

We took Harper to a paddock where you can let the dogs off the lead. He looked quite startled and just stood there. But then he wasn't very good on the lead either, and got all tangled up as we walked back to the kennel. He looked up at us as if to say, 'What do you want me to do now?'

'Looks like he just needs a good family, don't you think?' said Dad. 'And if you think he's right for you, Ben, let's go for it.'

I was so happy, I felt like I might burst. I gave Mum and Dad the biggest hug, and Harper too, of course. But this was only the beginning. Now we had to hope he would accept his new home with us.

Mum was nervous about taking him with us straight away, as it was Bonfire Night and she didn't want him to associate our house with the frightening noise of fireworks. So we waited until the following Sunday to collect him. The first thing we did on the way back was stop at the common near our house. We had bought one of those really long leads that stretches, and when we got out of the car, Harper was so shocked by the open space, after being in a kennel for so long, that he just went mad and ran off at top speed. We hauled him back in, but it was clear he had no idea what to do.

When we got home, we put his bed in the living room, and he settled down quickly.

'He seems to like it here, at least,' said Dad, as Harper nestled down in his new bed and slept until morning.

Ever since I had been ill I hadn't been able to get out of my own bed very easily. Mum would have to help me up when I was really weak. But the next day I leapt out of bed quicker than I ever had. I couldn't wait to see Harper, and for once I didn't think about the pain or my illness or anything else.

When Mum came down at about seven o'clock, I was already up, lying next to Harper on the floor.

'I don't believe it!' she said. 'You got down here on your own!'

'I wanted to see Harper,' I said, 'to check he was OK.' And from that day on, he was my main motivation. I finally had something else to think about, to care for, and, without me realizing it, I also had someone else to care for me.

When they diagnosed my illness, the doctors had given me an exercise routine to do every morning. It was supposed to help get me more physically fit, but some mornings I couldn't find the motivation to do it. It just felt like a horrible chore. When I started walking with Harper, though, that soon became part of my recovery routine. I was exercising my legs, and my muscles, and it was no longer a struggle. It was just something that I wanted to do.

We started Harper off on short walks of about fifteen minutes. We pretty quickly got him used to being on the lead, and then when we let him off, he would run about quite happily. But we soon found out that Harper was terrified of other dogs. As soon as we saw one, he would collapse, curl up into a really small ball and just sit there, shaking. But if the dog came up to us he would jump about and try desperately to get away. It was quite distressing to watch; he was obviously terrified.

'I wonder what happened to him, to make him so scared,' said Mum.

But we didn't know. We just knew that he'd been found wandering on the golf course, and that he had dog bites on his legs.

His other natural instinct was, when he saw a barbed wire fence, to make himself really small and try to fit underneath it. We wondered whether perhaps he had been trained as what they call a 'lamping dog', to go and fetch rabbits and things. And that maybe the bigger dogs had picked on him, but we'll never really know. Whatever his past, a big part of the early mission with Harper was trying to build up his confidence and socialize him.

But I still had problems of my own to deal with. Although the walks were helping me to get gradually stronger, I was still very ill. My morning routine consisted of taking loads of drugs to try to stabilize the disease. And though sometimes I would leap out of bed to see Harper, other days I simply didn't have the energy. Mum would have to come in and wake me up, and it could take hours just to get me up and dressed.

In the end, the doctors had decided to switch off my immune system and wait for my body to stop attacking itself. If they hadn't done this I would have died. But I was now much more vulnerable to general sickness because I had no immune system, and I was taking so many different pills, I'm sure I must have rattled when I walked.

Mum even had to inject me every week. She had to learn how to use a proper syringe, which I absolutely dreaded. I had already had so many blood tests that I wasn't really afraid of needles by now. But for some reason this particular injection was really painful. I would try everything I could to avoid it, hiding away from her under the duvet. It was a real battle for both of us.

In the end, Mum spoke to the consultant and he told her it was one of the most painful injections you can have. It's not just the needle, it actually hurts when the liquid goes into you, because it's so toxic. They had to give Mum all this special equipment, because if you spill anything it's so dangerous that it can even be harmful to others.

The side effects from all the drugs were sometimes just as bad as the illness itself, and I got terrible stomach aches and sickness. I even had to avoid the sun, because if you get a sun-tan your immune system thinks your skin is being attacked and this would cause my condition to flare up.

So, all in all, I was living a far from normal life for a nine-year-old boy.

I soon began to realize that my illness wasn't just affecting me. It was tough on our whole family. My parents were worried, Mum had given up work and my older sister Sophie was just starting grammar school. For about three weeks she was essentially living on her own, while I was in hospital. Mum spent all her time with me, and when Dad wasn't at work he was visiting me too, so after school Sophie was left to her own devices a lot. And when I got out, she had actually moved into my bedroom, which was quite funny (although I didn't think so at the time!). Having a dog brought us closer together, because it was like having a baby brother we could share. When we first got Harper home, Mum and Dad were out of the room when he came trotting in with a toilet roll in his mouth.

'Ha-ha! Look at him,' laughed Sophie. 'He looks like that dog in the adverts.'

It was too much to resist and we played with him on the floor, and he got more and more excited as the toilet roll started to unravel.

'Come on, Harper,' said my sister, and she started filming it on her mobile. 'Show us what you can do!'

The more excited he got, the more the toilet paper rolled out and around him and across the room, until in the end the dog and the whole living room were covered in toilet paper, with Harper just standing there in the middle of it all with his tongue hanging out. By that time we were in hysterics on the floor, and Mum and Dad heard us screaming with laughter.

'What's going on?' asked Dad, and he came in from the kitchen to have a look. But it was so funny even he couldn't get annoyed.

But most of the time, while Sophie was at school, I had all the hours of every day, and every week, to fill. I would do the walk with Harper in the morning if I was up to it, and schoolwork, but that would take it out of me. Then I would spend a lot of time watching movies, just to try to pass the time.

'You must have watched that film about twenty times by now. Aren't you bored of it?' asked Mum one afternoon.

'No.' I said. It was the Lord of the Rings trilogy and I knew most of the lines by now. But the truth was, I *was* bored. Bored of seeing the same four walls every day. I missed my school friends, too.

Harper was invaluable, of course. He didn't care what I looked like when I swelled up because of the steroids, and he always seemed to know when to be calm with me if I was weak, and when to energize me when I needed it. But it would have been nice to do something else, or at least be somewhere else.

'Why don't we take Harper for some training sessions?' suggested Mum. 'It would get you both out of the house. We could do it together.'

When we first brought Harper home he couldn't have handled going to training classes. He was just too scared of other dogs. But after a few months he began to get a bit more confident. So I said, OK, why not give it a try. We got the number of a local trainer from Battersea and we took Harper down to a nearby village hall where they took the dogs around a little course set up in the hall.

We soon realized how convenient it was that Harper was absolutely obsessed with food. We had already used this to train him to come back to us in the garden, and out on our walks. But when we went to dog training, the instructor cut up pieces of juicy sausage and very easily used them to teach Harper all the proper commands like 'sit' and 'lie down'. Although he would still sit apart from the other dogs, he was very well behaved. In fact, he was so chilled out that he didn't really want to learn any of the really fancy things they tried to teach him, like going left and right. But he got the hang of all the important basics.

In the end, we did the course three times, because it was so much fun.

One of the things I enjoyed about being there was that while I was out training Harper, I wasn't Ben the sick child. I was just Ben, training his dog. In the past, when people had found out about my illness, they would start talking to me as if I was about three years old, like I didn't understand what they were saying. But in those training sessions it was a real relief to be treated as just another student.

In the lead up to Christmas we were really pacing it with the training and the walks, and Harper had a real breakthrough.

On the way home from a walk, Ginny, the Retriever across the road, ran over to meet us. She wasn't aggressive at all, but I tried to get in quickly. I didn't want Harper to get stressed out. Amazingly, though, he was absolutely fine. They met each other, and both remained very calm. This was the first dog Harper hadn't reacted nervously to, and I knew then that we had really begun to socialize him.

When Christmas Day finally arrived, I pulled back my covers and took my stocking downstairs to open it with Harper. Snow was falling, which made it all doubly exciting.

'You're up early!' said Mum, coming in to the room. 'Did you find your stocking?'

But I hadn't even opened it yet, because I was too busy watching Harper and the snow.

'Look at that dog,' said Mum, equally fascinated. 'He doesn't look like he's ever seen snow before! And he's grown so much since we bought him, too.'

I looked across at Harper, leaning against the window, pawing at those amazing snowflakes. And it was true, he was quite a bit bigger. So perhaps he had been just a puppy when we first saw him, after all.

Later that day, as we walked through the local woods, there was a thin layer of snow on the ground. Sophie and I threw snowballs at each other, and ran around with the dog. I felt so completely happy to be there with my whole family on Harper's first Christmas Day.

By the time we'd had Harper for a year, I was so much better from all the walking I'd been doing, I could kick a football again. This was made all the more exciting by the fact that Harper turned out to be a great footballer too. He could even head the ball while I kicked at goal.

The other thing Harper turned out to be pretty good at was trampolining. One day I got on the trampoline in our garden while Mum threw balls for me to catch. And Harper seemed to wonder why he wasn't involved.

'Fine. I'll just get up on the trampoline and do it as well,' he seemed to say. And Mum ended up having to throw balls for both of us! After that, every time I got on the trampoline, Harper would jump up there too.

This first year together was a real period of recovery for me, and for Harper too. He made some dog friends on our walks, and even got himself a girlfriend, or so I'm sure he'd like to think. She's a huge Irish Setter called Kerry, who's absolutely mental. They're complete opposites in personality, but somehow they get on really well and sit and play together quite happily for hours. It was such a transformation from the quivering, nervous Harper we had first known. And after a while he also began to get a little bit famous.

The first thing was the local paper. I was due to start back at school in Year 6, and decided to do a 'walk a dog to school day' event with Harper. I got sponsorship from everyone on our street, and the local newspaper picked up on it. They came and took pictures and there was an article in the paper as we did the walk.

Unfortunately, after that I realized I wasn't actually quite well enough to go back to school. But the media attention continued. The phone rang one day and Mum answered.

'It's Battersea,' she whispered to me. '*GMTV* want us to go on the telly. "We'd love to get you on the sofa," they said.'

'Wow! What do you think, Harper?' I asked and he wagged his tail.

A few days later, we were waiting in the hall when the doorbell rang. It wasn't even light yet, because it was four o'clock in the morning.

'Quickly. Get your coat on. Have you got his lead? The food?' said Mum.

The car *GMTV* had sent all the way from London to come and collect us was waiting. It was a big posh black thing, but Harper was very good all the way there.

'What do you think they'll want me to say?' I asked Mum, feeling a bit nervous.

'I don't know! Remember what they told you, though, to call it Battersea Dogs & Cats Home.'

Battersea had changed the name of their charity some years back to include cats in the title, and I had to remember that in my interview.

'Well, I'm not going on that sofa, and that's for sure,' said Sophie. She was way too cool for breakfast television. 'I'll just wait in the wings and laugh at you lot.'

When we got to London, we drove right into the centre of town, along the Thames and past the Houses of Parliament, which was really exciting. They showed us through security and along lots of corridors towards the television studios, where people with walkie-talkies and headphones strode around urgently.

'This is the Green Room,' said a researcher, waving us into a room with lots of posh sofas and pot plants. 'You can relax in here for a bit before the show. There will be one little interview first, to get a bit of a feel for your story. Then we'll have a break, and then there'll be another main interview after that with the presenters. Help yourself to those pastries, by the way,' he said, pointing to an enormous bowl of croissants and cinnamon swirls on the table.

'Two interviews!' said Mum. 'What do they want us to talk about?'

'Oh, it'll be fine,' he said. 'They'll ask about you and the dog, and the boy, how it all happened. That kind of thing.'

When he left we all sat down, and poor Harper looked dolefully at the plate of croissants on the table. After a while he started to get a bit fidgety.

'I'll take him to somewhere he can do his business,' said Mum. 'Before we go on, so he doesn't do it on the set.'

'Where will you go?' I asked.

'I'll improvise!' she said, and smiled.

Sophie and I waited for what felt like ages, and I wondered where on earth they would go, in amongst all these corridors. Finally they came back just before we were due to go on.

'I had to take him all the way out to the Embankment!' Mum said, breathless from running.

Then the researcher came back. 'You're on. Follow me!' he said with a wave of his arm. But it was all too much for poor Harper, and he leapt up and grabbed one of the croissants on the table. He was still gobbling it down when they started filming!

I was a bit nervous, thinking I'd be in front of so many people with all those cameras and lights. But since my time in hospital, talking to all the doctors, I was used to speaking to adults. And as soon as we got on the sofa it was surprisingly fun and easy. I told them how I got ill and how we got Harper, and how that had helped me to get fitter. Harper was so well behaved the whole time, and stood there looking very 'handsome', as Dad would say, for the cameras.

After about five minutes, they broke for the news, and we were about to go off, but there was a sudden commotion among the production crew.

'What's going on?' mouthed Mum to me. 'No idea!' I whispered back. Then a man in headphones came over in a bit of a panic.

'So sorry, er, would you mind terribly staying on? It's just that it's such a good story, and we've got a bit of a gap to fill now, in the news. Lost a satellite link, that kind of thing. You know how it is.'

'Fine, no problem,' I said. I was quite enjoying it by now.

So instead of coming back later for our main interview, we ended up doing one really long interview there and then. And I got to say 'Battersea Dogs & Cats Home' on several occasions. But as the time dragged on, I could tell Harper was getting a bit annoyed. Who were all these people rabbiting on, and all these lights and cameras moving about, he must have been wondering. It was meant to be about both of us, but in the end, he just lay there looking bored. And because we were the last interview of that day, the closing credits were a close-up of Harper with his head on his paws, asleep. When you remember that he's a rescue dog, it was amazing how well he behaved that day.

It was fun to be in London and see a TV studio, but I was exhausted when we got home. It was probably the biggest thing I had done since I had been ill and I must have slept for Britain after that. And it wasn't long before reality kicked in again.

As I was starting to feel a bit better, I had to think about school properly again. I had been home tutored for a while now, but I missed having a group of friends, and amazingly I even missed going to school! I really wanted to go to the local grammar school, because my sister was there and she always talked about how good it was. So, just before Year 7, I took my Eleven Plus exam. It was hard work having missed so much school, and I waited nervously for the results.

I knew when the letter had arrived, because it had the school insignia on the envelope. I had been watching the post like a hawk, and as soon as I saw it I ran to the doormat, picked it up before anyone else could get there and ran upstairs to my room.

'I hope he got in,' I heard Mum say. 'After all he's been through.'

I slid the paper out of the envelope and, five minutes later, I ran downstairs in my sister's old school blazer. And they knew that I'd passed.

Starting at grammar school was great and I made some really good friends. Whereas my old primary school mates had seen me get ill, which I think was quite hard for them, here at this new school, this was just who I was. People accepted me and knew I couldn't do everything other kids could. They knew my limits and were really helpful and kind. On field trips they kept an eye on me, and they all knew what to do if I got into any difficulties. There were additional perks for them too. When we went to Thorpe Park, I was allowed to jump the queue with them all, because queuing was so tiring for me with my illness. I became very popular after that, I can tell you!

Of course, Harper has been my other great friend over the past few years. I remember one time when I got sick, just after I had started school again. I was crying, and he came over to me and leant against me and wanted me to stroke him. I went upstairs and he followed me and lay on the bed comforting me, as I cried into my pillow. As well as companionship he's done a lot with us too. We got him a dog passport and we took him to France on holiday. And he's even been centre stage at Crufts!

It was during Battersea's 150th anniversary year, and they wanted to get some stories about the dogs they've rescued, so we became one of the big stories of the event. I had to go right into the show ring and speak about Harper, and then we both did a big walk round the whole stadium. In the end we got a standing ovation, and I was so proud of how Harper held his own among all those pedigree dogs.

Since my childhood dreams of football stardom, I have had to face up to a few harsh realities. I know I won't be a professional footballer now, but I've done some work experience at the local vets and know I'd love to work with animals when I've finished my A levels.

I know I've missed out on a lot of things other kids have experienced. It's only a year since I stopped taking all the medication for my condition. Even now I miss a lot of school because I still get all kinds of infections and things. But I know one thing. If it wasn't for Harper I'd never have got where I am today. After all, we grew up together and he was with me through thick and thin. Even recently, as I was getting stressed revising for my A levels, there was Harper next to me, with his head in my books, just chilling, and I thought how lucky I was. It's no exaggeration to say that Harper has been the best thing that ever happened to me.

A few weeks ago I was on a school field trip. Harper hadn't been very well before I left, but Mum and Dad had been to the vets and they thought it was something viral. When I got back from the trip, though, they told me that the vet had discovered my beloved friend had an inoperable tumour. I couldn't believe there was nothing we could do and even went to the vets myself, because I just couldn't believe that was it. The vet was very kind, explaining the inevitable, and I had to try to come to terms with it. But I didn't and still haven't. Just a few days later we had to say goodbye to Harper. It was the hardest thing I have ever had to do.

Harper was my best friend. In fact, he was so much more than that I can't put it into words. Every day that passes without his gentle presence, I feel the loss more deeply. I remember him beside me when I was at my weakest, bounding in to give me that extra energy, or lying calmly beside me when I just needed his special company.

Thank you Harper, for everything.

Afterword from the Harrison family:

Harper brought so much joy to our everyday lives and his unique character and unbounded love for us all was something that we all fed off; he was always there for each of us in our moments of need. The way he dealt with any situation made him a great ambassador for Battersea, and the love and support he gave to Ben was priceless. He is and always will be our beautiful boy and we miss him so much.

Cocoa and Molly: The Two-Dog Family

We're no strangers to medical problems at Battersea Dogs &
Cats Home and have an on-site clinic team including six vets who
take care of our dogs and cats. As soon as an animal comes in it is
thoroughly checked by our experienced veterinary team and given
any treatment it needs.

Although many of the dogs who come in are in very good
condition, others do need medical care and have to be treated for
anything from joint problems and skin infections to more complicated
operations.

Medical issues are part of any animal's life, but once in a while,
when things go wrong for a pet, it's not only a Battersea vet who helps
out. At least one Battersea dog itself has also been a valuable lifeline
for a canine friend, as owner Jill Moss explains . . .

We've always been a one-dog family. When Henry died we
were devastated, but after a while we decided it was time
to replace him with another dog from a nearby rescue
centre.

'How about this one?' asked my husband, John, as we
scoured the website. The dog we had spotted was a hound
mix.

'He does look a bit like Henry. Look at his little paws.
OK, let's give it a go. We've just got time if we leave now.'

It was Maundy Thursday and we only had a few hours
before the centre would shut down for the holidays. When

we got there a woman called Susan showed us into the kennels, and pointed out the dog we had seen on the website, and waited as we read his papers.

'He's been returned twice,' I whispered to John.

'And never even been inside a house,' he said.

'He has been chained up a lot. That's quite clear,' said Susan, clasping her fingers together and waiting for our reaction.

We peered in at the poor animal, who was leaping about in his kennel and barking.

'He's nice enough natured. Bit of a handful, I suppose,' she continued. But before she had finished we both knew it wouldn't work.

We love training animals, but as we're retired now we're just not as capable of taking on a big, un-housetrained dog as we once were. It's never an easy thing to turn down a pet at a rescue shelter, but you also have to know your own limitations.

So, with some reluctance, we decided that he wasn't for us and turned to leave, somewhat disheartened. Just as we were about to walk out, John stopped in the corridor.

'Hang on a moment. How about this?' he said, peering at a notice on the wall.

'DOG OF THE WEEK' it said, and above it there was a blurry picture of a very furry brown dog, though I couldn't see its face at all clearly.

'Oh, yes. Cocoa,' said Susan. 'I take him home every night with me, in fact. He's so good with my other dogs. But we haven't been able to find him a good home yet.'

'Why not?'

'Well. He's very lovely natured and everything,' she said hesitantly, as if there was a 'but' coming. 'But there's just one thing . . .'

Here we go, I thought.

'Just be aware before you see him – if you want to see him – that he's got . . . it's a little awkward, but he's got no nose. It turns some people off.'

She waited for our reaction.

'What do you mean, no nose?' asked John.

'Well, you can have a quick look if you like. But there's another thing. When he gets excited, he pees on people.' She spoke quickly in one breath before letting out a little nervous laugh. 'That's why the previous owner brought him in. Her husband was in the RAF and she couldn't cope with him on her own. Peeing on people, that is.'

'Well, I think we can handle that,' I said, exchanging a little knowing look with John. We had a good deal of experience training dogs and something like that wouldn't faze us.

'Well, if you're sure, I'll take you to see him. He really is a very lovely animal.'

When we got to the kennel, a chocolate-brown dog with silver speckles sat in the corner, looking very nervous. The sign next to him said 'Cocoa'.

'He's not a breed I recognize,' said John.

Cocoa came over cautiously and crouched very low to the ground as we greeted him.

'He looks a bit nervous,' I said, and he put his head up to the gate as Susan let us in.

When I looked more closely at his face I saw what she had meant by 'no nose'. He didn't have a button on the end like most dogs.

'Oh, look. It's just a little snout.'

But I couldn't see what all the fuss had been. It wasn't off-putting at all and he was an adorable looking dog.

'We think he might have been the runt of the litter,' said Susan, ruffling his neck fur. 'You know, rejected by the breeder so as not to bring down the chance of selling the others.'

'What breed is he?' John asked.

'Australian Cattle Dog. Bit unusual here. He was taken to Battersea Dogs & Cats Home first, by the breeder, we suppose. Then the woman from the RAF took him. He's had a rabies jab and everything. Been moved about quite a bit. From base to base probably.'

As she spoke I was mesmerized by Cocoa's beautiful brown eyes. He was nervous but affectionate, and rubbed his head against my leg. I knew immediately that he was very loving and his fur was as soft as the softest teddy bear.

'I think I love him a bit,' I whispered to John. I always do go on my instincts with things like this.

'He is a sweet little thing, isn't he? Hello, you.'

Cocoa nuzzled us both.

'Does he chase people at all?' asked John.

'No, not that we know of. He does have a little ligament problem. In the leg. You might not get insurance for that, I'm afraid. And he has a little scratch on his eye that should soon clear up. But nothing else we know of.'

I could tell that Susan was beginning to get a little

anxious to shut the place up for Easter as she kept looking at her watch.

'Well, the nose thing isn't an issue at all for us,' I said firmly. 'Or the peeing on people. We can sort that out, can't we?'

'Yes, of course,' said John. 'I like a challenge.'

We stepped to one side to confer a bit more and take a good look at the papers Susan had handed us, but it wasn't a very tough decision.

'We'll take him,' we said simultaneously, and laughed. Cocoa's ears pricked up.

We were a one-dog family again. Little did we know, though, that events just around the corner were about to shake little Cocoa's world completely.

When we got Cocoa home that first week we invited our family round. We've got eight grandchildren of varying ages, so quite a brood. Cocoa was so happy to meet them, the first thing he did was, you guessed it, pee on the floor at their feet.

'We'll soon get him out of that,' laughed John as poor Cocoa looked back at us with such a sorry, guilty face. 'I couldn't help it, I'm just so excited,' he seemed to plead.

'He's got a funny nose,' said Katie, one of the youngest children.

'But it's sweet!' said one of the older ones, Jo, who loves dogs. She got down and ruffled his thick fur.

Despite Cocoa being an immediate hit with our family, he was still a very nervous dog around the house. For the first few weeks he would move around the carpet on his belly.

'He looks like a snake!' said John.

'That's really submissive, isn't it, crouching down like that?' I said, as Cocoa slithered over to us and then hid under my chair. 'Perhaps he used to get into lots of trouble for wetting around the house.'

'Yes, like he's almost apologizing in advance, before he's even done anything,' said John.

But as the weeks went on Cocoa gradually seemed to feel safer with us, once he realized we weren't going to shout at him. His bushy tail began to come up and up more and more as he grew in confidence.

Outside the house was another matter, though, and when it came to walks things were even worse. Our house is right next to the Grand Union Canal on what they call a 'redway'. It's a cycle and walking track, which is great for dogs because there are no cars to get in the way. We agreed that John was to take him out in the morning on his bicycle. The plan was that Cocoa would trot along beside him as our other dogs had done. I was to take him out in the afternoon.

On the first day, they weren't gone for more than about half an hour before John came back with a serious look on his face.

'You know she said Cocoa doesn't chase people?' he said as he put the lead on the hook. 'At the shelter.'

'Yes. What's up? He hasn't hurt anyone?'

I really didn't believe it, but you just never know.

'Of course not. But . . . well, he might not chase people, but he sure does hate cyclists.'

'Oh no!'

Cocoa came trotting back into the house as if nothing had happened.

'I wonder whether, being on an RAF base, with all the bikes going around the place, maybe he started to chase them when he was younger. Maybe the cyclists kicked out at him or something?' I suggested.

'You might be right. It certainly looks like he has a history with bikes. And not a good one.'

'What'll we do? How will you walk him?'

John needed to use his bike for our dogs because he had a spinal problem and could no longer manage long walks.

'We'll work out a way, but it might take some training.'

In the end it didn't take us long to train Cocoa out of the original problem of peeing on people. That had been the thing that had put off his last owners. But since all of our walking paths were shared with bicycle commuters on their way to work, the unexpected issue of chasing cyclists was a different matter. He really did look like he wanted to kill them.

We're both retired so luckily we had time to spend on Cocoa, but even so it took us three months of hard and constant training twice a day.

John went out in the morning and I took the afternoon shift, as planned. We went through a series of rigorous exercises, rewarding him for correct behaviour, and coaxing him this way and that to teach him how to behave when out on our walks.

At first we got a lot of abuse from cyclists who understandably didn't much like being pursued by a barking animal.

'Are you not going to train that bloody dog?' shouted one young woman in a day-glo jacket, as Cocoa ran up behind her with his tongue hanging out.

I went bright red with embarrassment, but then felt sad and deflated because I really was trying very hard and I wished I could have made them see that.

Cocoa never caught up with any bikes or injured anyone, and some of the cyclists were actually quite helpful and friendly.

'He's coming on, isn't he?' said a man on a bright green folding bike who we saw a lot. This was a few weeks into our training regime.

'I hope so,' I called back. 'You couldn't go past just one more time, so I can try again, could you?'

'Of course,' he said, and pedalled back past us to see Cocoa's response. This time Cocoa was a little less exuberant than usual with his chasing. So that was progress at least.

'Very good! Keep it up!' called the man as he sped off away down the path.

After three months of hard slog, we had eventually trained Cocoa to ignore passing bikes so John and I had a small glass of wine one afternoon to celebrate.

'To Cocoa,' we said. 'And long may it last!'

Cocoa was getting very confident around the house too. He no longer slithered along like a snake on his belly, and he hardly ever peed on anyone any more. He was, in fact, proving to be a lovely, lively and friendly family dog.

As an Australian Cattle Dog he ran about a lot on our walks, which was lovely to watch. It was as if he was hoping to do some real herding one day, a bit like a sheep dog would, but in his case it would have been cows. He would wheel round and round in tighter and tighter circles, herding imaginary cattle. It was hard work training him but as he was loving and enthusiastic it was very rewarding.

One morning, though, about six months after we had first brought Cocoa home I noticed things weren't quite right.

'Have you seen he keeps taking the weight off his back leg and limping?' I asked John one evening as we ate our dinner.

'No, I hadn't, but now you mention it . . .' We looked over at Cocoa who was walking awkwardly over to the door. After a week or so it became increasingly clear that it wasn't getting any better.

'We ought to take him to the vet.'

'Yes, but one thing. No insurance for leg problems, remember.'

'Better hope it's nothing serious then.'

When we had registered Cocoa originally, the first vet we saw had turned to a big chart on the surgery wall to identify him, but to our disappointment there was no Australian Cattle Dog on it. It was such a rare breed in the UK hardly anyone ever knew what he was. But this time we visited the vet, things were different.

We had been in reception for some time, Cocoa hiding under my seat as was usual in a strange building.

'You can go in now,' said the woman on the desk after about forty-five minutes of waiting.

As we walked into the neat little surgery there was a bench for the dogs to sit on, and various charts on the wall with pictures of animals on them. A tall young man with a shock of blond hair came over and shook my hand vigorously.

'Hey! A Red Speckled Aussie. G'day mate,' he said without a pause, and got down immediately on the floor to greet Cocoa with pats and strokes.

The dog had still been hovering about between my legs. But this time instead of cowering, it was almost as though Cocoa recognized the accent because he perked up straight away and rushed up to the Australian vet with his big bushy tail wagging madly.

Then, before I could do anything, Cocoa peed there and then on his shoes. I was mortified.

'I'm so sorry! He doesn't do that much any more. He's excited. He must like you.'

'Don't worry. I've had worse.'

And Cocoa seemed to relax with this vet like with no other stranger we had met so far.

'So you know the breed, and the colour too,' I said, impressed.

'Yeah, my dad has one on the farm to keep the roos off his land. I'm Phil, by the way.'

'I'm Jill and this is, well, you've met him now, haven't you, this is Cocoa.'

'Pleased to meet you, Cocoa.'

'Kangaroos? That explains a lot. He's definitely a natural herder,' I told the vet. 'Usually just other dogs, though. I daren't let him into a field with any cows in it. I'm sure he'd start herding them given half a chance.'

'So anyway, what's the problem, little man?' he asked, as if he really expected Cocoa to answer him.

'Oh, yes! Sorry. His legs. He's been limping a lot lately. Taking the weight off them and things.'

Phil looked at Cocoa for a while and moved his limbs about a bit.

'This one's not aligned properly,' he said after a while. 'So he'll get a lot of arthritis as he gets older.'

'Is there anything you can do?'

'Not really. There's no cure. But we can make his middle years pain-free. We might have to break his knee joint and realign it, though.'

Poor Cocoa, I thought. He's already had such a hard life, being abandoned, and now this.

I suppose if we'd known when we got him that eventually the leg problems would cost us £5,000, we might not have taken him on. But for us it was worth it once we had grown to love him like one of the family. After some to-ing and fro-ing back to the vets Cocoa had to have several operations and they eventually put in some metal plates. As part of his recovery we even took him to have hydrotherapy at a local unit in order to strengthen his legs again once the plates were out.

The therapy centre had a huge warm bath with a ramp going into the water. The therapist put Cocoa in a little life-jacket with a handle on it, so that he could carry him into the water and let him swim about. It was quite amusing to watch as they both got into the water – no sooner were they in than the dog would paddle and splash about for dear life to get back to the ramp and out again. The therapist would put him right back in the water, and the whole process would repeat itself again and again for about half an hour, back and forth, until Cocoa was tired out.

After about two months of this exercise we noticed that his legs were nowhere near as stiff as they had been, and eventually, three months after his first operation, he wasn't limping at all. With Cocoa back on form, finally confident and not chasing bikes any more, things were looking up.

Surely nothing else could go wrong . . .

Like nearly all dogs, Cocoa loves chasing sticks. One sunny afternoon, I was out with my grandson, Matt. Cocoa loved him to bits. Matt had more energy than I did and he could throw sticks a lot further too. Finding a good one, he took aim and swung his arm back to get a good distance but as he swung back Cocoa moved at the last minute and got behind him. The stick knocked him sharply on the head.

'Oh my goodness. I'm so sorry.' Matt looked mortified and got down to have a look.

'Oh, I'm sure it's fine. He's a tough cookie. Aren't you, Cocoa?' I rubbed his nose and he let out a playful whine as if to say, 'I'm fine! Just get on with throwing that stick.'

I didn't want to make a big deal, because Matt looked so worried that he might have hurt him. And Cocoa seemed OK, but we called it a day and went home.

Although we'd been to the vets with Cocoa so much, I don't think that at any stage anybody had looked into his eyes. After all, with his leg problems they had no reason to, did they?

Over breakfast the next morning, though, John peered over the top of his newspaper.

'I'm not sure about that eye. It looks a bit puffy, don't you think?'

I got down to Cocoa's level on the floor and had a look. Sure enough it had swelled up a lot since the day before and he had been pawing it a bit.

'Could be a black eye or something, maybe? Shall we take him to the vets just in case?'

When we arrived back at Phil's surgery Cocoa ran up to him as before with his tail wagging.

'Hey, mate. You're not going to pee on my shoes again, are you?' he laughed. But to my relief Cocoa just sat looking up at him with his tongue hanging out. I told Phil what had happened and he took out his eye instrument to have a look.

'Ooh, he's had a nasty knock, hasn't he? I can't see a thing at the moment, it's that swelled up. Some steroids should sort that out, though. Then I'll take another look in a couple of days, OK?'

We were a bit worried, but it turned out Phil was an eye expert, so this was his area. And he didn't sound too concerned at this stage. The swelling eventually went down and we trooped back to the specially equipped eye surgery. It was a tiny little room, completely blacked out so the vet could see inside the eye properly.

'We don't want to stress him by putting him on the table,' said Phil, and he got down to Cocoa's level.

Cocoa was always very quiet and obedient at the vets. He would never snarl or pull away. But this also meant that it was difficult to tell what he was really feeling.

'That's better. I can see now. Still a bit puffy but should be OK.'

I relaxed a little, until Phil suddenly stopped and leant back.

'Hang on a mo.'

'What is it?' I asked, clutching Cocoa's lead tightly.

'He's got . . . I think. Yes. He's got no lens. In his eye.'

'What does that mean? Is that bad?'

'Well. We'll have to wait and see but it's not exactly . . . good.'

All the while Cocoa just sat there silently, not giving us a clue what he was thinking.

'He's got a lens in the other eye. Look, you can see it here.'

He handed me the optical instrument, but I wasn't sure what to look for.

'Here, look at this one and you'll see.'

He showed me the good eye and I could see there was a clear difference.

'Oh, yes, there's a sort of . . . bulbous part in the good one, isn't there, but in the other eye it's just hollow.'

'Yes. A bit like a dewdrop sitting in a hole. I think the lens is what they call "luxated", that is dropped away. It's still a bit swollen, so it's hard to see, but I'm pretty sure that's what we've got.'

I didn't know what to think and Phil wasn't exactly reassuring me that everything would be OK, but he didn't seem too concerned either.

'I'll test the pressure, just in case,' he said, and puffed a little bit of air at the eyes. Cocoa shook his head then put his paw up on to Phil's shoulders.

'Good boy. That's a bit high, too,' he said, looking down. 'Definitely some pressure building up, but it's a bit soon to tell how bad. I think what's best is if you take him home until I can get a real look. Then, in a week or so, once the swelling has gone down a bit more, we'll see how it looks then.'

As I left the surgery I felt deflated and powerless. It was all so up in the air, so much new medical information to take in: lenses, luxating . . .

'How did it go?' asked John when I got home.

As I told him the news I was distracted with worry. The worst thing was that I couldn't ask Cocoa what was wrong and how he felt.

Over the next few days the dog gave us mixed messages. Out and about on his walks he was absolutely fine, running around and jumping up as usual. In the house it was a different story, though. He was obviously in pain, but not whimpering. He was just very restless, panting and breathing very rapidly.

'He just doesn't know what to do with himself, does he?' said John, as we sat doing the crossword one afternoon.

Cocoa got up and walked over to the door, then almost immediately came back to us, then walked back over to the patio door, so I let him out, but then he came straight back in and just sat by the radiator, sort of pressed up against it.

Later that evening he still didn't know what to do, whether to go and sit on his bed, sit with us near the sofa, or hang about by the front door. No sooner was he in one place than he would shift about and then move again.

'This isn't like him at all, is it? He usually has his nap about this time,' said John.

'Yes. It's almost as if he's trying to find a room where the pain will go away.'

But there was no room where the pain would go away. A week later John and I went back to the vet with Cocoa.

'G'day, mate,' said Phil. But this time, as he took up the optical instruments, he stopped almost straight away.

'This is not good.'

'What?'

'Extremely high. Hasn't gone down at all. He's definitely got glaucoma.'

'Too much pressure in the eye, isn't that?' asked John.

'Exactly. But this is high, and I mean *high*. Pressure at this rate in humans is incredibly painful, almost impossible to bear.'

'Oh my god. Poor Cocoa,' I said.

'Yes. It's pretty bad. And I won't beat around the bush. The only way I can stop this is to take the eye out.'

'Take it out! But . . . he won't be able to see,' I said, quite shocked by this sudden turn of events.

'Well, he won't be able to see out of this eye, no. But there is one big consolation. He'll be a different dog once it's done, he'll be that relieved, I'm telling you.'

I looked down at Cocoa. He was definitely more reserved than usual. By now it must have been so bad that he couldn't even tell where the pain was coming from.

John and I looked at each other and we both knew Phil was right.

'So I'll book him in tomorrow, then?'

'That soon? Well, yes. I suppose . . . whatever you think is best.'

'He'll only be in for one night. Bring him back here first

thing in the morning at eight o'clock sharpish. And don't give him any food from midnight. He can't eat before the operation.'

'But won't he be hungry?'

'He'll be all right.'

'Will you knock him out?' asked John. 'Oh, of course you will, I suppose!'

'Don't worry. He won't feel a thing. It'll all be over before you can say Red Speckled Aussie.'

I smiled faintly. It was a comfort that Phil always managed to maintain good humour even in the most serious situations. I suppose this was just a day's work for him. But I was sick to my stomach with worry.

In some ways it's even worse with a dog than with a human. You can't talk to them. And with a rescue dog it's even worse still, because you never know what's going on in their heads. I couldn't bear for him to think, 'Oh, here we go again. I don't like the smell of this. They're leaving me. I'm going to be put into a kennel or abandoned again.' At least even with children you can explain you'll be back and it will all be all right, but not with a dog.

I hardly slept a wink that night and at 7 a.m. we both got up and got ready for the hospital.

'He'll be so hungry,' I said to John again, as I looked down at his empty food bowl on the floor.

'Come on. Skipping a meal's not going to kill him.'

Cocoa didn't seem to mind, but he was still restless, perhaps sensing something wasn't quite right.

It was a grey morning with a light drizzle as we walked from the car to the animal hospital in town. In the noisy reception hall there were all kinds of animals about the

47

place and lots of barking and miaowing. Over by the desk, we caught sight of Phil talking to a nurse.

'Morning, morning,' he said, walking over to us, as jolly as ever. 'Did you bring his pyjamas?'

I couldn't bring myself to be too light-hearted about it just yet.

'The operation will be at about two o'clock this afternoon, OK?' he said as he took hold of Cocoa's collar. 'Hello, mate.'

'That late?' I said, still worried that he wouldn't be eating all day. 'He so loves his food.'

'Don't worry. We'll give you a tinkle when it's all done and you can come back and collect him first thing tomorrow.'

With that, the nurse who had been standing with Phil came and took Cocoa away and he walked off with her without any problems. He didn't even look back at us, we just saw his big bushy tail wagging back and forth as he disappeared. They walked down the corridor, through a set of double doors and in a moment they were gone.

John and I stood for a while quietly as other people's dogs barked around us: a small Yorkshire Terrier with stitches down one side trotted past us yapping, and a girl clutching a sleepy rabbit sat on a chair nearby whispering words of comfort in its ear.

'Come on, let's get some cake or something and cheer you up,' said John, turning to leave.

'This early?'

'Well, call it elevenses? Anyway, Cocoa's not eating so we might as well eat for three.'

I just about managed a smile this time. But as I turned

to leave, I looked down and realized I still had Cocoa's lead in my hand. Just seeing it there, all slack and empty with no dog on the end, was too much and my eyes filled up with tears.

'It's just that . . . it's all happened so quickly. And Cocoa will only have one eye and . . .'

'I know. But Phil knows what he's doing.'

'You're right. It's just . . . I hope he'll be OK.'

As we walked to the car John put his arm gently around my shoulders. We were both quiet on the drive until we stopped outside the bakery in town and John got out.

'Won't be long.'

While he was gone I watched the world go by. Other people with their own thoughts and lives, and of course dogs, seemed to be everywhere. A very tall skinny woman with two Lurchers who looked just like her walked past. Then an adorable little German Shepherd puppy leaping about on its lead seemed to be taking its owner for a walk.

'Apple turnovers and macaroons,' said John, slamming the door and putting the paper bags on my lap. But I could hardly touch them. All I could think was 'What am I going to do now?' We couldn't visit Cocoa like you would a human in hospital and the prospect of the day without him stretched out ahead of me.

When we got home John went off and did some things in the garage. He was always good at keeping busy. Then he came back in and cooked me a bit of lunch. I could tell he was doing his best to cheer me up, keep me upbeat. But I just sat and looked at the plate and moved a bit of ham around with my fork. It was no good, I just had no appetite.

After lunch was even worse. That's when I would normally walk Cocoa.

I couldn't bring myself to go out without him and instead I tried to read my book. I read the same sentence about ten times, then watched the clock on the wall tick away the time I would normally be out.

'Oh, this is no good,' I said and tried to do something more useful.

I sat at the computer for a while and looked at some emails, one trying to sell me a wonder drug and another asking me to wire some money to what was probably a fictitious charity. I also had an email to write, so I tried that, but thoughts kept flooding in. I looked at the clock. It was 2.30 p.m.

'He's probably having the operation right at this moment,' I called out to John but he didn't hear me.

What if the anaesthetic doesn't work and he wakes up in agony? What if they can't get the eye out properly or something gets stuck? These and all manner of disastrous scenarios whizzed through my mind. When I looked back at the computer screen I had written two words in an hour. This was useless. Eventually the phone rang and I jumped up.

'John, it's them, probably,' I called out. He popped his head round the door as I answered.

'Hello?'

'G'day, Jill? It's Phil.'

The vet's voice crackled over the line and I listened to the tone of his voice for clues.

'How is he? Is it out? Is he OK?'

'Yes, it's all fine. No need to worry. He's on a drip. You can pick him up first thing.'

'On a drip?' I said. It all sounded so serious. But at least he's OK, I thought, and breathed a small sigh of relief.

So that was that. Cocoa had lost an eye. He was awake again and we would collect him in the morning. I didn't sleep very well that night. This time I was more concerned about getting there as soon as the vets opened.

In the end, we got there so early we had to wait outside in the car for about twenty minutes until it opened at eight o'clock.

When we were finally let in, Phil, the nurse and Cocoa came back through the double doors where we had left them the day before. The dog ran right over to us with a big white collar around his neck and I could see his little eye all neatly sewn up.

'Hello, Cokey,' I said and gave him the biggest hug ever. 'Did you miss us?'

'He's just a bit pleased to see you, then,' said Phil as Cocoa smothered us in licks.

Then he showed us just how pleased he was in the best way he knows, by peeing right there on the floor by my feet. But of course we couldn't get cross with him, we were just so happy he was all right.

When we got him home, it became immediately clear that the big white collar round his neck was causing him problems. Because he only had one eye he couldn't judge distances, and he kept banging the collar against the door. Feeding time was even worse. The collar was so long, poor Cocoa couldn't reach his bowl to eat. When it became clear that it was really stressing him out I rang Phil.

'OK, well, if he doesn't bother with the wound, then if you're with him take it off. But if you go out, put it back on.'

As soon as we took the collar off Cocoa was more comfortable straight away, and he never scratched at the eye at all. Best of all, he was no longer in pain.

When we went back about ten days later for a check-up, Phil was very excited.

'I've been to this big conference in London, on canine ophthalmology,' he said, with his eyes shining. 'And there was this bloke there knew all about primary lens luxation. That was his presentation.'

'Really,' I said, still a little confused about what primary lens luxation was. 'Did he tell you any more about Cocoa's problem?' I still wasn't entirely sure what all this medical jargon meant.

'Maybe. So this bloke had a list of dogs genetically predisposed to primary lens luxation. And you'll never guess. On his list was an Aussie dog.'

'What does that mean?'

'Well, we're not sure yet, but when I told him about Cocoa, this bloke said he wanted him to take part in a DNA sampling. Because he's itemized the genetic code for this problem, he says. It won't help Cocoa, exactly, but it might help research into his problem. And we might find out what caused his eye to go. Also, if Cocoa is genetically predisposed, then there's the possibility his other lens is going to fall out too. And it would be good to be prepared for that.'

'My goodness. So there's the possibility Cocoa could go completely blind?' I thought. This was the first time this had dawned on me.

'What does it involve, this sampling?' I asked.

'It's just a simple DNA test. With a cotton bud. It's not painful.'

'Sounds like a good idea, if only to help this man, I suppose.'

'That's great,' said Phil, with the smile of someone who is about to contribute to the advancement of medical science.

He wiped the inside of Cocoa's mouth with the cotton bud and took the sample away. We took Cocoa home and waited for the results.

'What if Cocoa does lose his other eye?' I said to John that afternoon when I came in from my walk. I couldn't get this thought out of my mind.

'I don't know. We'll just have to train him to use his nose better, I suppose. He's a survivor.'

'Yes, he is, but . . .'

I looked down at Cocoa. He was so much better now that he wasn't in pain, but I could tell he was also becoming a little less confident out and about on his walks. It was gradual but he was staying closer to me than usual, not straying so far away.

Would another dog help, perhaps, I wondered to myself. But I quickly pushed the thought out of my mind. John would never have another pet in the house, after all the trouble and expense we'd had with Cocoa.

'I've got the results,' said Phil excitedly a week later.

'And?'

'Turns out Cocoa is predisposed to primary lens lux-ation. The bloke identified it, which means his breed is more likely to get this problem. This was just a ticking time-bomb. So you can tell your grandson who threw the stick that it wasn't his fault.'

'He will be relieved,' I said, remembering how upset Matt had been.

'Let's have a look at how it's going anyway,' said Phil, and went down to Cocoa with his optical instruments.

There was a long pause while he looked into Cocoa's eye, then he looked up at me with a serious expression on his face.

'This isn't good. He's dropped the lens in the other eye now. And it's behind the eye. Last time I looked the lens was there, but it's moved. It's floating loose behind the pupil, and we really don't want it to fall through an open pupil. That would block the drainage in the outer eye, and we'd get another case of glaucoma, like before.'

'Is he in pain again?' I asked, dreading the prospect that Cocoa would have to have his other eye out so soon.

'No, not yet. The pressure's OK. But you'll need to give him some drops. For the rest of his life, really, if it comes to it. Two drops a day should help minimize the risk.'

'At least there's something we can do.'

'Yes, but you also have to be aware that, even with this, there's still a fifty-fifty chance that the other eye will go.'

Now that I knew that the lens in Cocoa's other eye had gone, this explained why he had been less confident lately. His field of vision had soon become very small indeed. The eye drops narrowed his pupil, so that he could see shapes, but not much light. Phil told us that if he was a human he'd be registered blind.

'Well, dogs do use their nose and ears more than us, don't they?' said John, as we watched Cocoa awkwardly working his way across the room.

'Yes, but imagine being in the dark the whole time. Perhaps he needs a guide dog or something.'

Since our visit to the vets, the idea of another dog for Cocoa kept coming back to me with increasing persistence, and this time it wouldn't go away.

'What? Are you joking?' was John's response to the idea. 'We don't need any more pets or any more problems, thank you very much.'

Because we had no insurance for Cocoa's leg or eye problems it had cost us a small fortune to get the dog better; even now we still had to pay for the drops, plus there was the possibility of his other eye going.

'Well. You might be right. It's just that, if he had another dog on our walks, I'm sure it would help. To have the company. Someone to follow.'

Over the next few weeks we tried very hard to train Cocoa's hearing and scent detection. We gave him a denture chew to sniff and told him to sit while we hid it, then got him to find it. It worked quite well and after a while we were confident that he was able to follow a scent better than ever, even though his sight was so poor.

But somehow it didn't seem to be enough.

One afternoon, when John was out with him on their walk, I remembered that Cocoa had originally been sent to Battersea Dogs & Cats Home by his breeder. No harm in just looking at their website, I thought. I might find a nice companion for Cocoa. I did feel a bit guilty as I knew John was far from on board with the idea, but I loaded up the website and clicked around on it a bit. No harm in just looking, I told myself again.

After a few minutes I heard the door shut and quickly hid the Battersea site behind my emails.

'We're back,' shouted John, and came in and flopped on to the sofa outside my office. I continued to write away on the computer.

'I think I know what you mean,' he shouted through after a while.

'What?'

'About Cocoa. He only went a few metres from me today. It was like he really couldn't see much. You know, he usually runs right round the perimeter of the field, but he wouldn't go near it.'

'I know. He's losing his confidence again. I knew it.'

It was horrible to see this happen to Cocoa, when we had spent so long helping him to become such a happy dog.

'Maybe you're right. About getting another one. Maybe,' said John cautiously. 'Perhaps if we can find someone he can follow. Who is not too big. Not bigger than him. And can be careful with him.'

'Well, as it happens . . .' I said, clicking back on to the website, 'there are some lovely dogs on the Battersea web-site. Not that I've been looking, of course . . .'

John smiled.

'All right, then. Let's have a look.'

We clicked around the site a bit, looking at some of the featured dogs and their photos and descriptions. Next we put into the search engine that we wanted a medium dog who got on with children and other dogs.

'Look at this one,' said John, after a while. 'Looks like an Aussie Cattle Dog. Like Cocoa. Fits the bill perfectly.'

There was a small photo of an animal who did look a bit like Cocoa, a female with a lovely coat and a nice face.

'Perhaps it's meant to be,' I said.

So we rang up Battersea and arranged a visit the next day to their Old Windsor site, about an hour and a half's drive from us. We took Cocoa in the car with us to have a look.

The site is built on the edge of the Thames with a lovely wooded area around it for walking the dogs. When we arrived we filled out all the forms about our suitability as dog owners, and were met by one of the staff there in the rehoming department who was to show us the dog we had spotted on the website.

'They're just bringing Honey over to meet you now,' said the rehomer. 'She's very vocal, this one. A lovely dog, though.'

When she arrived we could see that she was indeed very lively. So lively, in fact, that she needed two kennel maids to fetch her out. And she kept barking and pulling on her lead like mad.

'She's not selling herself, is she?' said the woman, a little exasperated.

She looked nice enough, and a little like Cocoa as we had expected, but I was already a bit worried about how this bumptious animal would accommodate our dog's poor vision.

'We'll take them into the play area together, if you like?' offered the woman.

There was a nice outdoor area with lots of space for them to run about in, but when I threw a ball for them both, Honey wanted to get it so much that she barged right past Cocoa on his blind side and made him jump.

Obviously this dog was full of fun, but we needed an animal who would be much more gentle and considerate.

'I don't like to say this,' I said after a while, 'but I don't think it's going to work. She's just not taking enough care with Cocoa.'

'Fair enough. She's not for everyone, I suppose.'

It was heartbreaking saying no to this dog, and seeing her being taken back into the kennels, to wait who knows how long for another family. It was also hard that we had come all this way, got so excited about the whole thing, but not found the right companion for Cocoa.

'We ought to have a look, you know, at what other dogs there are. Don't you think?' I said to John as we were about to leave.

'But we know what they've got, from the website. That dog was the only one.'

It was a very hot day and I knew John and Cocoa were both getting a bit restless.

'I know, but just a quick look, through the kennels. You never know. Can't hurt.'

'All right. I'll wait here with Cocoa,' said John and he sat on a bench in a courtyard between the kennels. 'But don't be too long. And remember, we don't want anything bigger than Cocoa. And not a Staffie.'

Because we had seen Staffordshire Bull Terriers around us being used as trophy dogs by some owners, we believed their ill-gotten reputation for being aggressive. In fact we knew nothing about the breed, and had wrongly assumed them to be fighting dogs.

'Righto. Not a Staffie. Won't be long.'

I went through into the kennel area, which was surprisingly quiet. I had expected lots of barking but it was quite calm. There was a sign up on the wall saying 'Please Don't Forget Me in the Corner'.

I walked along and looked into Kennel 1 but it was empty; the dog must be out for exercise, I thought. When I got to Kennel 2 there was a little dog sitting in there. She jumped off the bench, came running up to the gate and put her paws up so I could put my hand on her nose. Then she gave me a lovely little gentle lick.

'You're beautiful, aren't you?' I said. 'Who are you? What's your name?'

I looked up, and to my dismay the sign above said: 'Princess – Staffie Cross'.

'Oh no!'

I felt sure that I'd found the dog I wanted. She was so gentle. I couldn't imagine she'd ever be aggressive or pushy with Cocoa and she had such a lovely shiny coat. But I was only at Kennel 2, and I still had John's last words ringing in my ears: 'Not a Staffie.'

'But this is a Staffie Cross,' I thought. 'Does that count?'

We hadn't seen Princess on the website because she was labelled as a small dog and we had only searched for medium dogs. Plus we would have discounted her as a Staffie, anyway. She was short-haired, was slightly small and strongly marked in black, tan and white, with tall pricked, bat-like ears, unlike the floppy ears of a pure bred Staffordshire Bull Terrier.

She looked back at me with her lovely gentle eyes and my heart melted.

I tried to pull myself together.

'I owe it to Cocoa and the family, and the other dogs here, to look at them all,' I thought.

True to my quest and knowing that I had dozens more kennels to visit, I continued along the corridor, all the time looking over my shoulder at the little white paws that were still draped through the door of Kennel 2.

There were some nice dogs, but after about half an hour, I emerged at the other end of the semi-circle of kennels adamant that Princess was the one.

'Where have you been? Thought you'd been kidnapped by one of the dogs. Dognapped,' said John. 'It's boiling out here.'

Cocoa was panting and they both looked hot and bothered.

'Sorry. I got a bit . . . waylaid.'

'Here you go, you take Cocoa. He's fed up, sitting out here.'

But all I could think about was Princess. I needed to see her again. One more time, just to make sure.

'Wait. I'll be back in a minute,' I said, and ran right back to the entrance, leaving John bewildered again.

I needed time to get my head right. What could I say in order to sell this lovely little dog to him?

As I approached the kennel again, to my horror another couple were looking at her adoringly. She was standing up at the gate again, looking at them with that sweet little face which had not long before thoroughly won me over.

'She'll be just right for Sally, don't you think?' said the woman, petting her on the head and stroking her nose.

'Yes. She's a beauty all right,' said the man.

They must be talking about giving the dog to their daughter, I thought. No way. This is my dog. Don't you dare say she's right for you. She's right for me!

I didn't say this out loud, of course, but my head was buzzing with the fear that I would lose her. I ran back towards the entrance and charged back through the 'In' door.

'What on earth did you go back for? We're sweltering here. And I'm starving.'

Again John got up and tried to pass me the lead. But I ran past at high speed – or as high a speed as one can at seventy.

'Where are you off to now?' he said, almost shouting.

'Sorry. Can't stop. I think I've seen the one I want.'

I ran downstairs to the reception hall as fast as I could and up to the woman at the desk who was filling out some forms.

'Can I help?' she asked calmly, without looking up.

'I don't know what to do. I think I've found the dog I want, but there's another couple up there now and they want her too, probably. But I really want her. John hasn't seen her yet, though. My husband, John. So I can't say yes yet, but I'm sure it is yes.'

I didn't stop for breath until I'd finished, then waited for her response.

'Don't worry. That often happens,' she said, looking up and smiling. 'I'll put her on hold for you, if you like. While you decide?'

She was so calm, as though it was all completely normal, but my heart was pounding.

'Thank you so much!'

I was so relieved, but then, as I walked back up the stairs, I remembered I still had to persuade John to accept a Staffie. Well, she was only a Staffie Cross, right?

When I got to the top I nearly bumped into the couple who had been looking at Princess after me. They were chatting and laughing together.

I bet they want her too, I thought. And I couldn't look the woman in the eye as we passed. I wanted to apologize for putting the dog on hold, but I had to keep going.

'What on earth was all that about?' asked John. He was by now sounding pretty cross and Cocoa was whining from the heat.

'I'm sorry. I've fallen in love with a little dog. But she's a Staffie. But only a crossbreed. She's so gentle. Lovely ears. Oh, you must see her. Please. Go and have a look at her. Just a look.'

I knew as I poured out this great torrent that I should have handled the whole thing better, but I couldn't stop the words from coming out.

'She's in Kennel 2. Please.'

John sighed.

'All right. But then we're going home.'

The next few minutes were agony. I couldn't bear the thought that he would say no. I just sat waiting anxiously with Cocoa and gave him a gentle hug.

'We might have found you a friend,' I whispered in his ear, and he licked my hand and quietly nuzzled up to me.

About ten minutes later, John came back through the door. He had a grim look on his face at first and I thought the worst. Then he smiled.

'You win. She's perfect.'

I have never felt so relieved in my life, and we both rushed back down to reception to tell the woman at the desk.

The couple who had also been interested were sitting very upright in their chairs, waiting to see what we thought. They were talking quietly to each other and looking at us out of the corner of their eyes. I couldn't look at them again.

But once we had told the woman at the desk that we wanted the dog, I soon forgot about all that. It was time for Cocoa and his new friend to meet. I loved her, but then, of course, they might not get on with each other, it suddenly occurred to me. My throat tightened. That would be too much.

'We'll take them into the play area again, introduce them and let them both off the lead,' said the woman who had shown us the other dog.

As we let them in to play together they were not at all wary of one another and I immediately relaxed.

'They seem to have a great respect for each other, don't they?' said John.

It was true, they didn't follow each other, but just seemed to allow each other space.

'Here, Cocoa,' I said. 'Here, Princess,' and I threw a ball for them both.

Instead of barging past Cocoa like the other dog had, Princess was courteous and only took the ball if Cocoa didn't want it. In fact, Princess was not interested in ball throwing and not particularly interested in what Cocoa was doing.

She ran round the pen, pleased to be out of her kennel. What I did like was the fact that if they found themselves in the same bit of ground she'd stop and defer to Cocoa in a very polite fashion. So far, so good.

The next stage was to see how they reacted to one another in a room inside. We did this back in the interview room, where there were toys all over the place. We let them both in and then sat on a chair and left them to it. Cocoa seemed a bit stressed because there were other dogs barking outside. He'd also been outside all that time, waiting, and was hot and bothered. But Princess looked OK with this, and sat quite quietly by him.

Princess would gently defer to Cocoa but neither was intimidated by the other; there was no lip curling, no lifted tails, no raised hackles, just the usual interested sniffing.

'She hasn't really interacted with toys much yet. But I'm sure you can help her with that,' said the rehomer after a while. 'You can get down on the floor with her now, if you like.'

I got down on the floor to play with Princess, but also to reassure Cocoa, who was nervous of the barking going on around him. When I'd given him a cuddle, up came Princess, who put one paw on each shoulder and gave me a long, gentle lick on the side of my face. My heart soared.

You're choosing me. I know you're choosing me, I thought. You're the dog we want.

'Where are the forms?' I said. 'She's the one.'

'Where is she from, do you know?' John asked.

'She was a stray, found wandering along the Thames,' said the rehomer. 'She was chipped, but the family who owned her were evicted. Landlord doesn't know where they are now. She might have escaped or been abandoned. We don't know. We don't even know if she's house-trained. I'm afraid we don't know anything much about her at all.'

But for us she had passed the test. She was a lovely dog and she was gentle with Cocoa and that was what mattered.

As well as Cocoa, of course, we had to consider our grandchildren, and we have since found out that Staffies, far from being aggressive animals, are actually sometimes called 'nanny dogs' because they are such good family pets.

'I'm afraid you can't take her home for a bit,' said the rehomer. 'She has to be spayed. She'll be in for a while yet. But you can visit her, so she doesn't forget you.'

So that day, we left happy, but without Princess.

'I'm so pleased,' I said to John as we got back in the car with a very tired Cocoa. 'It was worth it, wasn't it?'

'Yes. Shame we can't take her home now, really. But there is one thing.'

'What?'

'Princess. I'm just not sure I can stand in the middle of a field and shout that out.'

He looked so serious I laughed out loud.

'You might be right. Doesn't really suit us, does it? How about a jolly name like . . . Molly, or something?'

'Much better.'

So that was decided, we had chosen our little Molly, and she had chosen us, and we couldn't wait to see her again.

When we returned to visit her, she ran over to us so excitedly that the staff member said, 'Look at her. She knows you.'

I was pleased Molly was happy to see us again, though she had developed a little kennel cough while in clinic. But we knew she'd soon be right as rain once we got her home.

Not long after our second visit we were allowed to collect Molly for good. We left Cocoa at home so they could meet in a more careful manner later, but we took our granddaughter Jo with us, as she always loves our dogs and was keen to meet the new addition to our family.

We had no idea how Molly was going to manage being in the back of the car, though we knew she wasn't car sick when the dog warden had picked her up in the first place, so we were hopeful.

As we drove to Old Windsor for the third time, I tried to picture little Molly in my mind again.

I remembered that she had the most beautiful glossy coat, and even though she had been found wandering by the Thames, she looked very healthy and happy.

As soon as we got there, Jo leapt out of the car. The Battersea handler was coming round the corner with Molly on a lead. She was so bouncy, I was even more convinced that she had been loved by her former owners, and I felt sorry that they had felt the need to leave her somewhere, or worse, that she had run away and they were still pining for her.

'She's quite a runner, this one,' said the woman bringing her over.

'Hello, you. She's beautiful!' said Jo, getting down to meet her. Molly wagged her tail and licked Jo's hands.

'She likes you,' said the handler, smiling. 'I never get tired of seeing them find a new home.'

'What did you say she was, again?' asked John.

'Part Staffie, as you know, but we think maybe a bit of Basenji in her too. The ears are pointy like a Basenji, and she's got that independent streak. Natural hunting dog.'

But in the end it didn't really matter what she was. She was Molly.

The next challenge was to introduce her to Cocoa properly, and we knew this had to be on neutral territory. So John dropped Jo and me off at the bottom of our road.

'Why don't you take her to the park while I go home and fetch Cocoa?'

'Righto. You hold her lead, Jo,' I said. 'I'll open the boot. Just so she doesn't run out into the road.'

But we had nothing to fear. She just sat there, sort of smiling, while Jo stroked her head until we clicked our fingers and she jumped out.

This was crunch time, though, and we had all our fingers crossed that the two dogs would get on – after all, they would be spending a lot of time together!

We walked round the lake once or twice. It was a beautiful day, with the green leaves on the trees in full bloom.

'She loves it here,' said Jo, and then she ran around the lake again to give Molly a good burst after the long car journey. When they came back, Jo had spotted something by the gate and squinted in that direction.

'It's them. They're here!'

'Gosh, you have got good eyesight,' I said, but I could gradually make out Cocoa and John coming towards us. 'He can't see us, though, Cocoa, can he? Let's go a bit closer.'

As we walked towards them I smiled at John, and eventually, when he got really close, Cocoa did recognize me and started to wag his tail. We didn't say anything at first, just walked past them with Molly to see how Cocoa would react.

'Let's turn around and do it again,' I said to Jo, and we swung Molly back for a second walk past.

'Cocoa, meet Molly. Molly, meet Cocoa,' said John, as we both stopped and stood next to the lake.

The two dogs sniffed each other and walked about each other, as they had before when they met at Battersea.

'They'll probably think they're just part of the same pack in the end, don't you think?' I said.

'Hope so.'

A pair of ducks flew past and skidded into the lake. The sun was just dipping down below the trees.

'I think it's time we took them home, don't you?'

As we walked with them together it was clear the two dogs got along just fine. Molly didn't push Cocoa, and they didn't bother each other too much, just trotted along beside us.

When we got home, from the off it was important for us to allow Cocoa to be top dog in their relationship. We didn't want his fox-like tail to disappear between his legs again if there was a dog who bullied or bossed him about. When it was dinner time, we put Cocoa's food down first, then Molly's. We made sure he was the first to be greeted in the morning and when returning from a walk, and Molly accepted her position in the pack with exceptional grace.

Next came Molly's toilet training. We'd been told that you should choose an area you want a dog to use, and show them that area. Cocoa always used the pebbled area in the corner of the garden – good for us because it's easy to wash it down! We even call it the dunny (Australian slang for toilet) in honour of his antipodean heritage.

'Molly should use the dunny too, don't you think?' said John as we took her out for the first time.

But we just could not get her to go there.

'Looks like she's only ever used grass,' I said, as she emphatically refused to use the pebbles.

We spent about fifteen minutes walking around the pebbled area, and although it was obvious Molly wanted to go she made it very clear there was no way she was going to do it there.

With Cocoa's increasingly poor sight he was choosing to sleep downstairs in the lounge. He could get upstairs, but to come down again, the gaping black hole that he perceived was terrifying, so it seemed right that Molly should also sleep downstairs. Not as easy as it sounds, however, as most of our ground floor is open plan.

We had got hold of a dog crate so, for the first night, we could put Molly away from Cocoa in the kitchen. We really had no idea if she was going to foul the bed, scratch the kitchen cupboards or chew the place up. We put the bedding in there and she seemed very happy.

'Perhaps it reminds her of Battersea?' said John.

In the morning she hadn't wet or fouled anything, and when we let her out she ran into the lounge and everything was fine.

Next we put the crate in the lounge, so she could see Cocoa, and they seemed to be happy close to each other.

In the end, despite our fears, Molly was very easy to train, and she has never touched anything in the house that isn't her own. One thing we did notice, though, is that she is totally obsessed with food.

On our first walks she pestered fishermen for their bait and people having picnics.

'When you've been a stray you know what it's like to be hungry, I suppose,' we'd say, and had to get on with training her out of the habit.

We walked the dogs separately for two weeks. Then John and I would take them out separately, but meet up and bring them back together. After a few weeks, we took them out together. And because Molly had been trained well she was fine with John on the bike. She didn't cross over the wheels and it was fairly easy. They even chose their own places, Molly on the outside, Cocoa in the middle.

So what about Molly helping Cocoa gain more confidence? After all, that was why we got her in the first place.

Before Molly arrived, Cocoa would walk behind us to catch our scent, and he wouldn't stray very far away – he would go less than a metre from us. He certainly wouldn't run off to find things. But since she arrived, that has completely changed.

We put a little tinkly tag on Molly's collar, so Cocoa can hear her as they run about together. They don't follow each other, but just knowing where she is seems to give Cocoa new confidence. When Molly finds an interesting scent he will go and investigate with her. He plays with her when he finds a plastic bottle (a favourite of his), whacking her over the head with it and asking her to take the other end for a game of tug. Molly doesn't shove Cocoa under her wing, but it's reassuring to him to have her there and smell her.

When it comes to the house, Molly is always kind to Cocoa too. When he needs to go out, Cocoa sits and waits by the patio door and Molly barks, loudly and insistent, but just the once. We open the door for them and Cocoa struggles to his feet (the operation on his knee means this takes a few seconds). Meanwhile, Molly waits patiently until he's outside and then follows him.

We're still not sure, but we do think Molly is a Staffie crossed with a Basenji. Would this make her a Staffenji? Who knows. Whatever she is, it would not have been possible to find a more gentle, loving and reliable dog.

Molly and Cocoa's friendship grew gradually, over six months, but each week we'd notice them sitting closer, occasionally nuzzling each other and even copying one another. Their beds were moved into the lounge, side by side, and we'd often notice that one dog's chosen sleeping position was mirrored exactly by the other. I'm told this is classic behaviour for dogs who are closely bonded.

Cocoa's vision does cause him problems. In the house he bangs into things, for instance if we move a table or something, but we hope beyond anything that Cocoa will be in the lucky 50 per cent of dogs with his condition who do not become totally blind. If that should happen, though, we feel confident that he will rely more and more on Molly's guidance, listening to the reassuring tinkle of her brass collar tag. We also know that, given Molly's gentle nature, she would never take advantage of the situation. Cocoa will always be top dog.

Milly and Lily: A Tale of Two Animals

Battersea Dogs & Cats Home first opened its doors in 1860 as the Temporary Home for Lost & Stray Dogs, and moved to the Battersea centre in 1871. Since then, 3.1 million dogs and cats have come through our gates, and we have expanded beyond London into Berkshire and Kent, looking after an average of 400 dogs and 190 cats at any one time.

As many people have experienced over its long history, Battersea dogs can make great family pets, getting the whole family out together walking and having fun. Some people come back throughout their lives to rehome several animals and their children grow up alongside a Battersea dog as part of their family.

We love nothing more than to hear from people whose dogs are thriving many years after being rehomed, as was the case with Jennifer Wood and her family . . .

'Come on, boy!' I shouted at the top of my voice. 'Where are you, Cookie?'

I was running full pelt through the bush. Twigs cracked under my feet and the air all around me was quivering in the afternoon heat.

My beloved Cookie, a beautiful silver Australian Silkie, had scampered off into the thick brush just outside our little town of Wollongong, New South Wales, Australia. He often did this, it was no surprise. He was such a natural hunter and we would spend hours out here together, just rambling and running in the wide-open landscape. But on this occasion he had been gone for just a little longer than usual. My mother would be frantic. It was nearly dinner-time, and besides which, I was starving.

'Cookie!' I yelled as loudly as I could. 'Don't mess about now. Where are you?'

When he didn't answer with his usual bark I started to panic a bit. I ran through the undergrowth batting it back with a big stick and kept expecting to see him round every corner, wagging his tail. But every time I shouted and listened out for his yelp, my voice just bounced around and back at me.

I've always had a dog. Everybody in my family knows me and my dogs. And Cookie was one of my favourites. We'd grown up together, and discovered this little world all of our own out on the edge of Wollongong.

I was almost at the limit of where my mother would allow me to play. The bush got so wide-open, with so few landmarks, you couldn't tell which direction was which, and quite a few people got lost out there. As I hunted for Cookie, a nearby cockatoo mocked me with a squawk and then a flock of beautiful yellow birds danced up and down against the deep blue sky.

That was when I heard it. A soft whining at first. Then more of a feeble yelp. Cookie! I followed the sound. By this time I really had strayed off the beaten track.

When I got to him, Cookie was lying stretched out and stiff on the dusty ground. He had his paws up around his head as if he had been trying to scratch something away. I knew immediately he'd been bitten by a tick. He was a long-haired dog, and he just loved burrowing about in the grasses. The same thing had happened to my last dog, Tiger, when I was just eight years old and all the old memories came flooding back. The ticks in Australia aren't like British ones. They can paralyse an animal, or worse . . .

Cookie looked up at me with his big brown eyes. When I tried to pick him up he was a dead weight, impossible for me to carry on my own. He must have been bitten a while ago, because the ticks take a while to release their poison.

'Don't worry, little thing,' I said softly in his ear. 'I'll get help. You just stay calm.'

But as I ran back to the house, I knew it was too late.

My dad carried Cookie and I could hear the dog's breathing slowing, gradually, until I could hardly make it out. By the time we got home Cookie had stopped breathing altogether. My hands were shaking as I got down on my knees and hugged him for the last time. I couldn't believe he was gone. After that, it all happened in a bit of a dream. Dad dug a hole and carefully placed Cookie in it. Then he started to shovel the earth in around my beloved friend and I let out a loud sob.

'He had a good life, though, didn't he?' said Dad, putting his arm around me. But it was little comfort. The thought of endless days without Cookie stretched out ahead. Once we had filled in the little grave and I had put a homemade cross in the earth in his memory, I ran off without a word and hid under my favourite eucalyptus tree, quietly crying.

My parents walked arm in arm back to the house and I heard my mother talking in a low voice.

'I just can't bear to see her like this again. It was bad enough the last time. And now look at her. She's in shreds.'

'She just gets so attached, that's all. Loves them too much,' said my dad. 'She'll get over it.'

'I just don't think she should have another dog, is what I'm saying. I know it's cruel. But it's cruel to be kind.'

I suppose I should have been annoyed by this, but I was too upset to care. And anyway, maybe she was right. No other dog could ever replace Cookie, or so I felt then.

The weeks went on, and I gradually got on with my life. I had school and exams to worry about, and all the trials of being a teenage girl. I had almost put dogs completely out of my mind when, one afternoon, after work, my dad came round the corner with a little creature scurrying along beside him. I squinted to get a better look.

'What have you got there?' asked my mother, coming out of the house and on to the porch.

'Sausage cross. Stray. Bob at work found her wandering out by the old riverbed. But he can't keep the little thing. He's got two dogs already. He wondered would Jennifer like her.'

'But I thought we agreed?' said my mother anxiously. 'After Cookie.'

'This one's a short-hair, though. She won't get ticks.'

I ran over as fast as I could and leapt on to the little Dachshund Cross, who immediately covered me in licks and paws.

And that was that. I've been a fully certified dog lover ever since.

I never thought I'd end up living in England when I grew up. It happened sort of by accident. I trained in midwifery aged twenty-three, and then, through a friend back in Australia, I heard about an oncology course at the Royal Marsden Hospital in London. I joined the course and then got a job at St Mary's, near Paddington, on a neuro-logical ward.

I hadn't really intended to stay for long, but after a year and a half I met Stephen and we got engaged. I was so happy to be in London, starting our new life together. I loved my job and we were in this beautiful city together. But I longed for aspects of my old life, too. Having a dog as a constant companion: someone who never judges, who gets you out of the house whatever the weather. I was really keen to meet more people in England too, and dogs are a great way to do that, I thought.

Stephen did like dogs – he had always had them in the family as a child – but he hadn't been as attached to them as I was to Cookie and to my little sausage dog, Penny, who had ended up living to a ripe old age. But he could see what it meant to me to have a dog, and agreed that we could get one.

Not long afterwards we heard about Battersea Dogs & Cats Home and all the great work they do rescuing animals. It wasn't too far from where we lived, so one weekend we decided to pop down there. Just for a look. We told them about our circumstances and took a walk around the kennels.

I didn't really expect much, but I was quite shocked by all the animals. Some were quite skinny and others just cowered in the corners. Although the staff were very kind to them, it looked as if some of the dogs had been treated badly in the past.

Just as we had almost given up hope of finding any-thing suitable, I spotted an adorable puppy. The sign said: 'Staffie Cross.'

'We think she's crossed with a Labrador, that one,' said the woman who was showing us around. 'Came with a lovely little note from a lady. Said she just couldn't cope with such a lively thing.'

The dog's name written on her kennel was Perdy, and she was a brindle brown dog, with a lovely little face.

'I'll go and get the letter,' said the woman. And she showed us the note from Perdy's previous owner. It was written in a frail, shaky hand on a piece of blue paper. It said, in quite simple and moving terms, that 'Perdy is a lovely dog but she needs a lot of exercise'. And that unfortunately, at her age, she couldn't give the dog what she needed for a full life.

'Oh, it must have been heartbreaking for her,' I said to Stephen as we peered in at Perdy. 'Giving her up so soon.'

'She's never been mistreated, though. She's not nervous of people at all. She's about six months old. Want to have a proper look?' the lady asked. I caught Stephen's eye to see his reaction.

'Yes, why not,' he said. 'She's quite sweet, actually.' She put her paws up on the bars as if she could hear what he had said and wagged her tail. I knew how much hard work puppies are before they're trained. They chew all your best shoes and get up to all kinds of mischief, but this little dog staring up at us was too much to resist.

We took her out for a walk and then into a little play-room, and eventually Stephen and I both agreed that we would love to give her a new home. When we got her back we decided to rename her Milly.

When we took her to our local vet's, in Chelsea, every-one there had all these little pedigree pooches on their laps, and when the vet saw Milly he ushered us right to the front of the queue – probably so that this Staffie wasn't in reception for too long. Another place where the difference between our Battersea dog and the pedigree show dogs all around us was most conspicuous was Kensington Gardens. It was a lovely place to walk, and when we first got there I was quite cautious, and waited until there was no one around before I let Milly off the lead. But as soon as I did she was so excited to be free she ran immediately up to this fawn-coloured whippet, which seemed to have come out of nowhere, and they started leaping about together. They were both fine, just playing, when the dog's owner, a very tall, elegant looking woman, her hair all neatly set, wearing clippity shoes and a white fur coat, came tottering over to fetch her pooch.

'Oh, Holly!' she screeched. 'Come away from that yard dog.'

Yard dog! I thought. This was a far cry from my home-town of Wollongong, where all our dogs were a mixture of who knows what, and nobody cared.

'Sorry, she's just a bit playful,' I called over, hoping to strike up a friendly conversation.

But Milly, thinking this woman wanted to join in the fun, immediately jumped up at her pristine, white fur coat and left muddy paw prints all over it.

'Oh my God, I am so sorry!' I said, absolutely mortified, and pulled the dog away, putting her on the lead immediately.

Milly didn't have an aggressive bone in her body, she was just very friendly, but the woman didn't see it that way. She didn't say anything, just made a lot of flustered and disgusted huffing sounds as she wiped her coat down.

Then she put her whippet back on its lead, looked at me, shook her head and pursed her lips.

'Come on, Holly. Let's get out of here.'

'I can pay for the dry-cleaning or something,' I called after her, but it was to no avail as she stalked off up the path.

'She was a bit stuck up, wasn't she?' said another woman, walking towards me with a big Boxer dog. She was quite a bit older than me, about fifty. 'Why would you wear a posh fur coat out with your dog anyway?' she said. 'Hardly the most practical.'

'I know! Did you see her face, though?'

The woman's Boxer and Milly sniffed each other a little and seemed to get on OK, so I relaxed. Perhaps there were a few friendly people round here after all.

'She called her a yard dog. Can you believe? What does that even mean?' I said, and we both collapsed into laughter.

'I'm Josie,' she said, and held out her hand. 'And this is Gen.'

'I'm Jenny. And, well, you've had quite an introduction to Milly. Is Gen short for something?' I asked, thinking maybe it was Jennifer, like me.

'General Motors!' she said. 'That's where my husband works, in Africa. So I live alone at the moment. Well, my daughter's with me, too. She's at school. Frieda. She's sixteen. And I've got you, haven't I, Gen?' she said and rubbed the Boxer's floppy ears.

After that Josie and I met in the park quite often.

It turned out our walking routines coincided about three to four times a week. She would tell me about her life. She was from Belgium originally, and really was a very sweet lady. She always listened to what I said, and we were good company for one another on our walks. It was also good for Milly to have a friend in Gen, to help socialize her in those early days.

As the weeks went by, I began to tell Josie about my wedding plans. I was getting a bit nervous. We were to have a very small wedding, just family, but it felt like a lot to organize.

'I'm wearing this yellow sash,' I said to her one morning on our walk. 'I hope it looks OK. Do you think yellow's a good idea?'

'You'll look lovely, I'm sure.'

'But I'm so nervous. Of tripping on the dress or something. Or what if I can't speak in front of everyone?'

'You'll be just fine.' I hoped she was right.

Eventually the big day came. When we got outside after the ceremony, everyone threw rose petals over us and took photos. I caught sight of a person carrying a big bunch of yellow roses just outside the porch of the church.

'Who's that?' I whispered to Stephen.

'Not sure,' he said.

Then a face appeared from behind the enormous bouquet.

'Congratulations, you two.'

It was Josie, with her dog, Gen, the Boxer. We hadn't been able to invite any friends, really, because we had to keep it so small, but she had come all the way to the church anyway, just to give us these beautiful roses as we came out.

'Yellow, to match your sash,' she said. 'I didn't forget.'

'Oh, they're absolutely beautiful,' I said, inhaling their scent.

I was so moved by her gesture I gave Josie a big hug.

Soon after the wedding, I got pregnant with my first child. Stephen was, of course, over the moon. Alexandra, my first little girl, was born, and then one and a half years later we had another daughter, Rachel. Finally we had our son, Alistair. Within eight years we had gone from just the two of us, to three children and a boisterous dog.

When I had the babies I stopped working to look after them, and having a dog became even more of a lifeline. It got me out and about with the children, which was great for them, too. And living where we did we even got the occasional glimpse of the high life on our dog walks.

One crisp February day, I was walking with Josie around Kensington Gardens. We were crunching in the frost, wrapped up in gloves and scarves. I had my eldest child, Alex, in the pushchair.

'Who's that glamorous woman?' I asked in a low whisper.

'I don't know, but more to the point, who's that handsome man with her?' said Josie.

The woman walking towards us really was striking, a shock of blonde hair and a clear, aquiline face. The man was dressed in a sharp suit and appeared to be talking into something on his collar. As we got closer I noticed that it was a little radio close to his ear, and I realized it was a bodyguard.

'Actually, you know who that is, don't you?' said Josie.

'Who?'

'Princess Diana, isn't it?'

I looked back at them; they were laughing in the winter sunshine. Sure enough, it was her, and she had her little boy with her in a pram, Prince William.

'You see it all here, don't you? Even royalty! It's so nice that she's just out walking, like us. Makes her seem more real somehow.'

Once we had our family, the flat in Notting Hill began to feel too small so we moved, first to Kew, and then to Twickenham, to the house we live in now, which fits us all in comfortably. We've always had lots of parks around us, and walking Milly became a really important part of the children's lives growing up. We would walk her together at the weekends in Bushy Park and it helped form a really strong family bond between us all.

When Milly got ill, after twelve years, it felt like an absolute tragedy. And when we agreed with the vet that she was in too much pain to go on, it was heartbreaking for the whole family. I felt strongly that I wanted to be there when the vet put her to sleep; even though it was difficult, I owed her that – she'd given us so much. And, in a way, I felt lucky to be able to do that for her. She was so weak and in so much pain she could hardly look up before they gave her the injection. But it was all very gentle and she went peacefully. Afterwards I was left with the image of her little face resting on the vet's bench, before I turned to go.

'We can't get another dog yet,' said Stephen, the next morning over breakfast. He really was very upset, and it sounded like he had been thinking about it a lot. 'Out of respect for Milly,' he went on. 'I think it's a mistake to try to replace her.'

I agreed with him. You can't just suddenly replace something you've loved that much. We ended up waiting for three years, though we did get a cat, Tosca, in the meantime. But after a while we longed for another dog.

When we went to Battersea for the second time, it had been completely modernized. The first time we had been it was the early eighties, now it was the mid nineties. They had new kennels, and a new selection process for finding suitable owners. We were taken into an interview room and a lady there took a look at a long form we had filled out about our lifestyle. It asked whether we had a garden, children, any pets we had owned, and so on.

When we went to look round at the dogs, we found Lily, who was a puppy at the time. She was an adorable little black and white thing, with a lot of Jack Russell in her, but she was a bit bigger than a pure Jack Russell pup would be.

When we got Lily home we introduced her to our cat, Tosca. As soon as they met, we knew the cat was going to be in charge. We have since found out that Lily has a tendency to chase cats, but she has never chased Tosca. I don't know whether they had a little scuffle at some point and the cat won, but we would often see Lily sitting at the bottom of the stairs, waiting for ages for the cat to move, just so she could go up there. Tosca really was the boss in that relationship.

Lily may have liked being playful, and chasing other cats, but she is not at all aggressive. She's never snapped or anything like that. In that sense, she is very similar to Milly. Not in looks – they were a different size, breed and colour – but both were very loyal and quite easy to train.

The kids all loved Lily instantly, and we even took her on holiday with us a few times. But once in a while she got into a bit of a scrape, like the time we were all on a family holiday together in Norfolk. My youngest child, Alistair, was nine years old, and we took Lily to a National Trust property called Oxburgh Hall on a long walk. We had taken Lily through a stream, and she was leaping about, shaking her wet fur all over the place. Alistair was throwing a stick, which was almost as big as him, and the dog was getting closer and closer to a fence with cattle grazing behind it.

'Don't throw that stick any more,' said Stephen. 'You're getting the dog over-excited, with all these cows around.' Alistair was quite a boisterous little boy.

'Oh, Dad. She likes it,' he said, with an impish smile. 'Just one more!' And he ran off, shouting at the top of his voice, completely ignoring us. I was worried about Lily running amongst the cattle, but that turned out to be the least of our worries.

We saw Alistair throwing the stick one more time, as far as he could, and he called out for Lily to go and fetch it. 'I said no more!' shouted Stephen. But it was too late. Lily had run right up to the fence. Then we heard a horrible yelping, the dog ran off in the other direction and then stopped.

'What's up with her? That didn't sound good,' said Stephen, and we all walked over quickly to see what had happened.

'I don't know,' said Alistair, who had come to meet us there, looking sheepish. 'I didn't do anything. Just threw the stick.' By the time we got to Lily she was standing, totally stiff, with her eyes staring out into the distance. Her legs were shaking quite a bit, so I stroked her coat gently.

'Are you all right, little pet? What happened?'

I looked up in desperation, and just behind Stephen I saw a big red and white sign: 'Danger: Electric Fence'.

'She's been electrocuted!'

'And she was wet, too,' said Stephen. 'That can't have helped. Look at her. She's in shock.'

'Let's get her back,' I said, and looked over at Alistair, who had gone quite quiet. 'You naughty boy,' I said weakly. 'We told you not to throw that stick.'

I felt absolutely sure Lily was going to die there and then, and was close to tears with worry. I was too concerned to scold Alistair properly at the time, but I think he must have felt terrible about it, as he hardly spoke all the way back to the holiday cottage. When we got there, we took Lily upstairs and she lay on our bed with the lights out.

'She just wants to be in the dark, I think,' I said, and I stroked her head as she lay there, breathing deeply in and out.

'Thank God she's a young dog, or she would have died, and that's for sure,' said Stephen. 'I don't know what voltage went through her, but it must have been high.'

'I know. She's not very big, and she was wet. The combination must have been awful.'

Even after a check-up at the vets it took Lily several weeks to get back to health after her shock that day. But as it turned out, Alistair would have a second chance to redeem himself for throwing that stick.

By the time we had moved to Twickenham, my friend Josie had gone to live in Germany. We used to write to each other quite often. I would tell her how the children were doing, and she would tell me about her daughter Frieda, who had stayed on in England after her schooling here.

One day, Frieda knocked on the door. I was delighted to see her. I remembered her when she was just a little girl. But it turned out she had come round to tell me the awful news that her mother had terminal cancer. I was so shocked I could hardly speak. Josie was only sixty. It was just too young.

I wrote Josie a long letter, and we chatted on the phone quite a lot as she got sicker. Then one day the inevitable news came that Josie had died. Even though I had known she was ill, it was devastating. She had been so kind to me when I was first in London. Before she died, she had asked me to look out for Frieda, who was still quite young at the time. And it was important to Frieda, too, that I had known her mother. We became great friends, and she still lives just round the corner from us.

Losing a good friend meant that it was even more important to me to have Lily there, always chirpy no matter how I was feeling; wagging her tail for a walk whatever the weather.

It was through Lily that I met another good friend. I used to walk Lily at a regular time on the way to school with Alistair, and there was a lady I saw every day with a black Labrador called Guinness. We got chatting, and when she found out I was Australian she told me about another Australian woman, who also had a Lab, that she knew who lived nearby.

'I think she's a bit lonely. You haven't met her, but I think you'd get on. I'll ask her to call you, if that's OK. She could use a friend.'

'Of course,' I said, and I gave her my number.

I waited for a while, but the woman never rang me, which is unusual for an Aussie, so I thought, I'll ring her instead, maybe she's a bit shy. When we eventually met up, Susie and I became great friends. We would go for long walks with Lily and her Labrador, Lolly. She told me about how she had lived here for five years but had hardly met anyone, and we were good company for one another, talking about back home and all the things about Australia we missed. I was very sad when she decided to move back to Adelaide, where she was originally from.

'We're going to take Lolly,' she said. 'Six months' quarantine it'll be. But I couldn't bear to be parted from her, so it's worth it.'

Not long after they had got Lolly back to Australia, though, the poor animal died. Susie was so upset, she swore she could never replace her. Some weeks later, however, we were chatting on the phone and she told me that she had got Lolly from a breeder in Petworth, and that, by chance, she had come across a dog breeder living in Melbourne with the same name. She had rung them, not expecting anything, but it turned out they had emigrated from Petworth and taken their Labradors with them and bred them there. It was the same breeder she had bought Lolly from.

'You'll never guess,' she said to me later, on the phone. 'They've got relatives of Lolly here! In Melbourne!'

Amazingly, these dogs they had were from the same gene pool, so the pups in Australia were probably cousins or something of Lolly from Petworth. Having thought she'd have no dog ever again, Susie decided it would be OK to replace Lolly with one of her relatives after all.

I know how hard it is to replace a dog, after losing my childhood dogs back home in Australia, and poor Milly. And it wasn't long before we thought we were facing the dilemma again, with Lily.

One place we loved to walk with her outside London was near to Stephen's mum and dad's house. They live in Sussex and we would always take Lily with us when we went to visit them. It was a very hot Easter weekend, and the whole family had gone together to their house for a nice Sunday dinner. Once the meat was roasting in the oven, we decided to go with the children and Stephen's dad for a long walk through the fields around the house to build up our appetites.

We had been walking for about two hours down a steep, rocky hill. We were about to set off back to the house when Lily started chasing something in the long grass.

'Look at her go!' said Alistair, who was by now about fourteen. 'She loves it here. She's a proper hunter.'

But there followed a horrible yelp, and then an ominous silence. It brought back to me memories of my own dogs when they had been bitten by ticks when I was a child. I knew that yelp and it meant pain. When we got to Lily she was sitting in the grass, unable to move, just as she had been after the electric fence incident.

'Could have been a wasp,' suggested Stephen's dad. 'Looks like her lips are a bit puffy.'

'Yes, it's probably that,' I said. 'I hope she doesn't get anaphylactic shock. We might have to get her injected.'

Then, without a word, Alistair pushed past us and picked her up. She was a dead weight, and must have been very heavy.

'What are you doing, love?' I asked him.

'Come on. Let's get you home,' he whispered in Lily's ear.

It was a scorching hot day, dusty and stifling, and it must have been quite an effort for Alistair walking for about half a mile, back up the steep hill, carrying the dog. He didn't make a fuss. He was so gentle with her. It was as if a friend had been injured in battle or something, and he just knew he had to get her home, and did whatever it took.

I suppose now, looking back on it, that Alistair may have been subconsciously making amends for his part in the previous incident with the electric fence, but it was also just the right thing for him to do at the time. As he spoke calmly to Lily to keep her alert, she just stared into space like a zombie.

'She's frothing at the mouth now,' said Stephen when we got to the top of the hill.

'That's not good,' said his dad. 'Not sure that's just a wasp. I'll get the tractor.'

And we used that to get her the rest of the way back across the rocky landscape to the house.

When we got there, Stephen's mum was already dishing things out for lunch. Alistair put Lily in her little dog bed by the dinner table, so we could keep an eye out for her.

But the whole time we were eating, we just kept looking over and couldn't concentrate at all.

'Her nose is swelling up,' I said, as her face began to puff up more and more.

'I know. It's getting worse. I think we should take her straight to the vet,' said Alistair. 'She's not right.'

We all agreed, and took her right away to an emergency vet in Midhurst. By the time we got there, her mouth had blown up like a football. It was so swollen she looked like a comical cartoon character, and it would have been quite funny if we weren't all so worried.

We had to carry Lily into the surgery because she still couldn't walk, and were greeted by a vet from New Zealand who took a good look at Lily's mouth.

'Can't see it clearly enough at the moment,' she said. Lily always was a bit of a drama queen, and as well as the swelling she was whining and whimpering on the table, making it quite difficult to get a look.

'I'll need to give her an IV, steroids, some painkillers and some antibiotics to keep down the swelling and the pain. Is that OK?' the vet asked.

We didn't have dog insurance, and in the end it cost about £300. Considering it was Easter Sunday, so an emergency appointment, this didn't seem too bad.

'Now, I know I said I can't see anything,' said the vet as she inspected Lily's head, 'but back home we see quite a lot of this kind of thing. And more often than not it's a snake bite. But I can't be sure yet.'

'Snake bite!' I said. This hadn't even occurred to me. I was familiar with snakes, of course, from Australia, but I had never associated them with England.

'Well, actually you do get adders in Sussex. I used to see them as a child sometimes. So it's not impossible, I suppose,' said Stephen. 'It's a very hot day. I wouldn't be surprised if they were out basking, just out of hibernation, and Lily ran up to play with one.'

'Yes, she does love to play with anything that moves. Squirrels or rabbits and things,' I said.

'Well, as I say, it's not definite,' said the vet. 'I should know in a while. If you leave Lily here overnight, we'll put her on a drip and do some tests and you can come back in the morning.'

'Perhaps it's best if we go then,' I said. Lily was really in a lot of pain, yelping and howling. 'The sooner we leave, the sooner you can get on with making her better, can't you?'

That evening was awful. We all sat round in Stephen's parents' house, trying to make conversation, but none of us could concentrate. We didn't know if the snake bite, or whatever it was, would be fatal. Would Lily even make it through the night? Eventually we all got an early night, and went back to the vets as soon as we could, first thing in the morning.

'She's lucky to be alive,' said the vet as we walked back through to the surgery.

I was relieved to hear at least that she was still alive. And there was Lily on the bench, still quite sedated, but definitely breathing.

'If you hadn't brought her in here when you did, she would almost certainly have died.'

'Goodness!' I said. 'Was it that bad?'

'Well, I got the swelling down, and, as I thought, I could

see the snake bite on her lip very clearly. Definitely an adder. I recognized it straight away. They're really very poisonous. She must be tough, this one.'

'She has at least two lives,' said Stephen, and told the vet about how Lily had survived the electric fence too.

We took her home and before long she was back on her feet and just as playful as ever. Since her two scrapes with death, Lily has gone on to live a long and healthy life.

A lot has happened since we collected her as a lively little pup from Battersea. She has become a real part of our family, and even featured in the Battersea magazine *Paws* recently, when we had a Jubilee party on our street. There was a dog-jumping competition. We took Lily up to the jump, but she took one look at it as if to say, 'No thanks!'

Well, you can't blame her. She is sixteen now. And having made it this far, after all she's been through, perhaps she's allowed to take it easy.

Benji: An Adventurous Adoptee

When dogs come in to Battersea Dogs & Cats Home they are cared for by our animal welfare team, which looks after the dogs on a daily basis. We also have many wonderful dog socializers and kennel volunteers who walk and socialize our dogs regularly. With around 400 dogs at Battersea at any one time, if you added up the total distance covered on walks by volunteers and our dogs last year, it would stretch for many thousands of miles.

You might also find it surprising to learn that many of our dogs enjoy listening to classical music in their kennels. Our staff do everything they can to make a stay at Battersea calm but interesting. Although we try to make their time in kennels as comfortable as possible, we want nothing more than to find a proper home for the dogs who come here. And, as was the case with Chris, who was dedicated to rehoming a Battersea dog, some people will also go to extraordinary lengths to take their new canine friends home.

Our house isn't exactly lacking inhabitants. We have six children, ranging from the eldest who's twenty-one years old down to little Harvey, who's seven. What with outlying grandparents to visit, two cats and a lively black Labrador, our life is far from quiet.

But there's always room for one more.

We – that's my wife Nichola and I, and our brood – live in a rural parish called Castel, on the island of Guernsey, in an old farmhouse about a fifteen-minute walk from the beach. Having a family of three girls and three boys is fine if you operate a buddy system. We have Lee and Augusta, Cecily and Geneve, Sam and Harvey.

Having moved into a new house, we decided that we must get a pal for dear old Daisy, our rescue Labrador. She was a victim of divorce, and came to us by chance when her previous owner moved into a small flat. We knew we didn't want another big dog – having six kids as well, one big dog is enough – so we wanted to find a smaller one.

'Two dogs are very companionable with each other,' I said to Nichola one morning. 'But I don't want another mad Beagle, like Monty.' One of our previous dogs had been a real handful.

'I like terriers,' said Nichola. 'They're intelligent, very family-orientated and quite naughty. I like that in a dog. I think we should try to find a dog we can give a chance to. Another rescue dog or a bit of a problem dog. So we can give them a good life,' she went on thoughtfully.

'We'll end up with thirty-six dogs if you have it your way,' I said. Then the children started coming down for breakfast and joining in the conversation.

'Why do we have to keep getting more animals, anyway?' asked Augusta. She can't bear smells or dirt or anything mucky.

'We need different kinds of animals as well as more dogs,' said Cecily. 'A goat, some ducks and . . . a tortoise?'

'A big one you can ride on,' chipped in her younger sister, Geneve.

'Tortoises don't do anything. They just sit there looking

ugly and sleep half the year. And goats smell and ducks poo everywhere,' said Augusta.

'If we do get another dog,' asked Harvey, 'can it live in my room? Under my bed? I'll make it a nest.'

'Dogs don't live in nests!' laughed Sam. 'They live in hides.'

'That's birdwatchers. Dogs live in dens. Like foxes,' said Augusta.

'No, they don't, they live in lairs. Like wolves,' I laughed, and began to clear away the plates. We were all about to be late for school if we kept up this debate.

'Well, either way,' said Augusta, 'I don't care as long as it doesn't leave hairs all over my bed. Or bits of food and bones everywhere.'

Lee, our eldest child, stayed quiet. He is more keen on his guitar than anything else, and if a person or an animal can't play it he's not that interested.

Once we'd all agreed we were getting a dog and decided we were looking for one that had a bit of a history, we realized that it's actually quite difficult, living on Guernsey, to get a dog. They're so popular they get snapped up quickly. Since we were willing to give a dog that hadn't had a good start an opportunity, we decided to look at the Battersea Dogs & Cats Home website. I worked in London every couple of weeks and had often been past it. There were one or two dogs on the website, but in the end we rang them and asked the woman there to keep an eye out for us. Over New Year they rang back.

'You'll have to go through our various procedures. Come and see us and so on,' said the woman there. 'And as you've got a dog, two cats and children, you'll have to bring them all along to see the dog as well, if you find one that's suitable. To check they all get along OK.'

'But we live in Guernsey,' I said, getting concerned. 'It would be a real upheaval for all of us to come. Not to mention the cost. But we really would like a rescue dog. Is there any other option?'

After a bit of discussion, the supervisor was satisfied that we knew what we were getting in to. I suggested that if we took on a dog and brought it back here and the dog didn't get on with our family, I would go to see the guys at GSPCA here in Guernsey, and we would rehome it and make sure everyone was happy. I felt determined we should get a dog from Battersea. They agreed to this and not long after that they rang back to say they'd found a dog in need of some TLC that might just suit us.

'He's a bit of a problem; he's not a dog who can be left closed up in a small space alone. He needs company and the outdoors,' the lady from Battersea said.

'Well, I do a lot of work from home and my wife is home most of the day, so he won't be alone. He'll have a companion in Daisy, and we've got a park nearby, so . . . it sounds fine. When can I come and see him?'

I thought I'd better check with the rest of the family first, though, so later that evening we looked on the website at the dog they had picked out and everyone burst out laughing.

'He looks funny!' said Cecily. 'I want him!'

He did look rather odd: really short legs, a long body and a straggly terrier face.

'He looks like trouble,' said Augusta.

'Has he got a name?' asked Harvey, prodding the screen.

'Benji,' I said.

Benji looked a bit like a cross between a Dachshund and a Yorkshire Terrier but we had no idea what he really was.

'Oh, it breaks the heart, though. To hear his story,' said Nichola. 'He's been returned about three times they said. And he's only a baby. Well. What's the worst that can happen?' she went on. 'When we had our menagerie at home, you know Mum and Dad had everything, and the only dog that wasn't a rescue was a Schnauzer who was as mad as a hatter and cost a fortune. So you can't guarantee anything anyway. You get what you get.'

'Yes. I think it would be a positive thing, to give him a new life. He obviously doesn't want to be by himself in a flat. Battersea were worried about that, weren't they? So he doesn't like being cooped up. But if he can't survive here with all this space, then I don't know where,' I said.

Nichola and I were obviously talking each other into getting this little dog. As so many had struggled with him it sounded like he needed us as much as we needed him. It seemed like a no-brainer. I brought a work trip to London closer and arranged to see Benji then.

When I arrived, they took me into a playroom where there was this trembling, nervous little thing waiting for me. He was obviously a bit of a desperate case.

'He has been back to us three times. I'm not sure why he was sent here the first time, but in one place he chewed the legs off the kitchen cabinet,' said the woman holding his lead. He was hiding behind her legs and shaking.

'I think because he was locked in the kitchen all day,' she went on, 'he was really unhappy. Then he went to another lady, but she brought him back after twenty-four hours because she couldn't leave him outside the bedroom. He would just bark and howl all night. He was lonely. And so here he is again . . . and we're at a bit of a loss now what to do about him.'

'Well, he looks a cutie to me,' I said, stroking his little face. He started to wag his tail and slowly emerge from his hiding place. I gave him a cuddle, and took some photos to show the family. When I left, I rang Nichola; everyone was crowded around the phone, asking about him. Even Augusta was curious.

'Bless him, he is cute. You'll all fall for him,' I told them. 'Ooh, one thing, though. They did a cat test and . . . turns out he doesn't like cats much. So, nothing like a challenge.'

'What do you think, then?' asked Nichola, once the kids had wandered off. 'Realistically?'

'I think – realistically – let's give Benji a new home.'

Now we just had to work out how to get this nervous little terrier, who nobody wanted, on the 200-mile journey to Guernsey in the dead of winter. The usual way would be via Condor Ferries, and we could do that without too much trouble on a good day. But during the winter the ferries don't run every day, and only the freight ferry runs in bad weather . . . and wouldn't you know it, the week I was due to go and collect Benji it was blowing up a proper gale and no passenger ferries were running.

'Eight hours of bouncing around. Well, if that's the only way, it's better than nothing.'

But the way our luck was running, the schedule meant I'd have to stay in a hotel for a couple of days.

What about a plane? I thought. 'I'll ring the chaps at the aero club.'

So I phoned round a few mates I know who were into flying small aircraft, and found a fellow called Alan, a private pilot, who'd done this kind of run to England a few times before.

'Hello, Alan?' I said. 'I need to go to London to collect a dog. But the ferries are off so I'm in a bit of a spot. Wondered if you could help out at all?'

'Oh, I get asked to do that all the time,' he said cheerfully. 'I'm very happy to. Keeps up my flying hours. You just pay for the fuel. I've done this for a few people actually. Dogs and Kennel Club, type of thing. I picked up one for old Tucker last year. Cracking little Pekingese. We landed there, got the dog, and flew back in no time.'

'Well, actually. I want to get near to Battersea. How close can you get?'

'Battersea?' There was something of a silence.

'Well, yes, actually I'm going to pick up this Heinz 57 Variety. From the Dogs' Home there.'

There was another pause at the end of the line. I could only imagine Alan was wondering whether he had been called up by a complete nutter or if a mate of his was pulling a prank.

'Well . . . if you're really serious,' he said eventually, 'I can get you to Biggin Hill. How's that?'

I'd have to get a cab and then a train to Battersea, and back again with the dog, but that would work. So we arranged it all there and then.

By this time it was over a week since we had decided on Benji, and Battersea were ringing up asking when we were coming to collect him. I called and reassured them, but the day before we were due to go the weather went from bad to worse. There were twelve-foot waves in the Channel, so we definitely couldn't use the boat. And then the fog came.

'Sorry, old chap. We can't go tomorrow. Visibility's just too poor,' said Alan.

'But the airlines are flying,' I said desperately. I had rearranged work and everything to make the trip.

'Trouble is, I'm not a commercial pilot. That's the thing. Let's see if we can go Thursday instead. OK?'

So I rearranged my diary again and phoned up Battersea to let them know. But on Wednesday night Alan called again.

'Still a no-go, I'm afraid, old chap. I'll keep you posted.'

I was getting desperate. Battersea were anxious for Benji to be collected, if not they would need to put him back up for adoption, and I was mucking my employer about too. And the bad weather could last for weeks.

I walked Daisy round the park, mulling it all over, when a figure appeared from nowhere. As he got closer, I realized it was Malcolm, the managing director of the local airline, Aurigny, out with his two little beautifully trimmed dogs. Guernsey's a small island, so you do bump into people like that.

'Malcolm!' I said, explaining my predicament. 'It must be fate. I'm in absolute desperate straits – the boats aren't running. Is there any chance you can help at all?'

'Well, as it happens, we are one of the few airlines who

do take animals,' he said. 'You can't take a dog on an ordinary airliner, but you can fly it back from Southampton with us on the trilander. It goes via Alderney.'

'That's great,' I said, slapping him on the back with relief. 'How do I book it?'

'Just get hold of the office and tell them you spoke to me and you want to bring a dog and they'll book a seat for him.'

'I don't suppose it's like with a child, where you get it for half price, is it?'

'Now you're pushing it, Chris,' he said with a raised eyebrow and a smile. And he strode off with his little dogs at his heels.

So I phoned Aurigny and said I'd like to bring a dog back to Guernsey. It was as easy as that. And the very next day I flew out to Gatwick on the ordinary flight, then took the train to Battersea.

'We were so glad you made it,' said the woman who brought him out. 'He's been getting really anxious. He's been jabbed and neutered, so he's all ready to go.' And there was little Benji, wagging his tail and waiting, though for what I doubt he had any idea.

I was fully prepared, with my backpack on, a new lead, a rubberized blanket for the aircraft, water bowl, treats, a muzzle and everything but the kitchen sink. Poor old Benji didn't know what he was in for that day. Then again, neither did I. I didn't know how well he would behave on our journey, especially on the plane. He might freak out. And we didn't know how he was going to behave when he got home, either. Would he get on with Daisy? And would he cope with all the children?

Once the paperwork was all signed, off we trotted through the gates. But just as I got outside, Benji at my side, all excited about what was happening, I realized I had forgotten to ask whether you can take a dog on a train! I hadn't even thought about it. I'm going to have to take a taxi all the way to Southampton, I thought. That's going to cost a small fortune. I quickly made some enquiries and, luckily, it turns out you can take a dog on a train, so Benji sat next to me on his blanket, looking out of the window as the world whizzed by. Then he curled up and dropped off to sleep. So far, so good.

When we got to Southampton Airport, the man at the desk looked at me, looked at the dog and then looked back at me.

'Hmm. You're flying to the Channel Islands, aren't you?'

'Yes, that's right,' I said, showing him my ticket which said 'Chris Oliver', and then, next to that, 'Dog Oliver'.

Taking a dog through airport security is one of the strangest things I've ever done. He even had to go through the scanner, but luckily he didn't try to smuggle anything through. Once that was all over, we went upstairs to the bar and sat down; he had a bowl of water and I had a pint. We both looked out of the window and watched planes taking off and landing. A few people came up and stroked him, but most people were very British and just observed slyly from afar. One man reading a magazine kept glancing up, looking at Benji, then putting his nose back down. The third time he did this I noticed that his magazine was upside down.

'You don't have the faintest idea what's in store, do

you?' I said to my canine companion. He looked up at me and wagged his tail. He knew one thing, at least: he wasn't in a kennel any more.

The trilander plane is a tiny sixteen-seater, with just a few steps up to board it. It has small wheels, two at the back and one at the front, and a couple of windows along each side, with a propeller on each wing and another one on the tail. There are no cabin crew on board, just the pilot.

Inside there were seven rows of two seats, the passengers all squeezed in. Benji had his own seat next to mine, but I don't think he paid much attention to the safety notices. And he was very lost and confused once we started flying. The plane, being so small, was bumpy and very noisy, like flying must have been in the 1930s. Outside, it was starting to get dark, but we got a good look at Southampton from the air, and as we flew across the Channel I could make out ship lights and faint trails of whipped up white sea, the sun sinking below the horizon with a flash of orange.

Alderney airstrip is just a thin piece of runway in a field. By the time we landed it was dark, and men came with lights and fluorescent jackets to open the door from the outside. Everyone else got off, but Benji was fast asleep, curled up in the seat next to me.

'Are you going on to Guernsey? It's a fifteen-minute wait. Do you want to get out?' asked a fellow with a yellow jacket on.

'We're really settled. Can we just stay here?' I said. So all of a sudden the little plane was completely empty. We sat there, just the two of us in the silence, waiting for the pilot and the new passengers to come on board. After another rocky take-off, we flew the final, noisy leg, and in just fifteen minutes we arrived on Guernsey.

Guernsey airport is very small, with a large bank of windows overlooking the runway. When we landed, the whole family were standing upstairs, looking down on the little trilander, while Benji had his nose up against the plane's window. The airport crew brought the steps round and I carried the little fluff bundle off the plane. As I put him down on the tarmac, he stood there for a while and looked as if he was thinking, 'Oh hell, where have you brought me now?'

'Come on, Benji,' I said. 'We're home!'

It was quite windy and he looked so vulnerable and nervous as he trotted across the tarmac. I walked through the door marked 'Nothing to Declare', and there they all were, Nichola and all the children crowding round and fighting to get in front, to get a look. Benji and I just stood in the doorway, blinking.

'Smile,' said Nichola and took a photo. 'Oh, look at him, he's such a little dear!' she said, rushing over.

Everyone was jostling to get the first cuddle, but Benji looked as though he wanted to get right back on the plane. 'Oh hell no, I can't do this,' he seemed to say, as they all stood there, grinning. He was shivering with little trembles all over.

'Keep back, you lot,' said Nichola. 'He's a nervous little thing, isn't he? Let's not frighten him.'

'It's been one heck of a journey,' I said. 'But he was all right, considering. He even had his own seat.'

In the end we had more trouble controlling the children

than the dog. But it was really exciting for them; they love anything new, and if it's a thing you can play with, even better. All the way home the girls just wanted to mother him and cuddle him. It was too much for Benji. He'd had such a lot going on that day that when we got home he was nervous, clinging to me and under my feet whenever I moved. We thought it best to leave him alone to calm down for a bit. He hid behind the sofa.

Daisy the Labrador was very curious, and kept going over to sniff him. Eventually he started to sniff around her a little bit too.

'Why don't we put down that old dog duvet Daisy uses? We can put it outside our bedroom door and leave Benji with her. See how they get on?' I suggested.

'Good idea,' said Nichola. 'And if it doesn't work out we can always put him in the crate in the dining room to settle down.'

So when it was bedtime we showed him to the duvet, and were all prepared for a night of howling. But Benji just looked around, sniffed a couple of times and then set-tled down with a little sigh. When we woke up the following morning, Benji and Daisy were pressed right up against the bedroom door, the pair of them curled up together asleep.

I had to go to Jersey for the day, so Nichola kept an eye on Benji and kept him company. He was fine, but when I came home he went mad and hid behind the sofa again.

'He must be used to being abandoned,' I said, peering round at his shivering face. 'He's probably used to seeing someone once, then leaving and not coming back.'

'You might be the harbinger of travel, too,' said Nichola.

'He probably thinks you're going to take him on another horrendous journey.'

We put together a bed and got his own blanket for him, and after a day or so Benji decided we were friends and started to hang about by my feet again.

We always have a lot of people dropping by, and we had told our friends we were getting this little dog, that he was a bit of a pickle and we were trying to keep things quiet for a while. We asked visitors to tap on the door instead of walking straight in the house, as they were used to doing, and when we herd someone at the door we'd pick up Benji and take him into another room, then introduce them carefully. He'd run away and hide a lot at first, go down on his haunches and make himself very small, sometimes peeing himself when we picked him up. It was a very threatened pose he adopted and was quite distressing to see.

'Dogs are easily cured,' I said. 'Let's get him outside for a walk with Daisy. He'll soon get into it.' And it was true, once we were outside, all the new sights and smells and running after Daisy soon distracted him from his nervousness.

Having Daisy made everything a lot easier. She is an extremely affectionate Labrador and Benji began to look on her as something of a role model. She is very laid back, not fazed at all and it didn't bother her that there was another dog in the house. She's the type of dog who will come up to you if you're on the sofa and put her head on your lap and look up, or when you're standing she'll come up to you, bang her head against your leg and hold it there to give you a cuddle and get some attention. Within a couple of days Benji was stuck to her like glue and imitating her movements. We didn't do anything. We just left them to it and they made their own relationship. He's been completely reliant on her ever since.

We also found out pretty soon that Benji especially loves people with red hair. If you're blonde it will take him a while. We don't know why, but with one of our friends, a blonde-haired girl, it took about half a dozen or so visits before he stopped running away when she came to the house. Girls with red hair he absolutely loves. He tends to be more reticent with boys, too. But slowly, as he got used to people, their voices, who they were and what they smelt like it became a lot easier.

Battersea hadn't known exactly how old he was – between one and two, perhaps – but we thought he looked and behaved very immaturely, so we decided he was no older than eighteen months old. And despite being returned so many times, he's not a bad dog at all.

'I just can't understand why anybody would give him back so quickly,' said Nichola, one afternoon when the dogs were outside running around. 'The way he was returned, anyone would think he was a terror.'

He is quite crazy, and he doesn't always know the limits, but he's the most affectionate dog you've ever met and a very good little housedog too. We think that if he had continued being returned again and again, he would have quite soon become a very unsociable dog, and his future would have been grim. So we were extremely happy we could take him in and give him a new home.

We had no idea how Benji would react in a car. Daisy has always been a companion dog and is very happy to go everywhere with us in the car. She'll sit in the passenger seat and look out of the front windscreen, as if she's doing the driving. But we didn't know what Benji would be like. The first time he came with us, we put them both in the back together. By the time we got to the petrol station, he was on the floor whining and whimpering. He didn't like it at all, so we turned round and took him home, by which time he'd been sick.

The next time we got in the car, we thought he'd hate it again. But he insisted on getting in with us anyway. He sat on the back seat, looking out of the window, then poked his head in the middle of the two front seats and tried to climb over the handbrake to the front, to see what was going on. When we got out of the car, both dogs jumped into the front seat as if they were going to take over.

'They think they're human!' laughed Nichola.

They did look like they were about to drive off and start a new life together somewhere.

It took a while before we could let Benji off the lead on our walks, and he can still be a bit of a scamp even now. But wherever we go, Daisy takes charge. Benji will sniff around of his own accord, then, if he looks up and she's on the move, he'll follow her. So if you control Daisy you control Benji.

Once, a rather prim lady stopped us in the park. She didn't like the fact that Daisy was off the lead.

'You have let your dog off the lead,' she said sharply. 'I don't think that's right, you know.'

'Well, you've got to let them have a run, haven't you?' I said. 'Anyway, she's not being naughty. They're both very well behaved, actually.'

Then she spotted Benji.

'What's that . . . thing?' she said, with a look of disdain. 'I've never seen a dog like that before.'

'Oh, him,' I said, unable to resist some fun. 'He's a long-haired, short-legged Alsatian. Very rare.' I only just managed to keep a straight face.

'Right. Oh, yes. Of course it is,' she said, taken aback, and trotted off with her little perfect dog in tow. It tickled me pink. You do get some funny people about.

Benji is a funny looking dog. Because he's so hairy and scruffy he looks quite bizarre when he sleeps; he's often wedged up against things, on his back, legs in the air, or twisted double with his head in our shoes or bags.

He can get quite over-excited on occasion. When the kids are all running around he jumps up and nips them, just gently, wanting to play. He likes to annoy Daisy too, and constantly pesters her for attention. If he wants to play, he nips her undercarriage. Or he'll literally walk under her body to get her to notice him. She can get quite annoyed by this, because she's an old girl now. After a while, she'll pick up a paw and put it on his head as if to say, 'Now that's enough', then walk away. Or, alternatively, she'll sit on him so that you can just see his little head poking out from under her bottom. 'OK, I've got the message,' he huffs and leaves her alone for a bit. But he can't bear being separated from her for too long.

Daisy absolutely loves the sea. She's always been a water dog, like lots of Labradors, and wherever it is, no matter how manky, even a puddle, she'll get in and you can't get her out. So we go down to the beach a lot and Daisy's straight in there. Eager to join in the fun, Benji will follow her. Of course, even a small ripple in the water is really high to him and the waves knock him straight over. Benji wants so much to carry on being with her but because of his short legs he ends up with water up his nose, scrabbling to stay afloat. He does love the wide flat space of the beach, though, and races up and down, picking up seaweed or dead crabs and throwing them in the air.

The way Benji runs with his little legs is hilarious. If the grass in the field is a bit too long, he'll bounce like a spring lamb across the top of it. Daisy just goes through it like a tank. But he's got to hop along behind her and will disappear for a while. Then you see him jumping up and down, trying to orientate himself and work out where we are.

Because he is very keen to please, Benji has been easy to train. He learnt very quickly about manners and that he should do as he's told. He's also very clever and an outrageous flirt. He begs – sitting on his hind legs with two front paws bent on his chest, his back straight, cocking his head slightly to one side with his ears down, looking unbelievably cute. No one taught him this but he likes the reaction he gets, so will do it all the time, for a very long time if need be.

He's a terrible thief, though, really shocking. He will unpack bags, taking out one bit at a time, leaving things on one side until he finds what he requires, which is invariably food, carefully removing the aluminium foil from around sandwiches if necessary. But he doesn't like lettuce, so we're constantly finding bits of green leaf in his lair on the middle landing. That's where he sits to eat things he's pilfered. He must have ruined at least a dozen sandwich boxes since we've had him. If the girls are sitting around on the floor eating, Benji will come up and sit there without them seeing him, then he'll slip a piece of pizza off a plate, so deftly and quietly that no one notices. He looks to one side as if to say, 'What?' when they realize what's happened.

He even got on the table at Christmas. There was some food on the dining table and one of the chairs was left out very slightly. The kids were in the kitchen doing something, and Benji climbed up on to the chair, on to the table, wolfed the food down and scrambled back under the table. When the kids went back in they found him with grease all round his mouth and the food all gone.

Benji doesn't limit himself to food either. He eats shoes, toys . . . in fact, you can never tell what he's going to eat, and we definitely can't afford to leave soft toys around. We have a number of 'war wounded' articles sewn-up or patched. He thinks a soft toy is his and sleeps on it and then chews it methodically to bits. He doesn't do this all the time, he just likes to keep us on our toes.

We're quite a loud, busy family but it doesn't bother the dogs at all, they just join in and go wherever we're going, or sit on the threshold, eagerly waiting for us to get home. These days, far from being the shy little thing he was when he arrived, Benji is a happy, bouncy chap – but one who still gets under our feet wherever we go. He even sneaks under the table and lies on our feet during mealtimes, because he doesn't like to be separated from us. And with the girls, Cecily and Geneve, following us around too, we end up with quite a little train of people and dogs trotting around the house.

Benji got on with the kids almost immediately, especially

the boys. Harvey, who's seven, is the joker of the family and like Benji is a bit mischievous too. (We actually mix their names up sometimes!) Sam, who is eleven, is a gentle, sweet boy who loves being active. Both boys run full-pelt in the park, Benji at their heels. They like to rough and tumble or play football with him. But if Benji can't get the ball he has nipped the occasional ankle. Sam has been known to sit on the skateboard and hold on to Benji's harness as he is pulled along, Harvey running in front.

Even Augusta came round to the new dog in the end, but she does chastise him in her own way. When she comes home and puts down her bag, Benji is there immediately, ready to eat whatever there is left of her lunch. And she stands there, with her hands on her hips, wagging her finger: 'That's not cool, little dude,' she says, while Benji just does his innocent, 'What did I do?' face.

Benji loves the kids. But with the cats, it's a different story. Rosie is an outdoor cat. She's rather imperious and doesn't particularly like any of us. Our other one, Violet, is a home cat and a bit on the peculiar side. When we first got him, Benji tried to attack her but Violet was quicker as she rounded on him, leaving scratches on his nose and wounding his pride. He doesn't bother much any more. He's given up on that sport. You can see he still wants to, but the pain was just too much.

One thing Benji really does love, we've discovered, is being brushed. He will fight you for the attention. He's even tried combing himself before. He holds the handle of his brush in his mouth and hits his leg with it. Or he climbs on top of Daisy when it's her go, to get between her and the brush. One thing he hates, however, is the postman. We didn't think he could get out of the garden, because it's surrounded with fencing, hedging and a wall. But, of course, he did. When he saw the postman's yellow jacket he squeezed through the hedge, around the fence, on to the wall and jumped down into the road, chasing the poor man up the lane. We were horrified, though fortunately the postman managed to get away.

We have to get to the post when it's delivered before Benji does, because he seems to know what is particularly important and go for that. He got hold of Augusta's passport, which now has teeth marks in one corner. And he's particularly fond of letters from the Tax Office. So every morning there's a race to beat Benji to it. Because there's a tiled floor in the hall we do have something of an advantage as he ends up like something from one of those cartoons, his claws sliding all over the tiles – he's like Scooby Doo unable to get started. He's also discovered that if he steps on the mat, the mat keeps going and he bangs his nose on the door. His cartoon tendencies are evident at other times too – if we're outside and he feels he should be in the house, he will trot to the far corner of the back garden, look over his shoulder like a footballer taking a corner shot, then run headlong into the door, making a loud crash. Benji really is a living, breathing comedy routine.

The other thing he hates, perhaps even more than postmen, is the petrol lawn mower. He'll come bounding over to bite the wheels and stand there poised for another sneaky attack, before running off again. He'll come back and try again, and in the end you just have to pick him up and put him out of the way. He is the same with the

Hoover. He obviously feels they are dangerous invaders that need dealing with.

If we go away we don't leave Benji at a kennels because we'd hate him to think we've abandoned him. So a nice man named Peter comes to our house and looks after both dogs. As you might expect, it took Benji a while to get used to this arrangement, but he is fine now, although he would rather we didn't go away at all. He is still a bit nervous with unknown people, noise or crowds but Benji has come such a long way since he was the shivering little creature I brought over on that trilander plane. He's even been featured in the Aurigny in-flight magazine, as one of their proud customers. Everyone loves him. We're really proud of him, would be lost without him and are delighted that we have been able to give him a happy island life.

Lucky: A Very Fortunate Moggie

The team at Battersea Dogs & Cats Home care for around 190 cats and kittens at any one time, and each year around 3,000 new feline friends come through our doors. Life in the cattery is an adventure. You never know what will turn up from one day to the next.

Some of our cats are given to us by people who can no longer keep them, either because of allergies, moving house, separation or divorce and so on. Many owners have to give them up reluctantly. But some are abandoned and left out in the cold. Although it's hard to imagine, we hear all too regularly of kittens being dumped in skips or sealed cardboard boxes, everywhere from recycling plants to local parks. When these cats are brought to Battersea they are given expert treatment by our clinic and nursed back to good health. And most will go on to find a new home, as one lucky little kitten discovered when Douglas Stroud spotted her.

A few things happened last summer that changed my life.

Firstly, just off a motorway outside London, a small bundle was thrown from a car on to a slip road. Inside was a three-week-old black kitten, no bigger than the palm of a hand, which somebody, somewhere, didn't want or couldn't keep any more. Thanks to the kindness of strangers, it ended up at Battersea.

At around the same time that this little kitten was entering the world and about to face the biggest trauma of its life, my wife of forty-three years, Jeanne, was about to leave the world. Her life-support machine was switched off at 2 p.m. on the twentieth of June. Three and a half hours later, she took her last breath.

I first set eyes on Jeanne across the room one night at a dancing club. We would do waltzes and foxtrots, but I couldn't dance very well, and I still can't. I've got three left feet. Anyhow, I asked her to dance and it can't have put her off that much, because after six months I asked her to marry me and she said yes. I'm not a romantic, but I knew she was the one for me. She was a real character. She could be stubborn and very independent, but she was so loving and loyal and we made each other laugh.

Jeanne already had two young children, Belinda and Collette, when we met, and once we were married I adopted them. The children got all this 'you've got a different name to your dad' stuff at school at the time, so I thought it was the right thing to do. Then, in 1973, our daughter Maria was born. I was there for her birth and it was the most miraculous thing I had ever seen, this little vulnerable creature, there in Jeanne's arms. A whole new person in our lives.

Before I met Jeanne I was in the Royal Air Force Air Crash rescue service, putting out fires and rescuing people from crashed fighter planes. When I came out of the RAF I had a few different jobs, first with British Airways fire service, then British AeroSpace, and then BAA Security, checking people going through the scanner at the airport. Finally, I worked for South West Trains, until last year when I retired due to ill health – I've had two knee replacements, cancer of the bowel, and I've just been diagnosed with lung and liver cancer. But at seventy-three I soldier on.

I come from Southend originally, so when we were younger, and the kids were growing up, we'd go down to the seaside together as a family. We took them to see my mother, had an ice cream on the beach and dinner there before coming back home.

Eventually we moved to a three-bedroom house in Surrey and got on with a normal family life: work, home, dinner; birthdays, wedding anniversaries; seeing friends and family, and not forgetting all the parties.

The parties were quite fun actually. We all used to take it in turns along the street to have one and we'd all check on each other's children. One day a bunch of people threw some keys into a pot in the middle of the table. Me and Jeanne just looked at each other, got up and went home. We giggled all the way back. We weren't having any of that rubbish. That was a bit too much.

Animals came into our lives pretty quickly, as Jeanne absolutely adored them. From the day I met her she'd be scouring the newspapers for dogs and cats in need of a new home. First we rescued a dog called Ginty, then Cindy – who had the puppies April and Tricky – and so it went on. After a while our youngest daughter, Maria, started to show dogs. She would spend hours every day learning about it all, and practising walking round showing the dogs with their 'legs square', learning how to keep still, and so on, around the arena. Maria's favourite was this rough-haired Collie she had, and she even got to Crufts with her one year. But unfortunately the Collie dropped her coat – moulted and lost her thick fur – just before the big day. Maria was so upset but there was nothing we could do.

On top of all the dogs, I should perhaps mention that we also had fourteen cats. All at the same time. There was Mummy Trudy, Suzie Ugly, Clara, Candy Snot Box, Sheba, Amy, Corinna, Pepe, Socks . . . and a few more besides. We just sort of accumulated them. One minute they weren't there – then they were. Then one would have kittens and we'd have a load more. They were very much outdoor cats, thankfully, and would spend hours roaming about the neighbourhood. When they came back for feeding time, though, it was madness. You had to split them up – three here, three there, a couple over there – they'd be clambering all over everything, and with the dogs as well it was chaos.

Jeanne was just an absolute sucker for animals, though. If someone said, 'We can't keep them any more,' she'd say, 'Oh, I'll take them.' She just couldn't see an animal hurt or abandoned. She had to protect them.

Mummy Trudy was the worst of the cats. She was a light tortoiseshell we rescued, and she would get pregnant at the drop of a hat. The next thing I knew she'd got a litter of kittens. She had about four or five litters in the end. The funny thing was she would have them in my wardrobe. I don't know how she got in there, but she did, and somehow she'd manage to shut the door too. I'd open it up to get my jacket and there would be a litter of new kittens, all tiny with their eyes shut, wiggling about. And this cheeky little white and ginger-brown cat looking up at me as if butter wouldn't melt.

'Jeanne!' I'd yell downstairs. 'Sort these kittens out, will you?'

Mummy Trudy became Jeanne's cat. In the end we had to physically keep her in so that we could get her spayed so she couldn't get pregnant again.

Suzie Ugly was another one. She was a rescue too. One day, not long after we had got her, my daughter Belinda came in devastated.

'Suzie's gone,' she said, tears streaming down her face. 'She hasn't been back for days.'

'Poor thing. Well, if she doesn't come back soon, she's probably gone to cat heaven. She'll be happy there.'

We had so many other cats to look after we couldn't mourn her for long and we soon acquired another cat that looked very like Suzie. Then, six months later, out of the blue, a strange looking animal turned up on the doorstep. Maria saw her first.

'There's a cat at the door. At least I think it's a cat,' she said warily. 'But it's all disfigured, one eye down here, one up there. Come and look. It's weird.'

We all followed her to the doorstep. I looked at this strange animal, and at first I thought it was the cat we had acquired who looked like Suzie.

'She must have had an accident,' I said. 'But, no, that's not her, she's a bit different. Hang on a mo, then, so where's this one come from?'

We were all very confused.

'But . . . that's Suzie!' said Belinda. The cat was so disfigured we had hardly recognized her.

'Hello, Suzie,' I said. 'You're back, then. You have been through the wars, haven't you?'

'She's Suzie Ugly now, poor thing,' said Maria. And that was how she got her new name.

We still don't know what happened to her. Perhaps she was run over, but she survived it and somehow got home again, after six months away. And she soon joined back in with the other cats as though nothing had ever happened.

Suzie Ugly wasn't the only cat that was in the wars. The girls saw out of the window a little black cat with white feet get hit by a fast-moving car. There was a terrible screeching, the girls screamed and we all ran out. I picked up the poor thing, and carried him limply back to the house.

'It's Socks,' said Maria, in tears. 'Is he . . . dead?'

I felt for his little heartbeat but there was nothing. He had been struck so hard he must have died immediately.

'I'm afraid so,' I said, and we dug a little hole for him in the garden.

Later that night I heard an awful scream from Belinda's bedroom. Then there was a patter of footsteps and the door was flung open.

'Socks! He's back from the dead!' she screamed. She was visibly shaking. 'I saw this white paw, under the stairs . . . and then he, well, he came out from under, but . . . how?'

'Oh my God,' I said. 'That *was* Socks I just buried, wasn't it?'

Just at that moment, Socks came sauntering in and looked at us all. 'What?' he seemed to say, and then wandered out again with his tail in the air.

'Oh no,' said Belinda. 'You've buried someone else's cat!'

We worked out it was our neighbour's cat; I'd only gone

and buried it six feet under. But it had looked so like Socks.

'Well, you'll have to go round there and tell her,' said Jeanne. So I knocked on the door and told her. I felt like a policeman giving someone bad news. 'Oh, by the way, I buried your cat. I'm so sorry, we thought it was ours.'

At least the poor little blighter got a proper send-off.

Although we stopped taking in as many strays, Jeanne still couldn't resist keeping a lookout for the odd one, even after the children had left home. 'Here, Douglas,' she'd say. '"Lovely cat wants a good home." We could have this one, couldn't we?' If we'd had a farm she'd have had about 400 cats and 200 dogs and goodness knows what else. She just loved rescuing animals and that was that.

Besides all the cats, we've always had dogs too. And when our old ones died, we decided to replace them with a couple more rescues. We knew what great work Battersea does, so we went there and found Lily first. She was a little black and white bitch, a cross between a Staffie and a Collie. Jeanne fell for her immediately.

'She was actually born in Battersea,' said the woman who was showing us around. It happens sometimes that a dog comes in pregnant and the team at Battersea have to deal with a whole litter of puppies.

'Ah, bless her little cotton socks,' said Jeanne.

The whole thing was very well processed. They really did a good job of vetting us. After we had spotted Lily they said they'd send someone to visit the house to make sure it was OK. We had a back garden with a six-foot fence, and when the man came and looked over the place he was quite satisfied. But then I suppose it wasn't like we hadn't had much experience with animals!

We were so pleased with Lily, we also got another dog from Battersea five years later, called Jake. He was a Lurcher-Greyhound Cross. We don't know his past, but he was rescued at just a few weeks old, so we had both dogs from pups. Both Lily and Jake are still going. They live with my daughter Belinda now, but we were so happy to give them a new home, and Battersea had done such a good job of taking them in in the first place.

Not long after we got Jake, Clara, Jeanne's favourite cat, died aged twenty-three. Jeanne was so upset. Clara had odd eyes. She was a pure white Cornish Rex and Jeanne doted on her. She was about two or three when we got her, and at first she wouldn't go near anyone. Somebody had been cruel to her, we think, and it took a long time for her to trust us. She went through a dog attack and all sorts, but she was a tough cookie. That cat had been special to Jeanne and had outlived all the other cats, despite all her hardships. We had no other cats left after that. Over the years they had passed away, and we had gradually stopped replacing them. With slightly fewer animals about, and the children leaving home, we had some more spare time on our hands.

'Barry can play the guitar like Hank Marvin,' Jeanne said to me one day. She was talking about her younger brother. 'He's brilliant. He could have gone with that big band, The Shadows. He was offered a chance to join them.'

'Yes, he was good, wasn't he?' I said.

'And David.' That was her elder brother. 'Well, he can paint on anything – even velvet. He's a genius with a paintbrush. But I can't do nothing. I'm useless.' She put her chin on her hands and looked sadly out of the window.

Then one day she surprised me. We were at a garden centre, and there was a lady teaching people how to do this thing with eggs. She was decorating them really beautifully. We wandered over to have a look and Jeanne said, 'Ooh, I'd like to try that.'

'Why not come and see my workshop? I work from home,' said the woman. So the next week Jeanne went off to this woman's house and she got hooked. The kids called it her 'egging', but she basically decorated real eggs – egg crafting, I think they call it – in a really ornate way, with all kinds of jewels, clasps, and little clocks and things. I have them all still, in a cabinet. There are duck eggs, goose eggs, even an ostrich egg, and they look just beautiful.

Because it was only the two of us in our three-bedroomed house, Jeanne eventually turned one of the bedrooms into her workshop and she would spend days and days up there, carefully making these things. Sometimes I would just sit and watch her. She was so meticulous about everything; she wanted them to be just right.

Once Jeanne had her new hobby and we had the two dogs for company, we didn't really think about getting another cat until a friend of mine from work said he knew somebody going to Australia who couldn't afford to take his cat with him.

'It costs too much money for them to take him over there,' I said to Jeanne later that evening, as she stuck a delicate little clock on to a duck egg. 'It's a Bengal, he says. The cat.'

When I'd heard that news my ears had pricked up. I

love tigers and I love Bengal cats too; with their markings they look just like mini tigers.

'Well, do you want him?' she asked me.

'Yes, I think I do.'

And that was how we acquired yet another cat: Reggie. He was a noisy little beggar, though. He didn't stop wailing and miaowing for weeks. We began to wonder what we had let ourselves in for. But he settled in eventually and became just another part of the family.

During the next few years, Jeanne became quite ill. She was diabetic. She had chronic obstructive pulmonary disease (COPD), which is a collection of horrible lung diseases, and she had quite a few other things wrong with her too. All in all she lived through some tough times, struggling with sickness. But she always got through with humour and her usual stubbornness in the face of adversity. Our eldest daughter, Collette, started coming round to help a lot and became Jeanne's main carer while I was at work. Eventually I got ill too, and had to give up my job. We were thankful we had Reggie and the dogs then, because it was company for us during the long evenings.

One night we were sitting in the lounge. Reggie had just headbutted me out of my seat so he could have it, and I was moving over to the sofa.

'I don't know why you let that cat boss you around,' said Jeanne, looking up from her magazine. 'I'd never let him get away with that.'

'He gets the hump if I don't move,' I said. 'Then there's hell to pay for days.'

Reggie settled himself down in my seat and licked his paws triumphantly.

'Well, I don't know. You're too soft on him. Maybe we should get another cat,' she said. 'A friend he can boss around instead of you.'

'An older one, perhaps. From Battersea,' I said. 'We'll have a look in the morning. See what they've got on the website.'

The next day I woke up with a start. Jeanne was moving about next to me, panicking and struggling. She couldn't get any air. I got her inhalers. But they didn't work.

'I can't breathe . . .' she said quietly.

'I'll call an ambulance,' I said, trying to stay calm, but I could see she was under a lot of stress. 'Don't worry. It's going to be OK,' I told her, stroking her arm gently. She looked back at me and on her face was a look of sheer terror.

The ambulance arrived pretty quickly, rushed in and gave her oxygen straight away. They did this, that and the other with pieces of equipment, put her on a stretcher and told me they thought that fluid had built up in her lungs. As they got her into the ambulance she lost consciousness, so they made me go in a paramedic car instead of with her.

'It looks serious, Mr Stroud. If you follow us in the paramedic car we can meet you at the hospital,' he said briskly. Then they shut the doors and the ambulance sped away with its blue lights flashing.

My head was spinning. His words were going round in my head. I didn't know what to do so I rang our daughter Maria. 'She had an asthma attack,' I told her. My hands were shaking.

'Where is she now?' asked Maria. She was about to go to work.

'She's in the ambulance. They rushed her on blues to St Peter's. But she's in danger they say. There's a paramedic car here which came first. They said I should go with them but I was just going to ring Collette and let her know . . .'

'No, you get in the flaming car!' said Maria. 'Get yourself down to the hospital. I'll ring Collette. I'll see you there.'

I met the ambulance at the hospital and the medic took me to one side.

'We really thought we'd lost her in the ambulance, Mr Stroud,' he said. 'We have managed to revive her, but we're not out of the woods yet. We brought her back after half an hour, but she appears to have no brain activity. So we'll have to run some more tests.'

No brain activity. What did it mean? Where was my Jeanne?

Everyone arrived at the hospital then: Belinda, Collette and Maria. Jeanne was in intensive care on a ward, and they said we could see her at visiting time.

We knew what was coming in a way, but until you get told officially you don't want to voice it. In case you've sort of doomed it.

'I had a hell of a time getting here through the traffic,' said Maria, while we all sat in the canteen. She was fiddling with a plastic spoon in her coffee cup.

'Did you come down the High Street?' asked Belinda.

'No, the other way,' Maria said, snapping the plastic spoon in half.

'How's the fish, Dad?' Collette asked.

'Fine,' I told her. 'Bit bony. How's your chicken?'

'Dry. But you know, better than a slap in the face with a wet kipper.'

We talked rubbish like this to fill the time. I suppose we were trying not to admit the real reason we were there. After that we had a long wait in a room just off the ward before they took us to see her.

'You know it's bad when you're in a side room,' said Belinda.

'No brain activity,' said Collette. 'I wonder what that . . .'

'Come this way, would you?' said a nurse.

And there she was in the bed, looking so small and vulnerable, all hooked up to the bleeping machinery. Her eyes were shut.

'Can she hear us, do you think?' asked Maria, as we crept in and sat down.

'She's deaf, silly,' said Belinda.

'They put her hearing aids in!'

'Well, she might then,' said Collette. 'Remember when she heard me call her a silly idiot, cos I thought her hearing aids weren't in? We'd had a row. But she heard me anyway and gave me a right evil look after that.'

'I do remember that! She hears when she wants to, all right. Don't you, Mum?' said Maria, looking over at Jeanne for a response. But there was none, just the *bleep bleep* of the life-support machine.

Every now and then Jeanne would have a kind of involuntary spasm, and her eyes would open. But it was like looking at glass. There was no one in there. Just blankness.

'Only last night I was talking to her. About the cats . . . And now she can't say a word,' I said quietly.

The girls chattered away about old times, trying to keep me upbeat. And I talked to Jeanne about the early days when we were courting, and going to the beach, the parties we used to have, all our cats and dogs, and when the children were little. I reminded her of her eggs and told her they were OK, safe in the cabinet at home.

The next day, the medics said there was no chance of any more brain activity. It sounded so clinical. What about the person I loved? Where was she?

At 2 p.m. on Wednesday her life-support machine was switched off.

The hospital staff said we could stay as long as we liked. We could have stayed all night if we had wanted to. It's what they call twenty-four-hour open order. We sat at her bedside as long as we had to. Gradually her breathing got weaker, her pulse slowing.

I wonder if she knew we were there at all during those final hours. For one brief moment, it was almost as if she was looking at us. She opened her eyes, without that strange spasm. Who knows? It could have been nothing . . . sheer coincidence. But perhaps she saw us all one last time.

Some people live for weeks and months like that, apparently, but thankfully Jeanne didn't suffer and it was quick. After three and a half hours, at 5.30 p.m. on Wednesday evening, she took her last, shallow breath. I pressed her hand. She was gone.

She had a good send-off. Lots of people came to the funeral, so she must have made a big impact on others in her life. We walked in to the Simon and Garfunkel song 'Bridge Over Troubled Water'. Belinda chose that one, because she kept hearing it on the radio just after Jeanne died and because her mum had had a lot of problems in life, but now they were all gone. Jeanne had always said she wanted 'My Heart Will Go On' by Celine Dion. So we played that during the service. And then we walked out to Elvis singing 'Crying In The Chapel'; Maria thought she'd like that. Jeanne was a massive Elvis fan.

Once the funeral was over, and everyone went back to their own homes, and their families, I went back to Reggie. He was sitting in the lounge, miaowing.

'Are you wondering where she's gone too? Because I certainly am,' I said, and stroked his neck.

And at just around the time I lost my Jeannie, that little kitten I told you about was being thrown out of a car somewhere. But I didn't know that yet. But I did know that we had talked about getting another cat, company for Reggie. And now I needed more company myself. The family were great, but the evenings were the worst. No Jeanne to chat to. No Jeanne to nag me about this and that. All her things were still there. That was the hardest part. Getting rid of everything.

In the end I moved into a small flat, in sheltered accommodation. It suited me better on my own.

And not long after I decided to go and look for that other cat at Battersea. Belinda came with me, with her partner, Graham, and Collette.

'What kind of thing do you want, Dad?' asked Belinda.

'I don't know. Something older. That Reggie can cope with. Nothing too boisterous.'

When we got to Battersea, they showed us into the cattery. There were beautiful new glass pens for the cats all lined up along a plush-looking corridor.

'Blimey, it's like The Ritz in here,' I said, looking at all the different animals.

'Yeah, I might check myself in,' said Collette.

Some cats were playing with their toys, others were just sleeping or lying on their beds. Some were even looking out of the window. Some were enormous fat things, others were tiny and skinny. There was every kind of cat you could imagine. A bit like our old house!

'They come to us from all over,' said the woman showing us around, 'given up because they don't get on with a new dog, or in a new house. Or a couple split up and what have you, and neither of them can keep the cat. Or they're just abandoned and we don't know why.'

'That's so sad,' said Collette, peering in at one cat who was chasing its tail round and round.

I looked at a few of the older ones, but most of them were asleep. Then, all of a sudden, Belinda's partner saw this black thing go *whooosh* right across its cage.

'What was that?' Graham said.

Then we all saw this little cat shoot across again like a rocket.

'Will you look at that?' I said.

She was so fast, we didn't realize at the time that she only had three legs.

'It's just a little moggie that one. Willow.'

'Can I look at her?' I asked.

So the woman got little Willow out, and I held her. She was only tiny. She could fit in my hand. But boy could she move. And there were her three legs, and a gap where the fourth leg used to be, the wound all neatly sewn up.

'Would she be all right with an older cat?' I asked. 'We've got a very stubborn Bengal.'

'She should be fine, yes. She's never been any trouble here.'

'What happened to her? For her to lose a leg?' asked Collette.

'Yes. Poor thing was thrown from a car. Or at least abandoned on the motorway slip road. The leg was badly damaged. We've had her here for three months in clinic trying to save it. They were trying to see if they'd get any movement on it, but nothing. So they thought it was better to amputate in the end.'

'Well, she can move on her other three pretty well, can't she?'

'She certainly can! Lucky someone picked her up and brought her in. She was only four weeks old. We had to hand rear her for a bit, but she's weaned now.'

'Who could have dumped her like that?' said Belinda. 'So cruel.'

'What do you think, Dad?' asked Collette.

'I like her,' I said. 'Feisty little thing. She's got spirit. I like that.'

I renamed her Lucky. It seemed fitting.

We went away for a few days, so that Battersea could sort out all the injections and things she needed, then we came in and collected Lucky and brought her back to my flat.

I realized, as I took her out of the cat carrier, that this was the first animal I had ever brought home without Jeanne.

'She would have fallen for you, Lucky,' I said. 'My Jeanne. Hook, line and sinker.'

When it came to introducing her to Reggie, I split them up for a day, and then gradually introduced her into the house. She's got a very quiet miaow compared to Reggie's great bawl. But I could tell Lucky was a boisterous one, because she wanted to play right away.

They get on very, very well together now. Reggie was a bit dubious to begin with – it took about a fortnight before they really started to interact. But now they'll play, or sit on my lap for a cuddle. Lucky is very energetic, and Reggie's getting a bit older, but they still play together well. Then when one or the other is tired they'll have a little spit and a spat. But she's not frightened of him one bit. After all, she's been through it.

As for her losing a leg, well, you'd think she's got four the way she moves. She's adapted really well. Since she's been like that almost from day one she's just got used to only having three legs. I'm sure it would have been worse if she'd kept the bad leg. She is growing gradually, though she's still small. But that's just Lucky.

Lucky was a bit distant with me at first, but now she'll come and sleep with me on the bed. Reggie'll be one side and she'll be on the other. When we're all sitting together, the two cats and me, Reggie still fights me for my seat and I have to say I do relent. I suppose I make a rod for my own back, as Jeanne would say. Every day I miss her, but I'm fortunate enough to have Reggie and Lucky for company during those long evenings. And I know if she was still around, Jeanne would have loved Lucky just as much as I do.

Star: The Shy Rottweiler

With over 300 permanent staff at Battersea, most of us are lucky enough to see the animals on a regular basis, not only those who work directly with them in the kennels. As part of our mission to keep the animals stimulated and well socialized, you will often see a dog in one of the Battersea offices. So I suppose it's inevitable that, at some point in our lives here, a few staff members, such as Caroline Stringer, will end up rehoming an animal . . . or two . . .

'I'm going to be editor of that magazine,' I said to my partner, Mercedes, as the latest edition of the Battersea magazine, *Paws*, landed on the doormat.

'Yes, so you always say,' she smiled.

I flicked through as usual, looked at all the articles . . . and then turned on the computer to scan the job section of the Battersea website. Nothing doing.

We're both dog people, Mercedes and I. She's always had dogs, and from birth onwards there's always been a dog in my life. My parents had them when I was growing up, and I got my own as soon as I left home. First a Terrier cross called Carey, who went everywhere with me. Then, when she died, a pure black mixed Retriever-Border Collie Cross called Harold. Followed swiftly by a small German Spitz (known as a Klein) called Spider, and then after that we got Ted, a medium (Mittel) Spitz.

Ted adapted really well to living in the London sub-urbs, so we decided to give another dog a home – and Ted a pal.

'Ted could do with a friend, don't you think?' I asked Mercedes. 'She's always lived with other dogs.'

'Yes, you're right. Twice the dogs, double the fun!'

Later that week we happened to be in a supermarket car park when we saw a dog waiting in a van in a parking bay opposite. It stuck its head up against the window and started wagging its tail, looking right at us.

'What's that, do you think?' I asked. 'It looks like a little gremlin. So sweet!' When the dog's owners returned with their shopping, I asked what the little dog was. She was a Jug, a Jack Russell-Pug cross. We found out lots about this crossbreed, thought long and hard, and decided a Jug and a Spitz could work really well together. So along came Sergei.

'Got to be Sergei. Like the meerkat from the advert. Don't you think?' I said, stroking the little Jug's furry face.

The two of us, and our two dogs, were settling into life in our new home. Sergei got on well with Ted, who is a gentle dog anyway. Mercedes had a good job and I was working in communications. But my current position was only maternity cover so I needed to come up with some-thing more permanent, and fast. I applied for a few jobs, and had plenty of interviews, including one for a charity, which looked OK. Whilst I was still waiting to hear from them, one morning, out of the blue, something came up which had the potential to change my life.

'Editor,' I said, as I scanned the Battersea website. I

had to do a double-take, though, as I couldn't quite believe it. 'They're looking for an editor! For the Battersea magazine.' I almost jumped up out of my chair.

'Well, you always did say you'd do it!' grinned Mercedes.

And I set about filling out the application straight away.

I'd been a Battersea supporter for years. And, as a journalist and a dog lover, I'd long thought this was my dream job. But I never really thought it would actually come up.

Not long after I had sent off the application I got a reply asking me in for an interview.

When I got to Battersea's London centre, I was very excited. There were dogs about the place, being walked, and I could see some in offices with the staff. It looked like the perfect place to work. I was a bit nervous, but I quite like interviews, and I was determined to give it my best shot. So I marched right into that room with the attitude that it was my job and the other candidates would have to be very good indeed to beat me to it.

After the interview a few days went by, and I began to have some niggling doubts. I had heard nothing from Battersea. Had it really gone well or had I just been caught up in the moment? Eventually I got a phone call.

'Caroline? We'd like to offer you the job.'

Great! I thought, for a moment. Then I realized it was the wrong job. It was the other charity I had applied to. I had almost forgotten about that, in the frenzy of the past few days.

Now I had a dilemma.

'Do I accept it, though? I do really need a job . . . but what about Battersea?' I said to Mercedes that evening as we were walking Sergei and Ted around the local park.

'Well, you haven't heard anything from them. You can't wait for too long, you might get nothing!'

'I know, and I keep thinking I'm going to get a letter any day saying "Thanks but no thanks" from Battersea. Maybe my interview technique wasn't so good after all.'

In the end, I felt I had to accept the other job. After all, you've got to pay the bills. But such is the mystifying hand of fate, that I got a phone call the very next day from, you've guessed it, Battersea.

'We'd like to offer you the post.'

I could hardly believe my ears. Yes! It had happened. I felt awful about the other job, but there was just no way I could pass up the chance to do what I do best – write – for Battersea and all the dogs and cats in its care. After all, it's not every day the dream job floats within reach. I was basking on cloud nine for weeks after that.

'My mum would have been so proud,' I said to Mercedes, as I got ready for my first day. 'That's what makes it so special. She would have loved that I'm going to work for Battersea Dogs & Cats Home.'

It felt wonderful walking through the gates that first morning. There was a lovely brindle Staffie being walked through the courtyard by one of the many volunteers who help to take the dogs out. I walked past the paddocks where they take the dogs to exercise, or to meet their new owners, all in the shadow of the great big Battersea Power Station chimneys.

'Your desk's here,' said my line manager as I walked into my new office. I still felt like I was in a dream. She handed me a list of jobs to get on with, and I couldn't wait to get my teeth into the magazine. I had loads of ideas about what articles to do, but also a lot to get to know about the ins and outs of Battersea. The team I was working with made me feel really welcome. But it wasn't only my colleagues I met on that first day.

In the office there was a very large, nervous-looking dog being calmly stroked by a soft-voiced man in a Battersea uniform.

'That's Star,' said my line manager. 'Don't look directly at her. Just ignore her and let her come to you in her own time. She's really, really nervous with people.'

'Oh, right,' I said, and looked away. I could see out of the corner of my eye that she was a black and tan Rottweiler, now fast asleep with her head in her giant paws.

'It helps them relax,' said the woman sitting at a computer opposite me, 'being in the office, with the staff. Gives the dogs a more home-like atmosphere and a chance to chill. And we love having them here too, of course. You wouldn't get that in many offices!'

I hadn't realized that, as magazine editor, I was going to be in such close contact with the dogs. It felt really exciting to have a dog in the office with us. It meant that the cause I was working for – the animals – were right there in front of me all the time as a great inspiration.

'What's her story?' I asked a colleague who was sitting nearby. 'Star?'

'She's been here for ten months. We never put a time limit on how long they stay. It takes as long as it takes. But she's so nervous, she's really found Battersea a terrifying experience. We all love her, though.'

'How did she end up here?' I asked, getting curious about this gentle giant.

'She was found wandering in Star Lane. That's why she's called Star. Abandoned, we think. She was ever so malnourished. Beaten, probably. She was about five years old when she arrived. But we don't know if she was a stray or escaped. She was picked up by a dog warden and brought to us.'

Dog wardens are employed by the local council, who have a statutory duty to deal with stray dogs, and they bring a lot of them to Battersea. In fact, during the year Star was at Battersea, 45 per cent of the dogs had arrived as strays, which means we didn't know their name, age, medical history, behavioural history or anything. Star was just one of those mysteries.

I imagined this poor animal, shivering on a London street, scrounging for scraps to stay alive. A story had been written for the magazine about Battersea's 'challenge to make Star shine', telling people all about her and asking for a good home for this shy dog, who had been at the Home for over 250 days when I started work there.

'To help her come out of her shell, Star has been spending some time in staff offices, where she has made remarkable progress,' said the story. 'At first she was very wary of her surroundings and new people, but with a little time and TLC Star has become much more confident with the people she's got to know, and once she is relaxed becomes a giggly and playful girl.'

'Star is a sweet and loving dog,' it went on, 'whose favourite things in life are cuddles, belly rubs, ragger toys and treats. She may always be sensitive, but once she gets to know you she is a different dog. She has shown staff and volunteers here what a wonderful, bubbly girl she is, but really needs to find someone special who can bring her on.'

Gradually, over the next few days, Star started to come up to me, out of curiosity, just for a few moments at a time. But even then, if I showed the slightest movement, or raised my hand, she would hurl herself to the floor, cowering in terror. We had many different dogs in our office during my first few weeks, and they were all lovely. But there was none quite like Star.

When the public come to Battersea looking for a dog they can visit the kennels, with the dogs all in a row along the corridor. Star had one of these kennels. But no one ever saw her, because when people came round she would always hide away in the little back area. There was a photo of her on the door, but it looked like there was no dog in there, because she just couldn't bear anybody to see her. So no one ever did, and we would hear person after person asking why the kennel was empty.

In the end, she got so stressed by her visitors that she had to be moved to kennels which the public didn't go round. Then there was even less chance of her being spotted by a loving family.

As I got stuck into my new job, Star gradually got more and more used to me, until one day I sat on the floor of the office near her, and waited to see what she'd do. Slowly but surely she came over to me and let me stroke her and she pressed up against my arm. It was an amazing moment. It felt like a real privilege that this great big, shy, damaged dog trusted me enough to let me touch her, and help her to feel loved in that moment.

'You're very loving really, aren't you?' I whispered gently.

'I wonder what you've been through. Who hurt you so much?'

She couldn't answer, of course, but she did let me carry on stroking her, which said enough.

After a while, Star trusted me enough to take her out on a lead around the Battersea site. There are some dogs that are able to go out to the park with our staff and volunteers, but Star was far too nervous for that. So I used to take her to the paddocks where we have agility equipment. One of them has a huge stone sink in it, and the moment she saw it the great big dog lumbered over and jumped in. Then she started splashing around like a giant unwieldy puppy. She was so happy I could have laughed and cried at the same time, to see her so transformed. She didn't swim, though, she was just submerged up to her armpits, moving back and forth, stately as a galleon!

Some dogs are chatterers and others are a little quieter. Star is of the quiet variety. At least most of the time.

One morning, somebody arrived in the office who Star didn't know. They were there to do some maintenance on one of the computers. She had been napping, but as soon as the man came in she jumped up and I heard this enormous, deep, echoing bark.

'The Rottie boom,' said my colleague, sitting opposite.

'Sounds more like a sonic boom!' I said.

After that, I found that Star would do the 'Rottie boom' if she got excited, too. Except that then it was also accompanied by the 'Rottie bounce', when she rose as if by magic from the floor, all four feet right off the ground, up to human eye level. It was quite an extraordinary sight to witness this enormous dog in full boom and bounce.

When she wasn't leaping and booming, though, Star was often very distressed. She showed all the typical signs of a stressed-out dog. When she was out for walks she liked to have something at her side, for comfort, and she'd stick close to the nearest wall or fence. I suppose it was so nobody could attack her from the side. There are lots of planes and train lines criss-crossing outside the Battersea site, which would frighten her a lot. I'd see her looking up, literally waiting in trepidation for the next train or aeroplane to come along. Most dogs at Battersea cope with this. But Star couldn't.

She was also quite nervous around some men. Despite that, one of her best friends at Battersea was Brian, one of our canine welfare trainers. He was the man I'd seen reassuring Star in the office on my first day. He did a lot of work with her, trying to build up her confidence. He would take her round the agility course and build up her interaction with people and help her to be less nervous. She also had a Rottie boyfriend, Goofy, who was eventually happily rehomed to a farm in Yorkshire.

Brian is part of a team called Service Dogs, which assesses dogs to see if they're suitable for working in the outside world – for the police or for the services, for instance. Star was assessed at one point, because Rottweillers make good service dogs, but she was too nervous to cope with it.

Brian did a great job of building up Star's confidence. Unfortunately, it didn't last.

'She's coping with things less well, for some reason,' he said to me one day, when I was walking her past the paddocks. 'It's awful to see. Time for her to go home, if she's going to be OK,' he said.

'After all the work you put in it must be really hard,' I said.

'Yes. But it's life. Some dogs are just so badly treated it takes a hell of a lot to get them back on track.'

That night, at home, I mulled it over. I'd never thought about getting a Rottie. But she was just so vulnerable I had to do something.

'You always do go for the needy, vulnerable ones, don't you?' sighed Mercedes.

'I know. It just appeals to me in a dog. The ones no one wants. I always want to protect them.'

I thought about Star and the first time she had let me stroke her. It was a magical moment.

'You're thinking about rehoming her, aren't you?' said Mercedes after a while.

'Well . . . I hadn't been, until now, but after what Brian said . . . she's just so . . . I just don't think anyone else is going to want her,' I said finally.

'You always knew you'd end up taking a dog home at some point, didn't you, from Battersea. But I wasn't quite expecting a Rottweiler . . .'

'You like big dogs, though, don't you?' I jumped in quickly. 'You said you wanted a Mastiff and they're even bigger than Star.'

We already had two dogs, Sergei and Ted, but we did have the space and time for another, so it certainly wasn't out of the question. But I could tell Mercedes was a bit unsure.

'Why don't you just come and see her?' I said. 'You know . . . just for a look.'

'All right. But no strings. I suppose it does feel a bit like we're her last best chance, though, doesn't it?'

The following Saturday we went to Star's kennel together. It was early summer and when we got there she was in her yard at the back of the kennel, soaking up the heat. By that stage she would sit on my lap, so I sat down and she clambered up and licked my face.

'Hello, Star, you big old thing,' I said, and Mercedes sat down carefully next to us.

Amazingly, Star seemed fine with her straight away. A little nervous, as usual, but not panicking or running away or anything. We sat there quietly like that for ages, in the dappled sunlight of the little paddock, wisps of white cloud drifting in the sky above us. Mercedes smiled. I could see there was a twinkle in her eye.

'You like her, don't you?' I asked.

And she couldn't very well deny it.

'I can see how stressed she is. And nervous. But she is a lovely one, all right.'

We talked it through when we got home, just so we were sure. But I knew in my heart Mercedes wasn't going to be able to say no. She'd given too much away when they had met.

In a few days, we started the rehoming process at Battersea for the first time. I'd already registered us as potential rehomers. But now Mercedes and I would have to have an interview together with the rehoming staff. Even as a staff member I couldn't just pick out a dog. It all had to be done properly. We had to tell them our home situation, whether we had a garden, whether we were allowed pets in our house, whether we had other animals, if we would have any visiting children and so on; then we were asked what kind of dog we thought would suit us – big or small, energetic or more passive, what age – all to check whether Star was a match for us. After that, we had a chat with the rehoming staff, which went well. And then we had to bring in our dogs, Ted and Sergei, to see if they would get along with Star.

Sergei, the little Jug, and Ted, our beautiful Spitz, were very excited about coming to Battersea. They were sniffing and leaping about all the way up to the paddock.

'They can smell all the dogs, probably,' I said to Mercedes.

The rehomer brought Star out, and although she was her usual nervous self, the dogs all sniffed each other, and we were quite happy with the way they interacted together.

'What do you think?' I asked Mercedes afterwards.

'I think Star needs a good home and I think we can give her one,' she said.

I forgot to mention that, on top of getting a third dog, we were also moving house that week. So we moved into our new house, and the next day we went to collect Star.

Lots of people at Battersea came to say goodbye to her. She had been there so long she was very popular and it was quite an emotional send-off. But Star didn't seem to mind at all.

'She looks eager, doesn't she?' I said, and amazingly she jumped straight up into the back of the car, without hesitation. 'It's almost as if she knows she's going home.'

I had been worried about the drive back, but she fell

fast asleep and stayed sleeping all the way there. It was as if she was finally relaxing and, just for a moment, letting go of all the stresses of her past life. When we got home, I took Star straight to the country park, while Mercedes went to pick up Ted and Sergei. You're supposed to introduce new dogs on neutral ground.

When we met up we had a walk round the park and the dogs played together a bit. I could tell Star was very excited and pleased to be out, even if she was on a long line. Then we took them up a big hill, where there's a lake at the top. When Star saw the water she was absolutely thrilled. She did her Rottie bounce and then jumped right in, like she used to at Battersea in the big stone sink. And she waded about up to her armpits again, like a giant cruise liner on the end of the lead.

'She's just so pleased to be home at last,' I said. And she was.

I must confess that all our dogs sleep in the bedroom and Star was no exception. We had to get a memory foam bed for her, all the way from America, because she's so big. But it was worth it because she loved it straight away.

I knew quite a lot about Rottweilers by then. They were a guarding breed originally, bred to protect herds of cattle and sheep in Germany. They were also used to pull carts. They're very loyal, strong, courageous, protective of their people and anything else that they love. They're called trotting dogs, and have a lot of stamina, which means she could go at the same easy pace for days and days and days. They're a very old breed too, and were even used by Roman armies as sentinel dogs.

Unfortunately, they're also used as status symbols in

the same way as Staffies and other bull terriers are. People sometimes get them because they look the part, and then train aggression into them.

Star would never hurt anybody. She's very good with other dogs. She'll either avoid them, or go straight up to sniff them and play with them. With people, though, she's so afraid she takes the biggest detour around them that she can. We have even seen her crashing through thick undergrowth to avoid a person she's afraid of. She doesn't want anything to do with people if she can avoid it. But she loved Mercedes from the off, which was great, and the feeling was mutual.

When we brought her home everything seemed to be going OK, until one day, a few weeks on, I noticed that Ted, my German Spitz, wasn't quite herself. She was usually a very outgoing and friendly dog, but she was looking withdrawn and showing signs of stress.

People would always stop in the street to ask what sort of dog Ted was. Cars have even been known to screech to a stop just to ask about her, she's so special. She's also a real character and a very 'human' dog. She loves to be the centre of attention, absolutely loves people and is wonderful with children. In fact, everyone adores her because she looks just like a teddy bear.

But after we got Star things changed. Ted started making new and strange noises, squeaking and squealing, crying and barking. She was constantly looking nervously at the ceiling and, where she used to be very confident, she started to hide, trying to get away from Star all the time. She also started licking her paws anxiously until they got really sore, and eventually she wasn't eating her food.

I was distraught and asked one of my colleagues to come round to see her. We consulted with a number of vets too. One suggestion was that we separate the dogs as much as we could. We bought Ted a thunder vest, which is a tight-fitting garment supposed to relieve stress. And we even got her DAP diffusers, which mimic the phero- mones a bitch gives off when she's got a puppy and are meant to make dogs feel relaxed and happy. We took videos of Ted and Star, so the experts could see how they were together, and I took Ted for days out on her own, so she could relax.

At Christmas, we went to Trafalgar Square to sing carols and raise money for Battersea. Ted loved it and was a big hit with the other members of the Battersea choir, especially my friend Maddy, who works in Fundraising. I have a great photo of Maddy, dressed in a Dalmatian costume, holding Ted and singing her heart out. They had only just met but they certainly look in tune, and Maddy often asked about Ted after that. When little Ted did some more fundraising volunteering for us, helping me shake a bucket at Elephant & Castle station, she came into the office with me and Maddy was overjoyed to see her again, so we all three went for a walk around Battersea Park during our lunch break.

But back at home, despite all the consultations, tech- niques and gizmos, Ted just couldn't cope with the new situation. Eventually, one of the behaviourists gave us the dreaded verdict. He believed it would never work out between them. Ted wasn't coming to terms with Star, and was highly unlikely ever to do so. We could mask her signs of stress with behavioural work, and maybe medication, but she would still be feeling distressed.

'The only thing you can do is to control her symptoms,' he explained. 'And that might make it better and easier for you, but not for Ted. Effectively, all you'd be doing is hiding what she's going through. Star and Ted are a mismatch – it happens to dogs as well as people, you know, and no one could have foreseen how bad it would be.'

'That's no good,' I said, 'we want her to be happy.'

We loved Star and we loved Ted, and we wanted to do right by both of them.

'It's a real Sophie's Choice, isn't it?' I said to Mercedes sadly, when the behaviourist had left.

'I know. But they just can't live together. We'll have to rehome one of them to give them both a good life.'

Most people said it would have to be Star, on the basis of 'last in, first out'. But with Star being the special needs dog that she is, it wouldn't be easy, either to find her a home or for her to cope with such a major change. And she was happy and safe with us. But then I had owned Ted since she was eight weeks old and I loved her so much the thought of not being able to share her life broke my heart.

Mercedes and I had lots of discussions about it, and people at work were amazing, giving us advice and support. Working at a place like Battersea, people know what it means; how things like this make you feel, and how important the decision is.

In the end, after much hard thought, we decided that beautiful, gentle, funny Ted would have lots of great families wanting to rehome her. Whereas we didn't think Star was likely to find a new home at all. She'd just been through too much already. It was an awful decision, but that was the truth. We were Star's last chance.

I was so upset, I was finding it hard to keep the emotion in. The next day I was weeping in the ladies' toilets, being comforted by my boss, who knew how hard this all was, when Maddy came in.

'Are you all right?' she asked.

'Well, not really,' I blurted.

Someone else being nice to me brought it all flooding back and I told her about Ted, and Star, and the awful decision we had made.

'Our cat has just died,' she said. 'So I know how it feels to face losing an animal you love. They really become one of the family, don't they?'

Then Maddy looked deep in thought for a moment.

'Hang on a mo,' she said. 'Well. If you don't want to make a decision just yet, about who to rehome her with, we could look after her. You know, while you sort things out. As a foster care type thing. I remember seeing her that first time at the Christmas concert when we all sang carols to raise money for the Home. Do you remember, at Trafalgar Square?'

We laughed for a moment at the memory, and for a split second I forgot about the tragedy of it all. Then reality hit again.

'But ... goodness. Are you sure? I mean, that's an amazingly kind offer.'

'Well. Let me double-check with my husband first!' she said. 'But really, I don't think it will be a problem at all. Over Christmas. Until you find her a permanent home.'

The following weekend we packed up Ted's bed, and her toys and treats, and took her to her new foster home in south London.

By the time we got there, Mercedes and I were both in bits. We got Ted out of the car and she trotted into the house, looked at Maddy, sniffed around, then went into the garden and had a wee. Then she came in for a treat and eventually curled up in her bed.

We didn't stay long, or make a big deal of it. There wouldn't have been any point in getting more and more upset and Ted needed to settle in. I knew she was going to be fine with Maddy. But watching her disappear from view as we drove away, the last glimpse of her little teddy bear fur and her wagging tail, was one of the hardest things I've ever done.

'Now I get it,' I said to Mercedes, my eyes red from crying. 'How it feels for people bringing their dog to Battersea, when they haven't got any other choice. They really don't want to do it, but they have to for whatever reason ... divorce, children, landlord won't let them have a pet.' The tears were welling up again at this point. 'I've seen them come in, absolutely broken up, but I never quite understood it before now. We didn't want to give Ted up, but we had no choice. That's how it is for them.'

When we got home, we were so sad we just sat on the sofa and looked around us. Ted's absence was tangible.

Two hours later, Maddy phoned.

'We went for a walk,' she said. 'And Ted's absolutely fine. And my husband loves her. So don't worry.'

As the days and then the weeks went on, Ted remained with Maddy while we thought about what to do. A couple of weeks later Maddy told me her husband, Brendon, had booked them a family holiday, but not to worry about Ted, as Maddy's mum and dad had offered to look after her. Tales came back daily of Ted's exploits – getting to know the Golden Retriever next door, rolling in fox poo, meeting more of Maddy and Brendon's families, including their young nephews, going to the pub for Sunday lunch and all the regulars ending up watching Princess Ted's antics instead of the Spurs match on the big screen . . .

What happened next was, happily, inevitable.

'We can't imagine Ted not being a part of the family,' said Maddy one day. 'We would love to keep her.'

'Well, that's wonderful,' I said. And, of course, it was amazing that Ted now had a proper family again. But it was also very upsetting when it became permanent. Because it was final then. Ted was no longer ours, she was Maddy and Brendon's dog now.

After about six months, we thought it wouldn't confuse Ted too much if we paid a visit, and we had a wonderful reunion. Ted was thrilled to bits to see us, but trotted off with Maddy after our walk with not a backward glance. So we meet up every now and then – we take Sergei to see her old pal, but not Star. Ted is quite happy to be an only dog now, actually, because she loves people and she loves being the centre of attention. It was a miracle that Maddy was there to help us when we needed it. She helped turn an awful situation into something positive and joyful, and I can't thank her enough for that.

Once Ted had moved in with Maddy and Brendon, Star and Sergei were fine. Star was more settled too without Ted there. But now we were one dog short, and wanted to bring our family back up to three.

Alf was gifted into Battersea by a lady who couldn't

cope with him when her husband died. This is just one of many sad reasons people have to give up their animals, often reluctantly. Alf (who used to be called Barney) is a Border-Lakeland Terrier cross with really high energy levels. He was originally at Battersea's Brands Hatch centre, but was then transferred to London to be rehomed. That was when I met him, in his kennel, and of course fell in love again. But we had never had a male dog before and so I hauled Mercedes over to Battersea again, to meet him. She got that look in her eye. The same twinkle she had had with Star.

We were already registered, but we had another interview and did another intro with the dogs, and they were all fine. So we brought Alf home last April and he loves his new home. He didn't have any issues to overcome because he's had a loving home before, so he's just a normal little terrier, albeit with a lot of character and energy.

So within twelve months of starting work at Battersea, I had been able to rehome two dogs. Our dogs are quite a sight together, giant Star, tiny Sergei, and Alf running circles round us. But we love them to bits.

'At this rate I'll have twenty-four Battersea dogs by the time I retire!' I said to Mercedes, as we took our three out for their walk. But given the look on her face, maybe not!

Like many animals who have been mistreated, Star has been through a lot. The mental scars of her old life are still plain – sometimes one of us will be doing something everyday like getting a saucepan out of the cupboard and she will throw herself to the ground in terror. Or I'll pick her lead off the back of the door and she'll cower and whimper with fear at the sudden movement. It's tragic to see how damaged she has been by whatever happened in her past. We found out recently that she has bone fragments in her shoulder, caused by a trauma injury, and that she may have to have an operation to remove them. It's likely somebody controlled her using violence.

Star was at Battersea for ten months and she's now been with us for two years. So it's been almost three years since whatever happened to her in her past stopped. Whatever it was, it must have been so bad that she'll never fully get over it. She could have enjoyed a life with us where we could take her to the pub to meet up with friends, a life where she would enjoy being around people. But Star can't do any of those things, although she does still make tiny leaps forward – we were thrilled when she got brave enough to push a door open with her nose!

Despite all this, though, Star loves being in the house with us, and going to the local parks. We took her on holiday to Scotland and she spent every day paddling in rock pools. She is very loved, and very happy, which just shows the power of rehoming, even for some of the most damaged of animals.

When people come to Battersea they are almost always either coming in to find the dog they're going to share their lives with, or are heartbroken that, for whatever reason, they cannot keep their cat or dog any longer. They may be moving house, or changing jobs, or perhaps they've just had a baby. There are some incredibly sad stories of owners who have had to go into care homes and can't take their dogs or cats with them. My own experience with Star and Ted means I have experienced this too, in a small way. Ted will always be Maddy's dog now.

She's not mine any more. But we have Star, and she has a good life. It's the whole cycle, in a way, rehoming a dog and then having to give a dog up. That's what happens every single day at Battersea.

It also reminds me that not all the dogs who arrive at Battersea's doors have been treated like Star. Yes, there are cases of abuse, neglect and abandonment, of course, but there are also people just trying to do their best and, for whatever reason, failing. I expected to have Ted from the start of her life to the end. That's what I've always done with my dogs, and felt proud and privileged to do so. But I couldn't do that with Ted, so I do understand the predicament these owners face.

I absolutely love every minute of my time working at Battersea. And I've learnt so much by rehoming dogs myself. Everybody who works here is so passionate, so good at what they do, and they love and care about all the animals deeply. And when I look at Star, and I can see every day she's pleased to be here with us and not in a kennel or on the streets, it's worth it.

Bryn: The Search and Rescue Collie

Some dogs just love to get out and about and go to work. At Battersea our staff work very hard to identify those dogs that would be best placed being out in the world, putting their natural skills and instincts to good use. Every now and again we even find a cat in our cattery that is very hard to place but goes on to enjoy a working life, such as a big fluffy ginger tom cat who recently found he could cope best living on a smallholding among horses, sheep and goats.

When we identify an animal who might be happier working than being a companion animal, we look for suitable placements for them. That might be on a livestock farm, where Border Collies are often used to herd sheep and cattle, or police training for dogs which can be used to locate drugs and explosives. There are also some dogs like German Shepherds and Rottweilers who can work as security animals for the police and other services. Last year, we successfully gave thirty dogs a new working life.

Occasionally, though, some of our dogs who have already been rehomed are encouraged to develop their natural skills by their new owners. And, once in a while, they can even end up saving a life or two, as Jo Kenny discovered . . .

I wasn't looking for a search and rescue dog. In fact, I didn't even know anything about search and rescue really, apart from having a vague idea about mountains and helicopters. I live in Kent, not the Highlands, so it had never even crossed my mind when I set about getting a new companion from Battersea Dogs & Cats Home that he'd end up as a search and rescue dog.

My first dog, Shadow, was a Labrador-Collie Cross. I was working with horses then, so he had the most wonderful lifestyle. He was literally outdoors with me and the horses from seven in the morning to ten o'clock at night. By the time Shadow passed away, however, I had moved on from the horses. I had an office job in probation and I couldn't bring myself to get another animal just to leave it at home all day on its own. Over the next seven years I moved on in my job, and met my husband Stuart. My life was great, but I missed having a dog. Then one day Stuart came home from work all excited.

'I had a brainwave,' he said. 'About the dog thing. I could take it to the office with me, couldn't I?'

'What?! Well . . . I suppose you could, yes. If you don't mind,' I said, uncertainly.

Stuart has a converted stable block for an office, right in the middle of fields with woods behind it. But this idea had never occurred to either of us before.

'Yeah, I can take it with me and it can just run about while I'm working. Have the run of the land.'

'Do you think it would be all right, though?'

'As long as you train it properly, I'm sure it'll be just fine. So we can get a dog,' he said. 'If you want one, that is . . .'

'Of course I want one!'

Since losing Shadow I was realizing more and more

that I needed an active dog in my life, one who would match my own temperament.

The next day, we decided to approach Battersea Dogs & Cats Home to see what they had. I was keen to get a rescue dog that needed a new home, and not a dog from a breeder. When I called, a woman in the rehoming department asked me questions about what my situation was, and what kind of dog I was after.

'I'm really keen on a Collie,' I said.

'Oh, our main London centre gets a lot of Collies,' she said brightly. 'If you come in and fill out our forms, and have a short interview, we can be on the lookout for one for you.'

So Stuart and I went to London and began the rehoming interview process. I was very impressed by the questions they asked and the thoroughness of the checks they made. They were vetting us, making sure that we understood about dogs, finding out what our home life was like and whether we had an idea of the cost of keeping a dog.

'I had a Labrador-Collie cross before,' I said, feeling quite confident about my knowledge of dogs, 'though he was more Collie than Labrador. It's the intelligence, the activity of that type of dog, the ease of training them, that's what I like.'

'How many hours a day would the dog be left on its own?' asked the woman doing the interview.

'Well, I've got my office, basically in fields with woodland,' said Stuart. 'So it'll have loads of space to run about most of the day. So it wouldn't really be left alone at all.'

'I'm a really outdoor active person too,' I said, 'so it would fit in with me. I love walking and working with animals.'

'Well, that all sounds fine,' she said after a while, shuffling her papers together.

I breathed a sigh of relief that we'd passed that test at least.

'But we don't actually have any Collies in right now,' she went on.

'Can we stay in touch and you can let us know what comes up?' I asked hopefully. We had come all this way and it would be disappointing to go home with nothing to hope for. The lady agreed that they'd keep us up to date on new arrivals. Then, just as we were about to leave, another staff member came running up to us.

'Were you the ones after a Collie?' she asked breathlessly. 'I'm glad I've caught you. Because we've got one literally just in. Only thing is, he's not been vetted or checked or done the behavioural tests or anything yet.'

'Oh, wow. That's amazing,' I said, not really knowing what any of that meant but thinking perhaps it was meant to be. 'What can I do? Can I see him?'

'Well, let's put a reserve on him. Give us a week to do all the tests and we'll be in touch then to tell you if it might be a goer.'

I couldn't concentrate all week, wondering whether this Collie would be the one. It was funny, because I had gone so long without a dog, and now that the system had started rolling, I couldn't wait to be out there walking with one again.

My great friend Estelle used to work for Battersea as a

dog behaviourist. So, while I was waiting for them to get back to me, I rang her up for a chat.

'How did it go?' she asked. She was keen for me to get a dog too, so we could go out together.

'They've got a Collie in,' I said excitedly. 'But they have to do some tests and things. I haven't even seen it yet. Hey, do you think you could give them a quick ring and just find out what these tests are? And what this dog seems like to you? You know, from an insider's perspective?'

She agreed, and came back to me later that day.

'From what I can tell, from speaking to a few people,' she said, 'he's a bit like my dogs. A good all-round, sensible temperament. Sounds like a really cracking animal, actually. Listen, Jo.' She paused and lowered her tone seriously. 'In my experience, you can search for years looking for a dog that will tick all the boxes – or a Collie that ticks all the boxes. But I can tell you, this is a good one.'

It turned out that this dog did check all the boxes, on the Battersea behavioural test at least. They check for sociability, getting on with other dogs, confidence and lots of other things. Hearing from Estelle, who has Collies of her own, that he seemed like a good one, made me feel even more confident I wanted to go to see him.

In a matter of days we were on our way to London.

'We'll just have a look, won't we? To get a feel for things. I don't think it would be sensible to go for the first dog I see,' I said to Stuart firmly.

We walked into the brightly lit reception and were immediately greeted by the woman from the rehoming department who had interviewed us originally. They are in charge of matching up the Battersea dogs with prospective owners, and seeing the whole process through smoothly.

'Hello, again,' she said. 'Come through into the interview room and we'll bring the dog in.'

As we sat in the little room, I felt anxious, wondering what the dog would be like.

'What if he doesn't like us?' I said nervously.

'I don't see why he wouldn't,' said Stuart. 'Unless he's got issues.'

'I hope he's not too young. I don't think we should get a puppy. Do you? I'm just not sure about the puppy stage. You know. Whether we could cope.'

'You might be right,' he said. Then the door opened.

'Meet Patch,' said the woman. She had an excitable black and white Collie on a lead; he didn't look like he had too many issues. He didn't look nervous at all.

'Patch? He hasn't even got a patch. On his eye or anywhere else,' laughed Stuart.

'I know! But that's what he was called by his previous owner. So there you are.'

Patch calmed down once he was in the room, and sat there quite politely, with his head cocked on one side. He was gangly and long-legged and I thought he looked like more of a Working Collie than a Border. He didn't have a big fluffy tail, more of a rat's tail, bless him. Working Collies are the ones you see out on the farms, so they tend to be taller and of a slimmer build. Border Collies are the show breed and tend to have really fluffed up, stocky builds.

'How old is he?' I asked, remembering my vow not to get a puppy. He did look quite young.

'About six or seven months.'

'Oh, right,' I said, feeling a bit disappointed. I thought he looked great, but maybe he was too young for us.

As we greeted the dog, we were being assessed as well as us assessing the dog. The rehomer wanted to see how we interacted with him. I went over and stroked him and held up one or two of the toys in the room for him to play with. He seemed fine with that so I relaxed a little and rubbed his back.

'The previous owners said it was due to ill health that they gave him up. And he's never been let off the lead, as far as we can tell. He's from London, so he might have been cooped up inside a bit. Collies need a lot of exercise, as you know. Anyway, he seems all right, so do you want to be left alone with him for a bit? See how you get on together?'

'Yes, please. If that's OK,' I said, still unsure whether I was rushing into things.

The rehoming woman left the room, and the dog immediately went straight over to the door and pined a little, as if he was saying, 'Don't leave me.'

'He's obviously formed a bit of an attachment to her,' I said. 'Hello, Patch. It's all right.'

'We won't bite,' said Stuart gently.

Eventually he came away from the door and started to hang around us and go into the play position, with his front paws out.

'That's a good sign, isn't it?'

'I think so.'

And it must have been, because after a while he really did want to play with us. We had been given lots of biscuits and doggy toys to use and he seemed to love them. But, even as I was falling for the dog, all the time I was also thinking, I shouldn't be doing this. Because he was the first one I had seen and I had made that promise to myself.

Although it was a big decision, and I'm quite reserved – I usually need to say no before I say yes – it didn't take long to make up my mind. As Estelle had suspected, he really was a cracking dog. And when our time was up, it felt too soon.

'You know what?' I whispered to Stuart. 'I don't think I want to leave him.'

'Well, don't then,' he smiled. And that was that.

Before we had left home, Estelle had warned me: 'If you're going to take the dog, think of a name now, because they do all the microchipping and they're going to register it as you leave.' So we'd gone through the internet looking at dog names. I'd made a list, and Stuart had picked his names too, and we went for a name we had both come up with, which was Bryn.

When the rehomer came back and we told her we loved the dog she was delighted.

'Well, that's great. He's had all his veterinary checks, treated for fleas and worms and things, so we'll just take him away and microchip and register him, give you your goody bag – a lead and a few others things – tie up all the paperwork. Then you can go.' They told us that they would visit us and Bryn in about three weeks to see how he had settled. I was impressed that they would come all the way from London to check on him in Kent. And so, after seven years, I was a dog owner again.

When we finally walked out of Battersea, on to the

main road, we discovered almost immediately that Bryn was absolutely petrified of traffic. The collar he had on was a little loose and he kept trying to run away. It was all we could do to stop him running into the road, he was pulling like mad, just trying to get away from all the chaos and cars.

'I don't know why he's so scared, if he's from London,' said Stuart, as we both tried to keep a hold on him.

'He obviously hasn't been socialized properly,' I said. 'Not ideal, having a Collie in London, I suppose. Unless you can walk it a lot. I know that from Shadow.'

Bryn just would not give up his antics and I was nearing exasperation point.

'We'll just have to pick him up,' I sighed. 'Carry him to the car. I can't afford to lose him now, can I?'

So we picked him up, and just about managed to get him in the car, and drove at last to his new home.

Because I'd worked with animals before, I had a basic idea of how to train them. I could do the commands – down, sit and that side of it. But I was less sure what to do if there were lots of distractions, like if a dog or a cat or other people came past. My first dog, Shadow, had been very easy to train. He was so obedient and keen to please he just did whatever I asked. But when I got Bryn, I realized I had no idea really how to train any other dog. Now I had to learn.

Bryn turned out to be very headstrong. He was a lovely but very bright and independent dog. I spent two or three weeks on a long line with him, and then I plucked up the courage to let him off in the woods near our house. The first few times I let him go he would every now and then just clear off into the trees, and I would be yelling at the top of my lungs. He would always come back eventually. But it would be, 'Yeah, I'll be back, but in a minute when I'm finished here.' I could get him to do basic commands and rules, such as you always walk out of a door first, and the dog goes second. But I needed him to be obedient when there were a lot of other dogs around too and not just on a one-to-one basis.

In the end, I decided to take him to dog-training classes, and do what they call a 'good citizen' award with him. The training sessions at a local village hall were very noisy and incredibly active. There were about eight dogs milling about, jumping and barking. Bryn was probably the oldest as the others were all fairly young puppies. How we got through that award I don't know, but we did. It probably helped quite a bit that I had so many treats for him in my pocket.

Training Bryn didn't happen overnight, of course. I had to really work at it, and my friend Estelle was a great help too. She's a dog-trainer herself and understands Collies really well. We would take Bryn to the woods together, with her two Collies, and he'd run off out of sight as usual, among the trees.

'Where is he?' I would ask anxiously, and start panicking and calling out.

'Just relax, Jo,' she would say, walking on. 'You know he'll come back.'

And, of course, he always did. Though it would feel like an eternity to me, in reality he'd be gone only a few minutes.

Estelle's eldest dog, Brock, was quite a role model for

my dog. Bryn would constantly want to play, and he was a real pain in the backside, constantly barking: 'Play with me! Play with me! Play with me!' Eventually Brock would put him in his place with a sharp bark: 'Back down, boy, I'm top dog here.' Once he had backed off a bit they started running around together, and it was learning that sort of behaviour from another dog which was really good for Bryn's discipline.

Once we had cracked the basics, I joined an agility club, where they have obstacle courses for the dogs with jumps for them to go over, A-frames, see-saws and tunnels. The instructor was very experienced, and had all kinds of dogs there: German Shepherds, Spaniels, Yorkshire Terriers, you name it. She absolutely loved Bryn from the off, but it absolutely blew his mind. He was hyperactive and frustrated waiting for his turn on the course. The other dogs would be lying around waiting patiently. They might even drop off to sleep. But Bryn was upright and eager, panting and wagging his tail. 'I'll do it! I'll do it! I'll do it! Let me do it! Let me do it! Let me do it!' With every single dog that went round the course, there he'd be, keen as mustard: 'I'll do it! I'll do it! I'll do it!' Nonstop barking, like a coiled-up spring.

'Don't worry,' said the instructor, laughing as I sank back with embarrassment. 'It's just because he's a Collie. They're like that. He'll settle. I promise, he'll get over it.'

I did worry, though, wondering if he'd ever calm down. He was starting to get quite snappy with the other dogs, because he was so tense and hyped up. He just couldn't contain himself.

Once it was his turn on the course, though, he was just

brilliant. So I persevered, and in the end it was very good for us to have that closer bonding of working together. And it prepared him for what came later.

At first, when I went for a walk, Bryn would go off and find his own entertainment. So after a while I started to provide the entertainment for him, like getting him to jump over fallen trees. Or if there were three or four trees in a row, I would get him to weave in and out of them. It was about working together, building our relationship, rather than just going for a walk where the dog does its own thing. I would also hide titbits out in the woods. I'd put him in a wait position, then go around and drop biscuits. Then I'd tell him to go and find them. Or if he cleared off in the woods, I'd clear off too, and hide from him. Then I'd watch him come back, looking for me; he'd shoot up the path and then skid to a halt, realizing that I hadn't gone that far. Then he'd come back and work out where I was. It was all about keeping his brain active, keeping him working. And I suppose, inadvertently, I was starting to teach him to search. One thing was clear, though: he absolutely loved it.

One day I was out with Estelle for a Sunday afternoon walk. She was buzzing and excited because she had been out for a day at Kent Search and Rescue with her younger dog.

'It was amazing,' she said. 'It was like an assessment day, kind of thing. They see how the dogs respond to all these activities in the wood, search exercises.'

'I didn't even know we had a search and rescue here,' I said. 'I thought it was all done on mountains and stuff.'

'Yeah, I thought that too. And obviously we don't have

them in Kent. But we went across these big fields and into the woods and did the exercises there. You know what, Jo?' she continued animatedly. 'I was thinking, the whole time I was there, this would be brilliant for Bryn. You should go and get him assessed.'

Estelle knew Bryn inside out after all our walks together. So I trusted her opinion on this. But I had no idea what it would involve.

'Well, it's worth a shot, I suppose,' I said. 'Bryn does love to be active and stimulated. And maybe the discipline would be good for him.'

The next morning I rang them up and booked us in for an assessment. On the day, I was told to turn up with Bryn in the local woods. It was a beautiful autumnal morning. There was a thick layer of golden-red leaves on the forest floor and a group of people dressed up for the cold.

'Welcome, everyone. Thanks for coming,' said a tall instructor in a tracksuit and woolly hat. 'I'm James, from the dog team. I'll be leading the course today. And this is Maria, one of our officers.'

'Hello,' she smiled.

There were three other people there; an older couple with a German Shepherd, and a woman with a large but soppy-looking Rottweiler.

'We'll do various tests, basic commands,' continued James, 'get the dogs to come back, sit down. That kind of thing. See whether you can stop the dog when it's over there somewhere. Basic stuff like that.'

James and Maria were both very energetic and enthusiastic, and they had a fully trained search and rescue dog with them, who showed us a few typical search techniques.

1. Harper and Ben clicked as soon as they went for a walk
around the Battersea grounds.

2. Ben's strict exercise regime
prescribed by his doctor was never
a chore with Harper by his side.

3. Harper soon became a member
of the Harrison family. This photo
was taken on one of their many
walks together.

4. After Cocoa tragically lost an eye, new dog Molly gave him
the confidence to run and explore again by her side.

5. Best of friends: Staffie Cross Molly and Cocoa.

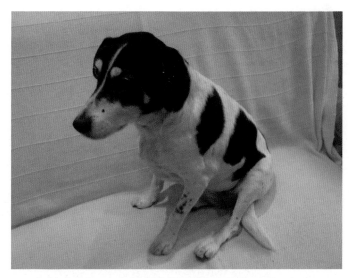

6. Little Lily was adopted as a lively pup from Battersea.

7. Owner Chris was relieved when his Battersea adoptee Benji instantly took to Labrador Daisy. Here they are enjoying the sun in their Guernsey garden.

8. Lucky lost a leg when she was thrown from a moving car at just a few weeks old, but she was given a new and loving home by Douglas Stroud.

9. Star the sensitive Rottweiler relaxes in the sun at her new home.

10. Bryn, the search and rescue Collie, is out in all weathers.

11. Bryn practising his search techniques in the woods: so important in helping to save lives.

12. Loyal and dependable Guinness helped her owner, Gill, through the hardest time of her life.

13. Stephanie couldn't resist the charms of happy little Terrier Johnny Reggae – or his unusual name!

14. Found on the day he was born on the grounds of Battersea, Wriggler needed constant love and care to keep him alive in his first few days.

15. As a tiny kitten Wriggler loved having his belly rubbed!

16. Owner Lisa says there's nothing she likes more than seeing her two Battersea cats, Wriggler and Johnson, curled up together by the fire.

17. English Bull Terrier Ice enjoying a weekend run on the beach in Denmark.

18. Ice lives up to her name; she's right at home in the Danish winter snow – it can be hard to spot her against all that white!

19. Jester the Staffie helped to bring someone very special into the life of his owner . . .

Then they got us to send our own dogs out, and call them back from around the woods.

Bryn was quite good with the basic commands, but my recall with him wasn't great. He was so excited that he kept running off into great piles of leaves and burrowing under them, looking for squirrels and rabbits, or getting distracted by the big Rottweiler and trying to play with him. Bryn was having a whale of a time with all the company but I was rather embarrassed.

'Sorry about Bryn. He's very good really,' I said to James.

'Don't worry. It's more about assessing the drive of the dog than anything else. It's not really meant to be an obedience test.'

'Really? Well, that's lucky!' I laughed.

'Yes. We find dogs that are too obedient, dogs that would really excel at an obedience test, don't necessarily make the best search dogs. We actually want them to use their own initiative.'

'Oh, right. I had expected it to be all about controlling the dog.'

'Well, it's no good having a dog that's constantly coming to you, asking "What do you want me to do next? Do you want me to go over there, or over there?" kind of thing. We want the dogs to be able to use their own initiative, but also to be under the control of the handler. It's getting that balance.'

This gave me a bit more confidence, as Bryn was nothing if not able to use his initiative. And it was wonderful to be out there in the woods, working with him.

'OK,' said Maria, rallying us all together again. 'We've

got another test. We want you to throw a ball and make sure it disappears from sight, then see if your dog keeps looking for it. Because, as James has said, what we need is a really strong working drive in our dogs. We don't want them to just say, "I can't find it," and give up.'

Bryn turned out to be very good at this. He would really keep searching for the ball, which I thought was a good sign. The final thing they tested was how you and your dog played together and interacted.

'So what's Bryn's favourite toy?' asked Maria, ruffling his fur.

'Tennis balls,' I said confidently. I knew Bryn did love them and I often used one as a reward for good behaviour.

'Are you sure?' she asked, and she started to play tug with him, with a piece of rope she had in her bag.

'I don't often play tug with him as a reward,' I said.

'Have a go,' she said as Bryn bit the end of the rope and shook it about. We pulled it back and forth between us for a while.

'Now your dog is really reacting to you,' she said, smiling. 'He wants to play with you. Whereas tossing a ball is just a passive throw-over-there. Does that make sense?'

'Yes!' I said. It was quite a revelation.

'The tug is like you and him having a little battle of who's gonna get that rope. And, look, he's in his element.'

It was true, Bryn was really enjoying pulling the rope back and forth, waiting for me to drop it then grab it again.

'You have to find out what your own dog prefers by way of a reward. So you should use this as the reward for the hardest things, and you'll find him a lot more responsive.'

I realized, after that, that I had made a fundamental flaw in my training with Bryn. I had been rewarding him with food, but he wasn't really that food-driven. Sometimes he would say 'Yes, thank you,' take the food and it was fine. But other times he would say, 'Actually, I'm very interested in that burrow down there.' I had to work out how to be more attractive than the rabbit, which is quite difficult!

By the end of the day we were all exhausted but totally exhilarated. I was absolutely buzzing and couldn't wait to do it again. But I still wasn't sure whether Bryn had passed his initial test. James came over, and I tried to tell from his expression whether Bryn had impressed them.

'He's a fast learner, that's for sure,' he said. 'And . . . yes, we'd love to take him on a probationary period to start with. Just to see how it works out.'

I couldn't stop grinning.

Not long after that, Bryn joined Kent Search and Rescue Dogs, and I also became a member of Kent Search and Rescue (KSAR), who have all kinds of other search teams including a boat team, foot team, flood rescue and even mountain bike teams. To do this, I had to go on a weekend course with about fifteen other people to learn general search and rescue skills; things like how to deal with the public, improve observation in the field, navigate with a map and compass, first aid, and how to operate a two-way radio.

Once I'd done that, and had a criminal records check, I started my training with the dog team. It's made up completely of volunteers, led by James who ran my assessment day. There's Maria, and of course my friend Estelle was now in the team too, plus the other qualified dog handlers to teach newbies like myself.

It was only a few weeks after I had finished my course, that I got my first call out. It was about two o'clock in the morning when I had a text from James saying they had been asked to look for an elderly gentleman who had gone missing from a local care home during the night.

'Are you going out now?' asked Stuart, rubbing his eyes and sitting up blearily.

'Yes,' I said. 'Go back to sleep. I'll be fine.'

I was still half asleep myself, and outside it was pitch black. After a cup of coffee and a splash of water to the face, I was surprisingly awake and alert, even a bit excited about what lay ahead. I said goodbye to Bryn, who was looking at me expectantly, as he had to stay behind, not being fully trained yet.

When I got to the meeting point, at a car park near the care home, everyone was standing in a circle with their torches on and wearing high-visibility jackets. The dog who was covering our area, a Hovawart called Venka, had her own harness with lights and a bell on it, so we could locate her easily in the dark.

As we stood huddled in the cold, ready to start our search, what hit me at that moment was the seriousness of the situation. Up until this point it had been me and Bryn running through the woods with balls, and playing tug with a piece of rope. Now it was someone's life we were talking about. There was a man out there, missing, who could actually die. And it was then the reality of what search and rescue was all about dawned on me. It wasn't about me and Bryn and our relationship, it was about finding real people.

'So the misper [missing person] was last seen here,' said James, pointing at his GPS. 'We'll cover this area, through the fields and sweeping across this way. Everyone know what they're doing?'

There was a chorus of yeses, though I was still unsure about what the night would hold. James was in charge of the dog and which direction we went and Maria was his support – she would do radio communications and act as medic. I was charged with carrying the bag with all the equipment in it.

'You've got spare GPS sat maps, a paper map, compass, first aid kit, water for the dog, and food and water for us,' said James. 'We also have disposable ponchos and silver foil insulator blankets, to put over the misper, a phone, notebook, umpteen spare torches and even dog boots, in case of having to go through really heavy brambles or debris like broken glass.'

'There's also a long-line for the dog, in case we go close to roads,' said Maria.

With all this stuff, we were quite laden down as we sent the dog off through the area closest to the care home. Not long after we started walking it began to rain, a fine drizzle that gets you really wet, and a cold easterly wind whipped through my coat. We entered a nearby field, the dog running off to one side and then another, basically covering as much ground as possible, trying to get a scent. It was so dark, I could only see as far as my flashlight beam.

'If we're this cold and wet I dread to think what it's like

for him,' I said to Maria. 'Out there on his own some-where. Confused probably.'

'Yes. Let's hope we find him soon. Sounds like he was only wearing a pair of slippers and a dressing gown,' she said, pulling her coat round her tightly.

After about an hour of searching we were all thoroughly soaked, and I was getting quite despondent, when the dog suddenly came back and gave James the signal, a bark that she'd found something. James followed her and we waited, hoping for good news but dreading the worst.

After about five minutes, he radioed through that he had found the man.

'He's tired and a bit confused and hypothermic, but he's alive,' the radio crackled.

I was so relieved.

When they emerged, James was walking with his arm around the man to keep him steady. We had called an ambulance to the nearest road and as they took the man away he was muttering in a confused way to himself. He looked so small and frail and vulnerable.

'You have no idea just how close you were to losing your life,' I thought to myself as the ambulance disappeared from view with its lights flashing.

When I got home, I couldn't sleep. My head was literally buzzing. I was happy we had found the man, but also sad that he had been so vulnerable. From now on I would see my search and rescue training in a completely different light. It was a serious job, not just a game of tug in the woods. And I was even more determined than ever for Bryn and me to get through our training, and become a real search and rescue team.

As well as going out on call with the search and rescue team, I went to fortnightly training sessions with the unit, and we would also train with one another in between times if we were available. In order to improve our observational skills, James and Maria would sometimes hide objects in the woods for me to find.

'In the field,' James told us, 'if you have rough ground, a body can look about the size of a rucksack, especially if it's a child.'

So he'd hide a dark rucksack and test at what point we trainees spotted it. It was amazing how many I didn't see at first, but I gradually began to pick it up.

It wasn't all about training me, though. I also had to work with Bryn and improve his search skills.

This started off with hiding behind a tree, as I'd done on our walks together, and seeing if he could find me. If he did I would give him a big reward, like a game of tug, then I would build up the distance. Sometimes another person would run in on the right-hand side, then I'd turn Bryn's head away. He thought he knew where they were, but whilst he couldn't see they would jump to the other side to confuse him, and give him a few feet of searching to do. This was called 'runaways'.

After this they showed me and Bryn how to do the next stage, which was to get Bryn to search for someone and then come back to the handler to tell them when he'd found them.

'It's no good having a dog find the person, but not tell you where they are,' said James. 'Nearly all dogs will do some sort of search and find. That's the fun bit, the hunting bit. But to get the dog to come back to the handler, bark, and then take them back to what they've just found – that's the hard part.'

Each dog has to learn an 'alert', and in Bryn's case, because he's so bossy, he would bark at me to tell me to follow him. After two months of training was up, Bryn was starting to get quite good at it. He was quick and he loved the challenge. He had calmed down a lot too. He was less aggressive, because he was using all the energy and pent-up frustration he had shown at agility club in a positive way. But he was still very wilful and independent and I wondered if this would count against us when it came to decision time.

One evening, after our training at the local TA centre, James took me into a side room. I knew our probation period was up and I was shaking. I was absolutely desperate to continue and I knew we could do it.

'OK,' said James, quietly rubbing his hands together.

Uh-oh, I thought. Doesn't sound good.

'But we're going to defer our decision until you have improved your recall a bit.'

'Oh. OK,' I said. I couldn't hide my disappointment, but in my heart I knew he was right. My recall wasn't good enough. Bryn was still too easily distracted and wouldn't always come back when I called him.

'Don't worry about it. There's another chance. We can't commit just yet, that's all.' James slapped me cheerfully on the back. 'But we'll all continue to support you both as much as we can. All right?'

After that I was absolutely determined to get through. And as soon as I could, I met up with Estelle to work on the problem areas Bryn and I had.

'I've got to work on this recall because they're going to chuck him out, otherwise,' I told her.

'I'm sure we can sort that out,' she laughed. 'Bryn's got some brains in him. And I bet he doesn't want to fail either.'

I immediately put him on a long line and let him out five metres away. He started sniffing something in the ground, I called him back and he totally ignored me!

'James was right,' I sighed. 'I haven't got the recall.'

But the next time, Bryn went off the lead, right across the field, and when I called he came running straight to me. So I was totally confused.

'He's just doing it when he wants to,' explained Estelle. 'He's doing it how he wants to. On his own terms. And we need to change that so you're more in control. That's all.'

We decided to use the tug game as a reward more often, like Maria had suggested. Estelle would be on the other side of the field and we'd call him between us. Bryn would go ballistic running to each of us. He'd bound up to Estelle: 'Yes, wahoo! A game of tug!' Then he'd run back to me: 'Yay, another game of tug!' And so on, back and forth, gradually building up his recall skills. Eventually, after a few weeks of hard slog, it seemed to be working.

One frosty afternoon, James came out with me to the woods, and I sent Bryn off, as we had practised. I called him back a few times, but I was still really nervous. After a while, James started nodding. Bryn was responding.

'Yep, he's got it now,' he said. 'It's finally clicked, hasn't it? That's great. I think you can come back on the training programme. If you're still interested.'

'Am I interested? Of course I am!' I said and almost jumped in the air I was so pleased.

It was nearly Christmas, and Stuart and I had a celebratory festive meal out. It was great to have a break from all the training. But I still couldn't help myself talking about it.

'I realize now I went in for the wrong reasons at the beginning,' I said to Stuart as we ate dinner. 'I thought it would be a good thing to do with my dog. But in fact it's so much more than that. The dog is just a tool for the task of finding someone.'

'I can see that. Well, it's certainly making you happy, anyway,' he said. 'And I love having Bryn with me during the day too.'

Stuart was very supportive of me spending all this time out with the dog. In fact, he had started to get involved too; he had joined KSAR and the dog unit, coming with me to training sessions with a view to becoming a 'support' for me and the other dog handlers during search and rescues.

'To Bryn,' we said that night, and clinked our glasses.

Once I was back on the course, the hard work really started. The first level of qualification then was called a 'hasty' or 'route and path', which meant the dogs were trained to search up to twenty-five metres either side of a path.

'If we go along a path like this,' said James on the first day, 'with woodland on either side, we can then tell police that we have cleared twenty-five metres down either side. And they know they can move on.'

'Why twenty-five metres?' I asked. 'It sounds very specific.'

'The statistics tell us that a lot of people who go missing

will be near a footpath, so they're actually likely to be less than twenty metres or so away. It makes sense to do that distance first, before a more wide-ranging search.'

The only problem was that when we sent Bryn off into the woods, he didn't seem to understand the concept of twenty-five metres. Two hundred metres, then he's your man (or your dog!) but twenty-five? That was a struggle. So for the first few months I had to work really hard to say, 'Actually, Bryn, can you just go down there and then come back?' He would just look at me as if to say, 'What, Mum? There's nothing down there – I'm going this way. It's much more fun.'

One of the other big challenges was getting him to do the four stages of a search for a 'misper' – that's the term we use for a missing person. The dogs have to learn to come back once they have found the person, return to the handler and give their 'alert' (barking, in Bryn's case) and then do the 'show me', which is to re-find where the misper is when the handler asks the dog to take them there. James and the team would set up sessions outdoors where we could hide for each other, pretending to be a misper for the dogs to look for.

'For the dogs to find us, they use air-scenting. They're trained to pick up the scent of humans, preferably in the wind,' said James.

'Is it all air scent or do they track too?' I asked. 'Will Bryn have to learn to recognize footprints or something?'

'Not really – a bit perhaps, but basically they are scenting most of the time. That's their forte. And that's what we've got to teach them.'

We started by putting whoever was pretending to be

the misper into the wind so that the dog could pick up the scent easily. I spent many an hour standing under some tree or other, while one of the dogs came looking for me. After they'd mastered that, we would put the misper downwind of the dog. That way the dog had to move in order to pick up the smell, and we gradually made it harder and harder for them.

'In a bigger area, like a large field, the dogs zigzag across, following what's called a scent cone, the way the scent fans out from the source,' said James, as we walked towards a particularly thick piece of woodland where one of our group was hiding. 'Here it's a bit trickier, because the scent gets bounced around everywhere. We have a lot of craters in the ground in Kent – we call them 'bomb holes' – and these obscure the scent.'

'Anything else I should know about that can get in the way of the scent?' I asked.

'If the temperature's dropping then the scent will fall down to the ground, if it's warming the scent will rise, or it might suddenly get blown up over a bank and deposited elsewhere. So, all in all, it's a complicated process. Not just picking up scent, but working out where the person is too, if they're moving, for example.'

You can only reward the dog if they get it right. At first we always knew where the misper was, so we could tell whether the dog had got it right, and we would tell each other by radio when they had been found correctly. By the end we were literally hiding in ditches, or burying ourselves into tree branches, fallen logs and all sorts, to make the dogs really work at it.

'Maria, you like climbing trees, don't you?' said James. 'You go up there and Bryn can find you.'

'I love climbing trees!' she said and scaled niftily up a tall oak. She hid perfectly silently amongst the branches while Bryn moved this way and that, sniffing out her scent. He eventually found the tree, but then took a while to realize he had to look up. Then he had a lightbulb moment: 'Oh yeah, she's up there!' he barked and ran back to me to let me know.

After the official sessions, I would continue training Bryn on our walks. Estelle would often help with this, by hiding for me somewhere in the woods. One afternoon, she went down a track and disappeared. I knew where she was hiding, and I took Bryn down another path, so he couldn't track her. But he was so fast, he picked up her scent before she'd even got into position, ran back and alerted me by literally running into my legs and barking.

I had been taught by James to react by saying 'Show me! Show me!' really energetically, to keep Bryn motivated and to get him to take me there. I summoned all my enthusiasm and he bombed off again and kept coming back to show me the way. Obviously I couldn't go as fast as him, or over the same rough terrain – trees and brambles, under logs and so on – so I had to make my own path through. The movement back and forth by the dog, to guide you, is called a 'shuttle' and 'reshuttle'.

I found it incredible. All of a sudden, Bryn was the boss. He knew where the person was, I didn't. 'Come on, Mum, it's this way,' he would say, until eventually he stopped. He had followed the scent, but couldn't find her.

Sometimes in real life, people will move around, so Estelle had replicated that by moving on. But Bryn is a smart dog, and in the end he found her new position, came back to tell me, and there was Estelle, huddled up under a big log.

'You found me!' she said, and we gave Bryn a very big reward.

Sometimes, in the early days, I wasn't sure if Bryn had really found someone or whether he was winding me up. He used to have fun, leading me on a bit of a merry dance on occasion. He'd say 'I found one, I found one' and then there'd be nobody there. After a few months of training, though, he started to get it more and more often. And when it was nearly time for our assessment, I thought he had it cracked.

Even though I had done a few mock practise sessions with James, I was an absolute wreck when it came to the real assessment. I've never been so nervous in my life, in fact. Partly because I knew Bryn could do it, and I was just thinking, 'God, if I mess this up I'll be letting him down.'

When it came to the actual day, I was so worried I over-did it a bit, overcompensating for my nerves. I kept telling him to go here and there, up that path, down that ditch. And he just kept looking at me: 'For God's sake, Mum, leave me alone, let me search.'

The assessment was an hour to an hour and a half, but it felt like longer. I had to navigate and keep track of where he'd gone, and manage all the communications over the radios, too.

'It's not just a matter of dog training or dog handling,' said James. 'From the moment you qualify, you could be out there on a search. You have to deal with finding a real person – what are you going to do? How are you going to handle that situation if they're injured, hypothermic? Calling an ambulance, working out how to get yourself out of that situation if they're in the middle of the woods, for instance. Do you need stretchers? What provisions do you need? All this as well as being able to do first aid. If somebody was stuck down a ditch, with a broken leg and unable to get out, in the middle of the woods somewhere, and you've got no obvious path in or out. There's a lot of decision-making to be done.'

My mind boggled. It was an emotional roller coaster, all this training and being tested. Although we had rehearsed all this many times, it was always going to be a challenge under pressure. In the end, I scraped through the assessment. I had been so nervous, I think it impaired my judgement a bit. But I knew in my heart that I was ready. And Bryn was definitely ready. I knew that if Bryn found a person he would tell me every time without fail.

Then, at two o'clock in the morning, a few weeks later, I got a text from James: 'Can you come to the rendezvous point? With Bryn. Despondent female missing.'

'On our way,' I replied.

Despondent is the technical search and rescue term for someone who is depressed, possibly suicidal. I was shaking. Now it was for real.

'What was that?' asked Stuart.

'Misper. Despondent female. They want Bryn to help with the search.'

So we got him kitted up in his harness with the lights and bell. Stuart was coming with me as my support: he would navigate, do the radio and act as medic. We would then search as a two-man team with the dog.

'She's written a note,' said James when we got there. 'Broken up with her boyfriend, apparently. The note said she'd gone out on one of their walks. So we have an idea of the route she may have used and it includes a popular viewpoint.'

As Bryn had been trained to go twenty-five metres from the path, we went off down the footpaths nearby. It was pitch black and the torchlight was picking up all the insects darting across my path. It was early summer now, and there was a fresh smell of honeysuckle on the air, which struck me as incongruous given the potentially tragic circumstances. Bryn ran off ahead and out of sight, while we climbed up the steps to the top of the bank, near the viewpoint. After about twenty minutes walking he ran back, ran into my legs and started barking madly. My heart was in my mouth.

'Show me! Show me!' I said, as I had practised so many times before.

It was a magic moment. But then I had the horrible thought.

'My goodness. I hope she's alive,' I said to Stuart. 'Let's get there quickly. Come on, Bryn, show the way.'

We left the others, and followed Bryn down the bank, which dropped off suddenly. He kept coming back to guide us down; I could hardly see a thing it was so dark. Eventually I could just make out a pile of really big stones, almost like a cave, dripping with water, way down below the viewpoint. Then, in the light of my torch, I saw a woman's leg.

'She's trapped between the stones,' I said. 'We've got to get down there.'

Bryn was already at the bottom, panting and excited to have made his find. We scrambled our way down amongst the big rocks. There was a young woman just lying there. She looked grey and her hair was plastered across her face. She was unconscious.

'Hello,' I said gently, 'can you hear me? Are you all right? We're here to help.'

Although you have to reward the dogs when they make a find, Bryn also seemed to sense the seriousness of the situation. He went quite quiet, and allowed me to get on with the job. I sat down beside the young woman and checked her pulse. I could hear Stuart on the radio, letting the team know we had found her.

'Let them know she's alive,' I said. 'She's breathing, but very faintly.'

I put the silver blanket over her to keep her warm and tucked it in. She came to and muttered something incoherent. I could smell alcohol on her breath.

'Looks like she might have overdosed,' I said. 'We'll need an ambulance. And a stretcher to get her out.'

Everything I had learnt in our training sessions came back to me and I went into a kind of automatic coping mode.

'What have you taken?' I asked the woman. 'Do you remember whether you took any pills or drink?'

While the foot team were on their way I had to keep her talking, although she wasn't able to say much. They arrived after about twenty minutes, though it felt like a lifetime to me, and we stretchered her out to the ambulance.

Once she had been taken away, mixed emotions hit me. It had been an awful and scary situation. But I was also really excited, and kind of ecstatic for Bryn who'd made his first find.

'The pain she must have been in emotionally, to try to take her own life like that,' I said to Stuart as we drove home. 'But I'm so proud of Bryn. He saved her.'

In the days after that I gave Bryn a lot of rewards, playing games and especially tug with him, so he knew I was pleased.

Before long, Bryn started to get a reputation for being really smart at finding people. Members of the unit even started having fun trying to outsmart him, though they rarely succeeded.

'I think you can start training for the next level,' said James, not long afterwards. 'Level Three – an area search of up to fifty acres.'

I was ecstatic, and since Bryn liked to range big distances anyway, he was a natural at area searches. We started preparing for the next assessment with eagerness. I had to work out his strengths and weaknesses, and make sure I had a really good strategy for approaching where the scent was. He had to learn to trust me too; sometimes he wouldn't believe me that someone was down in a deep ditch or a bomb hole, because he couldn't pick up the scent straight away. It was really a case of working out our relationship and trusting each other.

By the following spring we were being tested by James for Level Three.

It seemed to be going well on the day, and Bryn was absolutely brilliant. After about half an hour he came and barked at me to tell me that he'd found who was hiding. For some reason I panicked. I thought he was messing about with me. So I ignored his alert – three times! Eventually I found the misper crouched in a ditch.

'He's been in to you before, hasn't he?' I said.

'Yeah, three times actually.'

'That's a fail, then,' I said. 'And not because of you, Bryn, either.'

Bryn just looked at me and wagged his tail as if to say, 'I told you so!'

I was so disappointed that I had let him down. But I knew it was right not to get a pass, because when you're on a real search you've got to be able to completely trust your dog.

We retook the test a few weeks later, and Bryn was great as usual. I, however, did have one more panicky moment. I had almost finished my assessment and it had gone really well. We just had one last bit of woodland to cover when Bryn picked up the scent and started to go off. Then I saw the deer.

'Nooooo, it's my assessment!' I thought. 'Bryn, come back!'

I am always a bit afraid of coming across deer. They're a big distraction and it's happened before with Bryn that he's got sidetracked. But this time he hadn't picked up on the deer, and he waited when I called him. The deer went past and I thought, Right, you're in scent now, Bryn's going to pick up on you. But because he'd picked up on the person's scent first, thank goodness, he prioritized that instead.

I had nothing to worry about in the end. I managed to

trust him with the searches and, in spite of the deer, we sailed through it.

Bryn was now an area dog, and not long after that, I got another middle of the night text from James.

At the rendezvous point the search managers were huddled together again, planning the route when we got there.

'Two teenagers with learning disabilities haven't returned back home from the youth club. One of them is diabetic,' said James. 'The lad hasn't got his medication, either. So ... Well, anyway. Let's hope for the best. At least there are two of them together.'

We had been asked to cover the beach area, and we took Bryn up quite high along the cliff, pushing him up and down the bank. After a while, he disappeared into some beach huts then ran back and alerted me. I ran down the crumbling verge, but there was no one there.

'I think they're running away from us,' I said to Stuart. 'Probably think they're in trouble. Running away from the police or something.'

So Bryn had to re-find a few times; every time I got there the boys had always moved on. Bryn just kept finding them and they eventually gave in and stopped running. When I got there, they were both sitting down, exhausted, hungry and thirsty, leaning against a sandy piece of cliff. The lad with diabetes didn't look very well. He had his head in his hands.

'He needs his medication,' I said to James via the radio.

I think the lad was quite relieved, really, when we escorted them back and got him some medical help.

When I've got my high-vis jacket on, and he can sense the buzz of everybody else out there, Bryn always seems to know it's a real search. He can be a little bit stubborn and hot-headed when we're training, thinking he knows best. But when he's doing a real search he knows the seriousness of it and responds really well.

Sometimes it's very hard work for the dogs, searching for many hours at a time. Once we were searching through some really thick bluebell woods, knee-high in bluebells all day long. That was tiring, but after that we had to do another area search the same night, and this time we were knee-high in garlic! Bryn was absolutely exhausted, and now he stank of garlic, and I stank of it too.

'You'll never smell out a person in all this!' I said, although dogs' sense of smell is far more advanced than ours.

We'd been training all day, now we stank of garlic, and then, to top it all, I got a call to do another search. In the end, Bryn just lay down by the car and curled up. That is something active Collies very rarely do. So I radioed in. 'I think he's had enough,' I said to James. You've got to know when your dog needs a break.

Bryn has had one other search success since he qualified four years ago. A man had been missing for three nights, and everyone was really worried. He was despondent and high risk. We were asked to search an area that included a garden at the back of a hotel, and then lakes and fields and dense woodland on a really steep bank. I was a bit daunted by the terrain, and thought I'd start with the easy bit first: the hotel garden.

In two minutes, Bryn came running back at me.

'That was the fastest find you've ever done!' I said. 'Show me!'

After just a few minutes, I saw the guy we were looking for sitting on a bench at the bottom of the hotel garden. He had a brown overcoat on and his head had lolled to one side. When I got up to him it was clear that he had overdosed on something. His body temperature had dropped really low, and he was very dehydrated. But he was alive; once again Bryn had come up trumps.

Since getting Bryn from Battersea, and joining Kent Search and Rescue, I have not stopped being amazed by what my dog is capable of doing and finding. I am now a trainer myself, and absolutely love teaching the skills I've learnt to all the new dogs. The biggest thing I have discovered since joining the search and rescue team is that you've got to want to be out there looking for a vulnerable missing person. It's not just about the dog and having fun with them. You've got to be really committed to the whole thing. It has taken over my life really. Some days I've been out searching all night, and then I have to go to work the next day, and I pretty well look like death warmed up.

But it's an absolute privilege to work with such clever dogs, while also helping to save lives. And I couldn't have done any of it without Bryn.

Guinness: A Loyal Companion

The Staffordshire Bull Terrier makes up over 30 per cent of our intake. Despite being a loving, courageous and spirited breed, the Staffie is misunderstood, and for this reason is harder to rehome. Registered with the Kennel Club since 1935, with its breed standard stating 'affectionate especially with children', we at Battersea Dogs & Cats Home are dedicated to giving the Staffie a chance of being better understood.

The breed has its origins in nineteenth-century dog-fighting: bulldogs, known for their athleticism, were bred with faster terriers and despite dog-fighting being outlawed in 1835, the fashion for owning a dog to look tough has given the Staffie an unjust reputation as a dangerous animal. In just over a decade we have seen an incredible 326 per cent increase in the number of bull breeds arriving at Battersea. In large part this is due to the increasing popularity of these so-called 'status dogs'.

We believe that these misunderstood dogs should be given a better chance to find loving families. In fact, we probably take on more Staffordshire Bull Terriers than any other animal charity. And although they tend to stay with us longer, we also hear many success stories from owners, like Gill Rae, who are proud to say they have rehomed a Staffie.

I had my first Staffie, Jessie Dog, for seventeen years. I loved her so much, I was more upset when she died than when my ex-husband walked out after twenty-five years.

After bringing up our three children, my husband and I had grown apart, and it was for the best when we split up. Strangely, Jessie Dog seemed to know immediately that my husband had left, and made herself right at home on the sofa, where she'd never been allowed when he was around.

After the divorce, I got a job in an HIV/AIDS clinic. My son Nathan was living at home and working, my other son, Daniel, had moved out, and my daughter, Karli, was at university. With the kids all independent now, I had some newfound freedom and started to enjoy a bit of a social life. After a while, I met a new bloke, Mark. We seemed to get along well and eventually he moved in.

It was around this time that Jessie Dog started to go downhill.

'She's just not her usual self,' I said to Mark one day. She seemed thin and wouldn't respond to anything. We were back and forth to the vet's, trying all sorts of things to get her better: pills, medicines, changing her diet, but to no avail. In the end her quality of life had deteriorated so much that we agreed it would be best for her to be put to sleep. I was close to tears as I told Nathan that I was taking her to the vet's.

'She won't be coming back home,' I said.

'Why won't she?' he asked.

'I'm afraid she's in a lot of pain and . . .' The penny finally dropped and Nathan hugged her with tears in his eyes and said his goodbyes.

As hard as it was, you know when it's time if their life is so diminished and you've tried everything the vets have to offer. I had to love Jessie enough to let her go, no matter how tough it felt.

We were all heartbroken when Jessie died. She had been part of the family for so long, she left a real void in our lives. I went through a difficult period at work around this time, and a combination of stress from my job and grief at losing Jessie meant I sank into a depression and, in the end, I just couldn't return to work. I was also finding it increasingly hard to leave the house.

One afternoon, a friend came round. Her son had recently passed away and, just before he died, he had promised to get her a little dog. She was so upset, she decided to go and get one anyway, in his memory. I went along with her to the Battersea Old Windsor branch, more for moral support than anything.

We wandered around, looking at all the poor animals, and in the end my friend found a lovely little terrier. This sweet thing jumped up at us wagging its tail and, at that moment, I realized how much I missed having a dog in my life.

So I filled out a few forms too. Just in case.

A while passed, and I forgot all about it. Then, a few weeks later, I got a phone call.

'Gill? It's Battersea Dogs & Cats Home. We've got a dog you might like.'

I had to think for a moment before I realized what they were talking about.

'We're looking for an experienced owner, for this little Staffie we have. And we wondered, would you be able to come and have a look at her?'

'Well, yes, of course!' I said, delighted they might have

found a dog for me, and that I was classified as an experienced owner. I suppose, after seventeen years with Jessie Dog, I was!

The first thing they did was visit to check my house, to make sure it was dog friendly. They came round to where I was living and were satisfied with that, so next it was a trip down to Battersea to meet the dog. Mark and I and my friend Sam all went together in the car.

When we got there they were exercising this little black and white Staffie in the grounds and I bent down to stroke her. The first thing she did was nip the tip of my nose, she was so excited. But it was a friendly nip, and I was smitten.

'She's just a puppy. About six to twelve months,' said the handler. 'We've called her Connex, because she was found on the Connex South East railway line at Norwood Junction. Just wandering about, abandoned. Luckily one of our nurses was on the platform and picked her up and brought her here.'

'What do you know about her life, beforehand?' I asked.

'Well, she hasn't been chipped. We know that. And we think her previous owner must have shut her in a confined space, because she gets really stressed. She's got a real phobia about being shut in.'

'Oh, poor thing. Who could abandon you?' I said, stroking her little velvety head.

When we left the room to fill out some forms, she started to howl like a banshee. It was a really horrible and desperate noise. She just could not bear to be left alone, shut in. It meant I wouldn't be able to put her in a kennel, but I wasn't deterred by that at all. She was young, so I was confident she'd adapt to a new home. And I knew there and then she was the dog for me.

Battersea had named her Connex, but Mark said he thought she looked more like a half pint of Guinness, with her black body and white markings on her head. So that was what we named her. Guinness.

Once we had sorted out all the paperwork and were taking Guinness to the car, Mark kept saying 'sit', 'sit', 'sit', over and over again, in a serious voice. He had this notion he could train dogs, and was trying to get this little puppy to sit down till he was blue in the face. In the end, Sam and I had to sit on the curb we were laughing so much. Guinness just stood there looking at him with her head on one side, wagging her tail. We knew she wasn't going to do it. She was lovely, but very unruly, and completely untrained.

When we got her home I let her out into the garden, and she went absolutely ballistic, running round and round in circles. Then she came back into the house and ran up the stairs, and round all the bedrooms and back outside again in a matter of seconds.

'She must have a rocket up her bum!' I laughed.

Back in the garden she had managed to chew through the fence to next door.

'Oh my God, their cat!' I said. 'Come back, Guinness!'

Then I heard a most awful yelp. A moment later, our little dog came skulking back through the hole in the fence. She had a large scratch on her face where next-door's cat had clearly told her who was boss.

Guinness did wonders for my health. I had been feeling increasingly depressed since losing my job and, apart from the trip to Battersea, I'd been struggling to leave the house.

But once I had a dog again I had to get out and walk her, because she'd just look at me with her big soft eyes. I started to go out to the park near my house, and I soon remembered how good it felt to be out in the fresh air.

I started training her to come back when she was called. She was all right most of the time, but even now she can still be a bit wilful. She's also quite protective of me, so I only let her off the lead when I'm with dogs I know, or if no one's about. It's more for my security, really, knowing no one's going to hurt her.

'I think she may have been beaten in the past,' I said to Mark one day when we were out walking. 'If she sees a stick she seems compelled to take it away and then smash it into a million pieces!'

She's so enthusiastic she can be a bit of a handful at times, especially when visitors come round. She thinks they've come to see her, I'm sure. She adores the attention, and will go mad, running circuits around the house – up the stairs, round the bedrooms, you name it. What with this and her banshee howl, some people can be a bit daunted, but she's an absolute softie really. I've noticed that if people are scared of her, she'll make a point of going to them straight away, wagging her tail, as if to say, 'Don't be daft! I'm not vicious.'

Staffies are really misunderstood as a breed. They've got such a bad reputation, but I think they make ideal companions. They adapt well, and they're very good town dogs too. It's so sad that when they talk about dangerous dogs on the news, all the pictures they show are always Staffs. Any dog is capable of fighting and causing injury

– even small dogs – and really it's the owner's responsibility to train them well.

It's true Guinness can be a bit boisterous, but she's also very sensitive and I think she detected the depression in me. She was never quite as rowdy around me as with other people, and I don't think it was just my officious Barbara Woodhouse-type voice that calmed her down!

The biggest thing Guinness did for me at that time was give me more confidence. I took her to dog training classes in the evening, where I met some lovely people. And, step by step, I began to build my life back up again after the shock of having to leave my job.

Guinness also made me laugh like nothing else. On our walks, she'd pick up a great big log, take one look at me and shoot off with this enormous thing in her mouth that was twice as big as her. She knew I'd never let her take it home, and she'd be in such a hurry to run off with it that she'd get stuck between the park gateposts. Other times we would go to a gravel pit that had been filled in with water, and she loved paddling and chasing ducks there. She never caught one, but I think she had crispy aromatic on the brain. She enjoyed chasing squirrels too. Sometimes she would even try running up trees after them. I couldn't help laughing at the confused look on her face when she failed to scamper up the trunk like they did.

Once we found a rope swing someone had made and Mark was showing off on it, swinging back and forth. Guinness immediately clocked a stick on the swing, ran over and jumped up to get it. But unfortunately she got the stick and his private parts muddled up. There was the dog hanging on for dear life but I couldn't do anything about it – I have to admit, I was wetting myself laughing.

Years seemed to fly by once I had Guinness. Karli, my daughter, finished university and met and married her husband, Jason. When they had their first baby, a little girl called Nell, I was over the moon. When I looked after my granddaughter as a baby, I could leave Guinness by the pram and she wouldn't let anyone near it. Then, when Nell started to explore, Guinness would lie across the stairs to stop her crawling up, or lie at the bottom while the baby was sleeping upstairs and then come and tell me when she was awake. The Victorians called Staffs 'nanny dogs' because they are so good with children. When Nell's first words were 'no' and 'Guinness' we all laughed so much we nearly cried.

Soon afterwards, my son Daniel's girlfriend had a baby, Isabella, and the next year Karli had another daughter, Indy; then Nathan's girlfriend had Nathan Junior; Karli had a son, Eden; Daniel's girlfriend had James and finally Nathan had another son, Lucas. So I've had seven grand-children in seven years! They've all grown up with Guinness and Guinness absolutely loves them.

After a few years with Guinness I was pretty much clear of the depression. She had settled into her new home, and I had started to put my troubles behind me. I had great friends and a wonderful family. But you never know what's around the corner.

Aged fifty you get a mammogram automatically on the NHS. I had mine just before I went on holiday one year with my niece, Cher. We were visiting a friend in Ibiza, and we couldn't wait. We planned how we'd spend our holiday, lazing on the beach and partying and chilling with friends.

But I had this mammogram to get out of the way before we left. It was pretty routine, but afterwards they said they wanted me to come back in for some more checks. I didn't think much of it. I'd had a few harmless lumps and bumps in the past, and I had the holiday on my mind. We went and had a great time and the mammogram hardly crossed my thoughts. But as I made my way to the hospital the following week, I started to feel a bit nervous. Why had they asked me to come back?

'I'm afraid it's worse than we thought,' said the consultant in a grave voice. 'There are some abnormal cells and it definitely is breast cancer. But we need to do further investigations before we can tell you any more.'

Cancer. I was stunned. I didn't know what to think.

The thing that really upset me, though, was when he said, just before I left, 'Oh, and please try not to cry too much. Because it might upset the other women who are waiting to come in.' I was taken aback by that. I thought it was a bit insensitive, considering the news I'd just been given.

As it happened I was actually quite composed as I walked down the corridor. On the way out, I bumped into a consultant I'd worked with before. I told her what had happened, and we had a little chat about what it all meant.

It was only when I phoned my daughter that I broke down.

'I'll come and get you,' said Karli softly, when I started to cry. She met me at the station and really helped me to deal with those first moments.

When I got home, Guinness was ever so gentle too. She seemed to know something was up, and she also kept trying to nuzzle under my armpit; at the time, I didn't think much of it.

When I went back to the hospital, they told me I would need a lumpectomy, surgery to cut out the growth. Once that was done I thought it would all be over. But after the operation they announced that the consultant wanted to see me.

'The cancer has spread,' he said. And he told me that I had to have a mastectomy – where they remove the whole breast – and my lymph glands removed too.

Again, I thought that would be the end of it. But after the mastectomy it turned out I had what they called 'advanced aggressive cancer', and they said it was terminal.

So this is it, I thought. 'I'm on the cancer trail.'

When I got home, I realized that this was what Guinness had been trying to tell me all along, when she kept nuzzling my armpit. Dogs have a kind of sixth sense, and I'm sure they pick up on things that we don't. She was quite aware that something was amiss even before I was. From then on she was so sensitive and gentle, and she wouldn't leave my side. When I had to call an ambulance one day, she was so protective she wouldn't even let the paramedics in. In the end they called out a doctor as I just couldn't leave her.

Chemotherapy lasted for a year. I was wired up to a drip as a horrible concoction of freezing cold drugs went round my veins. Some of the treatment was so toxic they said I wasn't allowed to be around young or old people for twenty-four hours afterwards, because I was actually toxic myself.

One day I asked one of the nurses, 'Do these drugs make you hallucinate?' Cos I think . . . Elvis is in the building . . .'

I was feeling a bit woozy, and I was sure I had just seen Elvis Presley walking through the ward.

'Oh, that's just an impersonator!' said the nurse. And it turned out they had brought some actors into the hospital to come round the wards and sing, dressed up as famous people. As well as Elvis there was also Marilyn Monroe wandering about, so thankfully I wasn't seeing things after all.

Before I had my first treatment my friend Tiff came round to cut my long hair to shoulder length, to get me prepared.

'When it starts coming out in clumps, I'll shave it off for you,' said Tiff. 'So it's not such a shock. You know, rather than it all coming out on your pillow.'

And within three weeks I'd lost it all. In the end, though, I didn't mind so much losing my hair. It was losing my eyebrows and eyelashes that were the horrible thing. That gave me the 'I'm sick' look.

Then came the radiotherapy. They pinpoint an X-ray at the tumour site, but it kills good tissue as well as bad. At least with chemo you're in a room with other people. With radiotherapy you're completely alone, with this thing blasting your body.

My friends all really came up trumps supporting me when I was ill. Even people I didn't know that well rallied round. Deb and Michelle, my friends who lived round the corner, would drag me out to the pub to cheer me up. The cab drivers used to call us the Bermuda Triangle because we all visited each other so often. The people at the pub were great too. They used to look after my false boob behind the bar! I used to laugh with my Irish friends about the drugs in the chemo – the doctors and nurses shorten its name to FEC, and it always made me think of *Father Ted*. And another time my wig nearly caught fire on one of the heaters.

When I first lost my hair, my granddaughter Isabella asked me, 'Granny, where's your hair gone?' I said, 'I don't know, I must have lost it,' and she said, 'Well, have you looked under the bed?' Not long after that, she noticed my surgery, and said, 'Granny, where's your boobs gone?' I said, 'I've lost them.' She replied firmly, 'Well, you're really getting very forgetful in your old age, aren't you Granny?' It was the laughter that really got me through it in the end.

One thing which did hit me hard was when I found out Mark was cheating on me. Mark and I had been together on and off for nine years, but I hadn't realized things were so bad between us. I was too focused on staying alive, I suppose. I was so angry I could have burnt his clothes, like they do in films, but in the end I just threw him out. After that I tried to get on with my life, but a friend of mine phoned to tell me that a mate had just said to her, 'I'm so sorry about the loss of your friend Gill.' It turned out that not only had Mark had an affair, he'd taken compassionate leave from work, having told them I was dead! Well, that really takes the biscuit, I thought. I'm well rid of him.

Some days I was so ill, I didn't have the will to get up. That's why I was lucky to have Guinness. I didn't feel so lost having her there. When I came back from my treatments I always knew there would be a friendly face. She was such a character and always cheered me up. I was worried about her being walked, and would ask friends to help out. But there were times when she just wanted to stay near me and didn't want to go out at all.

After I was diagnosed, I had a friend, Paddy, move in to help me. I had known her since she came to England from Malaysia to train as a nurse, and she was between jobs. It was great having her around, because I didn't know how ill I was going to get. The one thing I didn't want was my kids to have to help me wash and go to the toilet; they all had young kids of their own and I thought it would be too much for them. My family were great, though. My nephew would come round and cook for me. But because of all the treatment, the worst thing was that I had lost my sense of taste. So he would cook for me to cheer me up, but I couldn't taste a thing. It was torture!

When I was really at my lowest ebb, my friends Michelle and Sam nominated me for a charity event called Caroline's Campaign. The charity had been set up by Caroline Monk, who had been a PA for Mike Oldfield. She had suffered with breast cancer and said she'd felt like she wasn't attractive, losing her hair and everything. So when she was in remission she founded a charity, which would choose a number of women to take to London and give a really glamorous treat. I was delighted when I got picked, along with five other women. They took us to Toni & Guy in London, did our hair or gave us fabulous wigs and got us all dressed up. It was such a giggle. Then a pink stretch Hummer, complete with a bar stocked with champagne, took us to a nightclub where our friends and family met us to see our new look. It was really wonderful, when I felt so rubbish, to be taken out and glammed up like that. It was a turning point for me – I even raised money for a hospice where I had spent some time by doing a sponsored parachute jump, which was an amazing experience.

My nieces promised that, as soon as I was well enough, we'd go on holiday to Barbados, to visit a friend, and that was my focus. I was lucky enough to begin a year's course of the drug Herceptin which, along with the chemo and radiotherapy, I responded well to. Then, before I knew it, I was saying goodbye to Guinness, who was being looked after by my son, as I flew off to the Caribbean. Barbados was amazing and we had great fun getting the lifeguards to rescue my fake breasts, which often floated away out of my swimming costume. Not so much shark attack as boob alert!

When all my treatment had finished I thought to myself, there's no point getting a second bite at the cherry if you're stuck with the same old stresses and strife. Life's too short. The house in Uxbridge was starting to feel a bit big for me and Guinness now the children had gone. It was time to buy something that suited the two of us.

I went on a day trip with my daughter to the beaches near Clacton-on-Sea. On the way back, we drove past a sign for Mersea Island, just off mainland Essex. I'd never been there, but a friend of mine had recently moved there so we had a quick look around. The island is connected to the mainland by a causeway that is impassable for a couple of hours at high tide, and I really fell in love with its remoteness.

I went back a couple of times after that, and I liked it even more each time. It was so nice to be so close to the sea. I started looking at houses on the internet, just casually at first, but then I saw one that suited me perfectly, and I thought, What the heck! I'll move there.

After that it all happened so quickly. I put my own house on the market and, amazingly, it sold the next day. It's meant to be, I thought, and I moved to Mersea in July 2010.

I'd never have been brave enough to move all that way on my own, miles away from friends and family, if it wasn't for Guinness. I'd always dreamt of living on the coast, but because Guinness doesn't like travelling she'd never actually seen the sea. My son Daniel, son-in-law Jason and my friend's husband, Peter, came round to help me move. Guinness cried in the car all the way down, even though she was sitting on my lap. I went to get the guys some fish and chips at one point, and she jumped out of the car window after me, she was so afraid I was going to leave her there. But when we got to the new house she was delighted and jumped straight into the fish pond. Her own personal swimming pool!

When I looked at all the boxes stacked on the pavement, I felt a bit sad for my old life. My son looked at me and said, 'Do you want me to stay the night, Mum?'

'Oh, all right. If you insist!' I said. I was glad to have that extra company on the first night.

In the end I felt really excited to be in my new home, in

this cosy little house, with Guinness at my side. The next morning, Daniel came in for breakfast.

'Did you sleep all right, love?' I asked him.

'No! I couldn't sleep at all! It was so quiet, I could hear the electricity buzzing in the wires.'

It certainly was a far cry from our old London home. It's so dark at night you can even see the Milky Way here.

My parents came from Park Royal in London, where my dad worked for the Guinness brewery. They used to tell me lovely stories about how nobody would lock their doors and everybody knew everybody there. It's a bit like that on Mersea, like going back in time, with no KFC or McDonalds or anything.

The only way on and off the thirteen-mile-round island is a causeway called the Strood that gets completely covered over at high tide. We sit there sometimes when it's covered and watch all the tourists getting stuck and having to call out the lifeboat.

I do miss my family and friends, but they visit a lot. When I moved, I think the grandkids were more upset I was taking the dog than about me leaving. I have to go on Skype so that they can see Guinness when we talk. Part of my inspiration for living by the sea was so they could have the sort of great experiences I remember having as a child. When my grandparents retired they moved out of London, to the countryside in Sussex, and we'd go out along the Downs, or to the beach. Some of my favourite memories are the good times I spent on holidays there, and I'm so happy I have been able to give my grandchildren these same kind of carefree memories.

They love going to the beach, where we build rafts, but

they love going crabbing especially. My grandson once caught fifty crabs in one go, he was very proud to announce. They always want to go adder hunting too. There's a big 'Danger! Adders!' sign up in a nearby field. Just the kind of thing that attracts children! Thankfully they've only found a couple of grass snakes so far.

I didn't know how Guinness would react to the sea at first, but she absolutely loves the beaches. And since I've been on Mersea, I've been out every day with Guinness, rain, shine or wind – and I mean lots of wind. We've even been surrounded by several feet of snow and still made it out for a walk. It's really dog-friendly here, too. Not everyone knows my name, but they all know Guinness. She even comes into the pub with me when it's raining; nobody minds, they even put out dog bowls. Perhaps they can't refuse because of her name.

Guinness is tiny, really, for a Staff, but that's good for me, since I've still got lymphoma in my left arm. And though she's still quite hyper for an old dog, she's a little bit slower and calmer than she used to be, which suits me. I've even thought about getting one of those little carriages to put on the back of my bike, for her to sit in. Then I remember that the point of a walk is to take her out for exercise, not for her to sit behind me in a little carriage, like a princess!

There's a lot going on in Mersea so I never get bored. There's a food and wine festival with local produce, bands playing sea shanties, and there's a jazz evening at the local pub called the Moondance Club.

The fresh fish here is incredible as well. Sometimes I take Guinness on the boat to get some fish and chips from a nearby town. She loves the wind in her fur as we speed along on the water. The fishermen email me the morning catch each day, and they even sell lobsters, but I don't like to cook them. I can't bring myself to boil them alive.

Jamie Oliver's favourite eatery, the Company Shed, is on the island, with all sorts of seafood. Sometimes he brings his kitchen caravan over and cooks up something on the beach. Mersea's famous for oysters too, which are supplied to the Ivy, Quaglino's and other posh restaurants in London. For ages I couldn't convince any of the family to try them, but my son's hooked now.

I've a beautiful little house, and even though I don't have a lot of money, I'm incredibly happy. My hobby is making stained glass. I took a course and now I've got a small workshop in the garden. Next to that is a little log cabin, all decked out with the grandkids' toys. And I recently got a wood burner, which completes the cosy cottage feel of my new home.

The only thing I haven't got here is a man. But I have lovely neighbours who help out with anything I ask, and I'd rather pay an odd-job man to come in and do a few jobs every now and then than look after a bloke who demands that I cook for him. I don't have to put my make-up on in the morning for Guinness either, and anyway, I don't think she'd share me with anybody else. We've been on our own for so long now, I'm sure she's got single dog syndrome. She has got herself two boyfriends on the island, though, lovely little Italian Greyhounds we walk along the beach with sometimes.

In October last year I was signed off, so I'm officially free from cancer. They can't say you're never going to get it again, but I'm feeling confident and positive. I'm quite conscious now about skin cancers and things, so when I go out I'm fully factor-fiftied up. And I won't be topless sunbathing!

Being ill made me re-evaluate what's important in life. It's twelve years since I first brought Guinness home, and we've been through a lot together. Through all the laughter and the tears, she's been the best friend anyone could wish for.

Johnny Reggae: The Old-Timer

All the dogs at Battersea are rehomed with the same amount of care and attention however, for obvious reasons, the younger dogs tend to get picked out more quickly. After all, everyone loves a puppy. However at Battersea we get many older dogs too and, although these more mature residents are frequently overlooked, they can actually be remarkably easy pets once they do find a new home. They are often settled into a routine, confident and house-trained. And they are also usually more relaxed than their energetic younger friends. As first-time dog owner Stephanie Fairbank discovered, our canine senior citizens can make really wonderful companions.

We weren't in the market for a dog at all, really. My husband works long hours as a lawyer, and I have a busy life working for a local charity and looking after my horse.

I was going through my emails one morning, and saw my friend had sent me a link to something or other. I wasn't even sure what it was, but I absentmindedly clicked on it while I was drinking my coffee. Suddenly there was an image of a beautiful little fluffy dog on the screen. The picture was sort of glowing in the sunshine and the dog looked healthy and happy, in the way animals can seem to smile back at you sometimes.

'Johnny Reggae,' the caption said. 'Johnny is typical of

so many dogs who come to Battersea Dogs & Cats Home because their owners can no longer look after them.'

My friend loves dogs, and this story had obviously touched her so I read on.

'A Jack Russell-Terrier cross, he's a happy chap with lots of character who loves his creature comforts.'

Don't we all? I thought.

'Johnny is the gentlest companion anyone could wish for. He could give so much happiness to a new owner. But at seventeen years old he's quite an elderly gentleman and it won't be easy to find him a new home . . . '

Seventeen years old! Poor little thing. I wondered why he was without a home. I read over the rest, which concluded with the words:

' . . . Johnny's looking for someone to share his passions for good company and food in his twilight years.'

I closed the browser window, still not quite sure why my friend had sent me the link. But as I got on with my work that day, I couldn't get the image out of my mind. And that funny name: Johnny Reggae.

When I got home I didn't tell my husband Nick about it. But I did keep going back and looking at the picture. Just to check. It became a little bit of an obsession after a while. I would click around the rest of the Battersea site and see that many of the other dogs who had arrived at the same time as Johnny or afterwards had been rehomed. But there was Johnny Reggae, that 'elderly gentleman', still up there, without a home.

Eventually I mentioned it to Nick, just casually, to see his reaction.

'Have you gone completely mad?' he said. He was bashing away at the piano, something loud by Bach.

'It was just something I saw on the internet. I thought it might be, you know, a good starter dog or something . . .' I trailed off.

'We'll be back and forth to the vets all the time, though, won't we?' Nick said. 'Anyway, if we're going to get a dog, I want a big healthy dog. For long walks. Not some poor creature who can hardly make it out of the house.'

I decided to leave it there for a while. But, as days became weeks, I kept checking the website and Johnny Reggae was always still there.

One evening we were out with some friends, on a bit of a drunken dinner, and I mentioned the link again.

'Oh, show me!' said my friend.

So I got the link up on my phone, and we all had a look.

'He's just too old though, isn't he?' said Nick. 'She'll just get upset when he dies.'

'I wish someone would look after me in my twilight years!' said Becky.

'I know! Tell me about it!' I said.

'Oh, you've got to get him,' she said, with the conviction that a few glasses of wine gives you, making it all sound so easy. But when we got home, Nick was still unconvinced.

'We could just go and look,' I said. 'I just feel so bad for him, at his age. He should be in a loving home.'

'You'll only get attached and then he'll die and you'll be devastated,' Nick said again.

'But at least we could have a look. Otherwise he might be stuck there and die without a proper home or a family.'

I showed Nick the picture on the website again, and his face did soften a little this time.

'Well, I suppose he is quite sweet, isn't he?'

In the end I think I wore him down, because he finally relented.

'All right. Let's see this Johnny Reggae you've become so obsessed with. But if we get a dog, you're doing the morning walks.'

'Of course!'

'And we'll have to set a limit. On how much we're prepared to spend on vets' fees on an older dog. We have to know where to draw the line if he gets ill.'

'Well, how much do you think?'

'I was thinking about sixty quid max?' he said, not entirely seriously.

'I think we might be prepared to spend a bit more than that!' I said. 'Anyway, first things first. Let's go and see him.'

So, six weeks after I had first seen the picture on the website, Nick and I went to Battersea. Just for a look, of course.

When we got to the Home we were given a form to fill in, and then met in reception by a rehoming staff member. She greeted us with an efficient smile and took us through to a small room to discuss our answers to the questions on the form about what our house was like and whether we had the time and space for a dog.

'Come through. Take a seat,' she said in a very professional manner. I got the impression that the rehoming process was pretty rigorous, with all the checks they make on your suitability.

'We've come to see Johnny Reggae,' I said.

The woman's face immediately softened. She went from being quite serious to very chatty and chirpy.

'Oh, really? Johnny! We all love him. But we just haven't been able to rehome him. Such a shame. It's because he's older. They're just less attractive to people who want a younger dog.'

'We have a walled garden and live right next to a park,' I said, 'and Nick works from home a lot, so there will be no problems of a dog being left alone or anything like that.'

'That sounds excellent,' said the woman, picking up her folder. 'Actually, though, there is one other woman looking at Johnny Reggae, right now as it happens. But you can have a look after that, if you like?'

I was stunned. I went from thinking 'We'll just see the dog' to 'I must have the dog' in a matter of minutes. All of a sudden I'd made my mind up that Johnny Reggae was mine. I was absolutely terrified that I'd lose out.

'What if somebody else gets him, after all this?' I said to Nick as we sat outside, waiting for the other woman to come out.

'Don't worry. He's been here this long. It'll be fine. And if it's not, it wasn't meant to be.'

I just sat there, almost rocking in my seat with worry. Eventually, the lady that had been in with him came out and disappeared round the corner, and by the time we went in ourselves I was so keen I could have just scooped him up and taken him with me there and then.

It was just as well I had built up this much enthusiasm, because in the flesh, Johnny Reggae looked nothing like he had in his picture. It must have been taken at a flattering angle or in good light or something, because he seemed very small and old and frail, shivering on the floor.

'What an ugly mutt!' whispered Nick.

'Oh, give him a chance!' I said, but I had to agree. He did look a bit frail and wobbly, compared to his photo.

'This is Johnny,' said the woman, smiling. 'We've all got quite attached to him here.'

Johnny didn't say much. He just peed up the filing cabinet. We waited for an uncomfortable few moments while he finished his business. Then Nick ventured awkwardly, 'Erm . . . he is house-trained, isn't he?'

'Oh, yes,' said the woman, laughing. 'He's just marking his spot. He doesn't always do that. He won't do it in a home, I mean. He spends hours in the office with our staff, during the day, and he's just fine. Why don't you play with him a bit?'

I picked up a great big ball that there was in the room and threw it vaguely in his direction. It bounced along the floor a bit and then came to a halt by his nose. But the dog completely ignored me. He just lay there with his head in his paws as though nothing had happened.

There was another slightly awkward pause. I looked at Nick, then at the woman.

'What do you know about his past? Did someone have to give him up or something? I mean, he's so old. Someone must have loved him.'

'Well, he's been with us for a couple of months now. But we don't know much, except that his previous owner got into financial difficulties. Just couldn't keep him any more. It happens. And when it does it's absolutely devastating.

People leave here in tears when they have to give up their animals after so long. But there you go. Sometimes they just have no choice. I think he came from Peckham.'

I decided there and then that I must have this dog. Not because he came from that part of London but because of the frailty of him, the sad story of how someone had had to give him up after seventeen years. It made me want to scoop him up and protect him. Even the fact he had peed up the furniture and completely ignored the ball didn't put me off. I couldn't leave him there a moment longer than necessary.

'What do you think?' I asked Nick cautiously.

'Well, we can't very well leave the little mutt here, can we?' he said and smiled.

I breathed a sigh of relief. 'Fancy coming home with us then, Johnny Reggae? To the wilds of Kent?'

He very briefly wagged his tail, which I took to be an affirmative.

'Oh, that's wonderful!' said the woman. She looked like she almost wanted to run over and give us a big hug. 'We were honestly beginning to wonder if we'd ever rehome him. It's the older dogs you see. It puts people off, unfortunately. But we find they're just great. Often easier, in fact, because they're already trained. Anyway, you can pick him up in two weeks. We need to fix up his teeth a bit, and get him neutered and chipped and so on. So he's in the best possible health for you when you take him home.'

After all that, I left on a bit of a high, if a little dazed.

'Don't do anything stupid, like go falling in love or anything though, will you?' said Nick on the way home. 'After all, he's only a dog.'

'You're getting a what?' asked my best friend Asha when I told her the news.

'I'm getting a seventeen-year-old Jack Russell from Battersea.'

Asha just loves dogs, but even she thought I was bonkers.

'Are you sure this dog isn't going to die on you any minute? You'll be heartbroken,' she said. 'Trust you to rescue a dog with no teeth! But I insist on being there when you collect the little beast. Wouldn't miss it for the world, in fact.'

Two weeks later, on a sunny Sunday morning, Nick, Asha and I piled into the car and made our way back to Battersea.

When we arrived, the rehoming woman came outside, with Johnny Reggae on his lead. My heart melted a bit. He was so frail. Like a little old man hobbling out, blinking, into the sunshine. Asha grabbed my arm and burst into tears.

'What's the matter, for heaven's sake?' I asked. 'Why are you crying? It's supposed to be a joyful moment!'

'He's so . . . old,' she spluttered, and broke into another explosive fit of tears.

The staff at Battersea must have been wondering what to make of all this. My husband was just standing there awkwardly, a woman on either side of him, one of them blubbing her eyes out.

'He might be old. But he's going to have a fantastic life now, isn't he?' I said.

Asha was right, though, in a way. He did look very small

and a bit pathetic. I hoped we weren't making a terrible mistake. We took Johnny Reggae out for a walk, although he couldn't go very far, but he seemed OK on the lead. Then we went in to see the nurse and the vet.

I was trying to listen to how much food to give him over snorts and snivels from Asha, who had still not recovered from her emotional ordeal. They gave us a brilliant rundown of the flea and worming procedures, which injections he'd had, and advised us when to have the neutering stitches out. It was all so new to us, they even explained what to do when we got home, about sleeping and walking arrangements and everything else. They also told us he gets a little bit car-sick. I wondered how much a 'little bit' was and whether I needed a 'doggy bag' for the car. Of course, as this was our first dog, we didn't have anything so we bought everything we needed from the shop at Battersea: bed, blanket, lead, bowls – armfuls of doggy stuff.

As we were about to leave, there was a sudden crackle over the tannoy system.

'Ahem . . . Johnny Reggae is leaving the building . . . Johnny Reggae is leaving the building . . . ' The announcement boomed around the corridors.

'What's all that about?' I asked. 'Do you do that every time?'

'Oh, no. Johnny was just so popular here. He's been here for a few months, so everyone will want to come and wave him off,' said the rehoming woman.

Sure enough, a send-off committee was gathering by the exit, eager to catch a last glimpse of my new dog. I think a couple of people may even have joined Asha, sniffing and dabbing their eyes with tissues. There was a lot of emotion at Battersea the day Johnny Reggae said goodbye.

I put him on my lap as we drove, and I waited for him to puke on me the whole way home. But he never did. And he has never had a problem with cars since, which is lucky. We dropped Asha off at home, and she plonked a big tearful kiss on his head.

'Good luck in your new home, little Johnny,' she said, and we drove off quickly, before she could get any more emotional.

By the time we got back I was exhausted and overwhelmed with everything that had happened. And by how much my life had suddenly changed. I now had an animal to take care of. I carried the dog out of the car and stood in the garden and soaked it all in. Before I went in, something caught my eye:

'WELCOME HOME, JOHNNY REGGAE!'

There was a huge, homemade banner strung up across the wall of our house. And finally, I, who had managed to hold it together all the time Asha was in tears, at last broke down too.

'This is amazing!' I said to Nick. 'Did you know about this?'

'Might have,' he said slyly.

We get on very well with all our neighbours, and they had organized a little party as a surprise for me and to welcome our new dog home. I was absolutely chuffed, but poor Johnny just stood there, bewildered by all the attention, looking smaller and frailer than ever.

The whole street fell in love with him that day, but it

was up to me to make sure he was happy with his new home too.

It was a really lovely summer day when we first took Johnny Reggae out into the park. He looked very small and a bit shrunken, a bit of an old man really. But he trotted along by us and was just fine. He had also obviously been trained to play with a ball, because as soon as I threw it he picked it up, brought it back and put it at my feet. It was a welcome change from the dog who had ignored my ball-throwing the first time we met.

Johnny had been with the same owner for seventeen years, and no matter what the background was, it must have been incredibly hard for them to give him up. But whoever it was had obviously cared for him well. He was completely house-trained, and he never even jumped on the furniture, let alone peed on it. In fact, we soon realized that he wasn't a lap dog at all, although he's quite small. If I tried to cuddle up to him he would humour me for a couple of minutes at the most, and then jump off.

For the first night, we had bought a cage, a really big crate meant for a Labrador, so he didn't rampage around the house and destroy anything. I was a bit worried about him chewing up the kitchen or peeing somewhere. I was new to dogs, and I guess that's the kind of thing you worry about as a novice. I thought he would probably spend about six weeks in it, but I don't think it was even a week before he had his own bed and we could get rid of the crate. We showed him the garden for the loo, his water and food, and quickly established a routine. So it really only took about two weeks for him to settle in.

I'd do the morning walk, as promised, and then he would sleep until about 3.30 p.m. and then we'd go for another walk. At first he could only do about fifteen minutes, perhaps because of his age, but also I suppose he was used to an urban life. But we soon worked him up to a nice walk of about forty-five minutes in the park or into Canterbury, our local town.

In fact, we soon took him everywhere with us, to friends' houses and everything. He would sit on my lap in the car and stare out of the window, looking for all the world as if he was driving. I did worry the first time we took him to a friend who had a cat, though. I had no idea how he would react. We were staying overnight so we took the crate, and in the morning, when I came down, the door was open.

'Oh my God! Johnny Reggae? Where are you?' I was fearing the worst.

But there he was, sitting by the radiator, the cat purring beside him. And he wasn't bothered at all.

'I suppose he's not a threat to cats, then,' said Nick.

'Yes. He's so old. And he just takes everything in his stride. Nothing seems to faze him, does it?'

For a Jack Russell he's not that noisy. The only time he barks is when we leave the house. He gets cross, hovers by the door and barks like a seal – *argh-argh*. But the neighbours say he stops after two or three minutes. But although he may not be very vocal, he can be extremely wilful and stubborn at times.

My husband Nick plays the piano a lot, and when he had finished playing one afternoon, I went in and sat on the sofa.

'That was nice,' I said.

'Bach. Goldberg Variations. Johnny Reggae seems to like it, anyway. Look at him.'

The dog was fast asleep, with his nose pressed up against the leg of the piano.

'Can he hear it, do you think?' I asked. Johnny Reggae's a bit deaf, because of his old age.

'I don't know. He can probably feel the vibrations,' Nick said.

'This must feel like the life of luxury compared to Peckham,' I said. 'Listening to Bach, garden on the doorstep.'

We both looked over at him; he did seem very contented.

'So . . . ' I said, after a while. 'Do you love the dog yet?'

'No,' said Nick quickly, opening up a new piece of music. 'He's just a dog.'

Not long after that, Johnny Reggae got ill. He wasn't eating much so we took him to the vet, and they told us it was his liver playing up.

'He'll have to take these pills,' said the vet. 'Once a day with food.'

'Oh, poor thing,' I said.

'But he's doing pretty well for his age! Seventeen, did you say?'

I glanced over at Nick. He had gone rather grey.

'Are you sure he'll be all right. I mean . . . could it get worse?' he asked, his voice quivering.

I could see a kind of look of panic on his face, and I knew at that point that Nick did love the dog. He just wouldn't admit it.

'You do love him, don't you?' I said when we got home. Nick was quiet. Still worried about Johnny's liver.

'All right,' he said after a while. 'You win. I love the dog.'

The pills pretty soon sorted out the liver problem, and after that, I would often come in and find Nick on the floor playing with Johnny, or with the dog sitting on his lap – or forcing the dog to sit on his lap, I should say.

'About those vets' fees,' I said one afternoon. 'You know, about only spending sixty pounds . . .'

'Oh yeah, that,' Nick laughed. 'Well, you know . . . give or take a few.'

Any thoughts of limits soon went out of the window, and whatever the vet says now, about buying this and that supplement for his leg, or whatever, Nick just says, 'Fine, we'll have that.' No expense spared. We joke that there's a Fairbank Wing at that vets now! Even so, he hasn't cost us much, only about £500, which isn't bad, considering he's an old dog. And, as you've probably guessed, we are both now disproportionately besotted with him.

After a while, I decided to train an old dog to do a few new tricks. It was something to do, and also, because Johnny Reggae's quite deaf, it wasn't easy to give him voice commands. So I thought I'd try to teach him some sign language. He's pretty much food obsessed, so it was actually quite easy. He's got a real sweet tooth, and in fact there's not much he won't eat apart from anything green, like rocket and lettuce. He likes cheese, even satsumas. He licks out yoghurt pots and then gets them stuck on his nose.

So bribing with food helped a lot when I was training him. Sitting was first. I made up a sign, crossing my arms, to ask him to sit and then rewarded him with a treat if he did it. I made sure he was looking, did the signal and pressed his bottom down. Then gave him the treat. With repetition it worked. Next I managed to get him to wait at the end of the kitchen, while I kept my hand out like the traffic police do. Then I'd clap and he'd come running. I tried to get him to give me his paw, but that was one step too far. It was a lights-on-but-no one's-home kind of response to that one!

'Well, that was a good day's work, anyway!' I said, and when Nick came home, I called Johnny into the room.

'Come on, you monkey,' I said. 'Let's show Daddy what you can do. Look at this, Nick.'

I crossed my arms and Johnny Reggae sat straight down.

'Oh my God! How have you done that?' asked Nick.

'It was amazingly simple actually,' I said, as I demonstrated the wait-and-come technique with my hand out.

'Wow! I'm impressed. Go, Johnny Reggae!'

'Lucky for us he's obsessed with food, I suppose.'

In fact, Johnny loves food so much that I call him my little meatball. And we do have to be careful. Seven kilos is his fighting weight, but over Christmas he gets ruined by our family, who all bring him lots of treats. In the new year we took him to the vet's and he weighed eight point one kilos!

'He's put some weight on,' said a stern nurse. She was looking over her glasses at me accusingly.

'Well, it was Christmas!' I laughed. 'We all put on a few pounds, don't we?'

She did not see the funny side.

'It's your responsibility, Mrs Fairbank,' she told me. She's ever so strict.

We know Johnny is happy and healthy, and we wouldn't let him get too overweight. But who's not allowed a treat in their old age?

You might be wondering about the name: Johnny Reggae. I know I certainly did when we got him. After some digging around on the internet, we eventually found out that it's the name of a song by a ska band called The Piglets. I can just imagine his previous owner playing it on a record player and dancing around with Johnny Reggae in his Peckham sitting room. The lyrics call him a 'real tasty geezer' and talk about him wearing a baseball cap. It's a funny image for our little dog.

I wonder whether he was owned by an older man, because Johnny will always gravitate towards older men and sit near them if he gets the chance. I imagine his previous owner as like someone out of *Only Fools and Horses*, living in a towerblock like Nelson Mandela House. He must have loved that song. But when I play it to Johnny I ask him if he likes it and he looks at me seriously as if to say, 'Not really, Mummy, no'.

I'm intrigued to know what happened to that guy. After a dog has been such a part of your life for so long, he must wonder what happened to Johnny Reggae. I wonder if he misses him. I even sent some pictures to Battersea, just in case the previous owner wanted to see them. But so far we don't know who or where he is. Battersea did put the pictures on Facebook and their Happy Endings website page, though, and they got some amazing comments. It makes you feel really fantastic to get that response from the public.

Since we've had him, Johnny Reggae has been everywhere with us. He's had a tour of several National Trust properties and heritage sites, including Dover Castle. And we take him down on the beaches at Whitstable and Camber Sands. He's not big on water, but he loves the beach. He might not like the sea much, but once, when I was carrying him over a little stream, his legs started to do the doggy paddle – even though he was in mid-air – so he must have a water instinct somewhere in the recesses of his genes. I carry him if it rains sometimes; we have a waterproof fluorescent coat for him and a little tweed coat too. He's not too sure about that. I think he's just humouring me by wearing it.

'You can take a dog out of Peckham, but you can't take Peckham out of the dog,' joked Nick one day as we trotted along the beach with Johnny Reggae, looking a little incongruous in his tweed coat.

Johnny Reggae has certainly travelled with us. He's been to Charing point-to-point races to watch the horses, and he's even seen the Archbishop of Canterbury in a shopping centre at a Christmas singsong. We take him with us for pub lunches regularly and he loves the Canterbury Cathedral cloisters for an evening walk, though I sometimes have to carry him to get there! In the summer we have barbecues on the beach with him, or if it's really hot he just lies for hours in the garden, baking.

There are three people Johnny loves best: Annette,

Nick's piano teacher, and Carla and Charmaine, the two cleaning ladies who come to our house. They say they never give him any treats ... but I'm not so sure. Either way, he really loves them. When they arrive he goes berserk, wagging his tail – which he doesn't normally do – and traipses around after them for hours.

Johnny Reggae will be nineteen this year. And although he's a bit deaf, with a touch of arthritis in the legs, he still gets around. He has featured in a lot of Battersea's publicity material too. He was even Mr April in their calendar one year and we were sent some stickers, address labels and bookmarks with his face on. Since then we've even had a few letters from children who must have seen his face as Mr April. One of them was so sweet, in a child's scrawly handwriting:

> To Johnny Reggae – mery crismas,
> love from chloe and Ellie xxx

It was bonkers really, deciding to take on our first dog the way we did, but we've absolutely loved the experience. We love it so much, in fact, that we tell everyone about Battersea. I'm sure sometimes people think we're on their marketing committee! But I'd much rather go there to rescue an animal than get a flash pedigree puppy any day. Everyone loves Johnny Reggae and he's really been the easiest, most wonderful little dog. He's living the life of Reilly in his twilight years!

Wriggler: A Winter Surprise

At Battersea we love the challenge of matching people looking for their ideal pet with the animals we have here. And as well as dogs we also get every kind of cat in the cattery. From those looking for a calm life with a laid-back moggie to families in search of a more active animal who is able to live with a two-year-old child, we know there is a cat out there for every potential owner. Cats and kittens come to Battersea for all kinds of reasons, but last winter we received a very unusual delivery on the Battersea site, as staff member Lisa Graham recalls . . .

It was one of those really bitter winter nights. The kind when the wind bites so hard, you just want to huddle up in front of the fire and hibernate. By the following morning, icicles were hanging from eaves, frozen spider webs were hidden in corners and it seemed so cold that frosty patches of grass threatened to glisten for weeks without thawing.

I spent that freezing November night at home with my fiancé, Phil, and our gorgeous old Battersea rescue cat, Johnson. We had dinner and then tucked up together on the sofa to watch a movie. Around the time we switched off the lights and headed for bed, a lean and hungry tortoiseshell cat stood miaowing in the shadows behind Battersea Power Station just south of the Thames. She stopped, sniffed the air for a moment, then scampered off into the darkness. Just a few metres away, eight little bundles of fluff, no bigger than a family of field mice, were taking their first, startled breaths.

I've always had cats growing up and, like many children do, I'd thought I would work with animals some day. But by the time I left college it was just a fantasy, and in the end I started working for Fujifilm, doing PR. I hankered after my dream, though, and started dog walking as a volunteer at a local rescue centre. After a while, I realized they didn't have anyone to do PR for them, and volunteered to work on that as well. It was fine, but I knew there was more out there for me, so every day I would take a sneaky peek at the Battersea website. I was broody for a dog anyway, and loved looking at all the dogs in need of a home. 'Ahh, that one's cute,' I'd think, really torturing myself. I'd also take a look at the jobs section too, just in case.

One day, I saw a job for a Communications Officer at Battersea. This would involve reacting to media enquiries, writing press releases and placing features in magazines and so on. It was my ideal job! I applied and, amazingly, I was asked in for an interview and offered the position. It was a dream come true.

After that, I suppose it was inevitable that I would end up getting a Battersea cat. There was just too much temptation. We take in an average of seven cats a day and I knew I wouldn't be able to resist for ever.

The first cat I rehomed was a ten-year-old black cat called Pepsi Ann, who was really undersocialized. She'd been living with a woman who had loads of other cats and was the stereotype of a crazy cat lady, and so she was extremely nervous and shy. Pepsi Ann was so nervous of people it was really hard to rehome her, and she ended up living at our Old Windsor site for a year. I kept seeing her on the website, week after week, still there. And after a while I thought I had to do something about it.

I mentioned it to Phil one night, and told him how adorable she was.

'I think she really just needs a good home,' I said, and loaded up the website for him to take a look.

He wasn't much of an animal person at that point, but I persuaded him in the end, and we went through all the Battersea rehoming procedures. They knew I was an experienced cat owner, so that was fine. And when Phil met her he fell in love too. After a year, she finally had a home to go to.

Pepsi Ann came on in leaps and bounds with us, but she was always very shy, and if anyone came round she would scamper off, hide under the bed and not come out for hours. She was really lovely though, and we had her for two years before she sadly passed away.

I didn't rush to get another Battersea animal after that; it was so sad losing my lovely Pepsi Ann. But eventually, inevitably, another moggie caught my eye.

Johnson was twenty years old when he came to Battersea as a stray. I've always been a bit of a sucker for an animal in need, and Johnson certainly fitted that bill. Being such a ripe old age, he had medical problems galore. He had so much wrong with him, in fact, that it was very difficult to rehome him in the end. You couldn't get insurance, for a start, and that put a lot of people off. If animals are really hard to rehome, Battersea will sometimes ask staff if they can provide a foster home. Johnson was so rickety and difficult to place that, in the end, the cattery started looking for a staff home for him, which is how I heard of him.

We don't know much about Johnson's past, except that he was found wandering as a stray by a member of the public, and brought in to Battersea. Forty-six per cent of the cats that come in are strays, so we always recommend that owners get their cat microchipped and give them a collar with a tag on it. If your cat doesn't have any ID, someone might think it's a stray and bring it in, and we have no way of knowing it's actually a much-loved pet. Johnson might have wandered off and got lost, or been abandoned, but as he had no collar or microchip we didn't have a clue.

But not all cats brought in are strays, like Johnson. Others are brought in by owners who can't keep them for whatever reason – allergies, a new baby, no permission from their landlord to keep a pet and so on. It's a familiar story. There might also be a litter of unwanted kittens, if their cat hasn't been neutered. Sometimes we even get a box of kittens just left on the Battersea doorstep, and we know nothing about them at all.

When I saw Johnson's picture on the website, I immediately knew I wanted him. He's black and white, with a little bald nose, and he looked very gangly and manky in the picture. I thought he was just really gorgeous.

'Exactly my cup of tea,' I said to my colleague. So I went to see him in the cattery.

When I got there, he was lying casually on his bed. He looked up at me nonchalantly with these glazed and dreamy eyes. Then he got up and hobbled over.

'He looks just like John Wayne!' I said to the woman in the cattery. 'Slinking around with that funny walk. He's so cool and chilled out.'

Then he let out this really loud, *MIAOW!*, which I just loved.

'He's got a bit of arthritis,' she said. 'He's a bit deaf too, and he has a heart murmur, and an overactive thyroid gland . . .'

But I could tell Johnson had the most beautiful temperament, so I rang Phil.

'Yes, another old cat. But he's so gorgeous. You have to see him.'

'I don't have much choice, do I?' he laughed. 'Well, all right, if you're sure.'

So Johnson came to live with us. Battersea cat number two.

I didn't feel comfortable letting him out on his own, because he was so old and confused.

I'd been told he had a form of cat dementia, and would probably get lost and wander into the road or something. He's not very streetwise and would just be disorientated. As he's deaf, he wouldn't hear the traffic either. Or someone might think he's a stray again, because due to his hyperthyroidism he looks really skinny. We feed him loads, but he just doesn't put any weight on, so he looks a little neglected, although he's certainly not!

I did pluck up the courage to take him out into the garden for supervised outings, though, to get him used to being out in the fresh air. Occasionally he would even get a burst of energy from somewhere and peg it into next door's garden. He can actually be quite fast when he wants, despite all his ailments. He dashes off and makes a beeline for their cat flap, to steal their cat's food.

'Sorry! Johnson's at the food again!' I have to confess, as I go round to drag him back.

It's nice having an old cat, though, because they're pretty easy really. Kittens can be quite hard work, chewing or shredding things and climbing everywhere. But Johnson's just really chilled out most of the time.

The following November, one frosty morning nearly a year after we'd got Johnson, one of the staff at Battersea came up to me all excited.

'Guess what?' she said. 'They found a whole litter of kittens this morning. Eight of them! At Keen's Yard. Someone heard this squeaking noise, apparently, and went to investigate.'

'What, actually on the Battersea site?' I asked.

'Yes, a cat must have come here and given birth last night then wandered off. The kittens were found in one of the old buildings, the ones we use for storage. They were all in an insulation pipe! Can you imagine? The maintenance staff had to cut a hole into the floor area to get them out in the end. They're in clinic at the moment; they're trying to keep them all alive.'

'Wow! Well, she couldn't have chosen a better place to leave them, I suppose, if she was going to leave them anywhere,' I said. 'What with a whole team of cat experts within a few hundred yards.'

All morning I couldn't stop thinking about those poor little kittens, and it wasn't long before I found an excuse to go over to the clinic.

'Hi, Lisa,' said the head veterinary nurse.

I went over to where she was tending to something in the corner of the clinic. 'Are these them? Can I have a look?' I asked, tentatively. I didn't want to disturb them, but I was desperate to see the poor little mites.

'Of course. We're just feeding them and keeping them warm. In here,' the head vet nurse said, pointing to a little cat holder they were being kept in together. 'We've already given them some warm fluids and have been using heat discs to help give them some body warmth.'

The clinic staff had put them in amongst lots of comfy bedding, and I was absolutely amazed by how tiny they were. I was so overwhelmed by it that I nearly burst into tears. They looked so incredibly vulnerable. Seven small creatures that didn't even look much like kittens yet. Their eyes were tightly shut, they had such tiny skinny claws, and were no bigger than little mice.

'They are so tiny,' I said quietly, looking at these defence-less little things, so close to the edge of their short life.

'They can't see or hear anything yet,' said the head vet nurse, stroking one on its little head. All kittens and puppies are blind and deaf until about ten days or so.'

'We're just keeping them warm,' she said, 'and seeing what happens. We're so sad, but one of them had already died before we got them in here. One of the little boys. So there's only seven now. They are just so fragile. Very hypo-thermic – abnormally cold, that is. The mum was nowhere to be seen, I'm afraid to say. They really were that close to death. I don't think they would have made it for much longer in that cold if we hadn't found them.'

There was one black kitten, three ginger and three tortoiseshells.

'The three tortoiseshells are female,' she continued, 'and the gingers and the black are male.'

'How are you going to keep these ones alive?' I asked. 'Without their mum?'

'Well, we're going to hand-rear them. We've divided them up into pairs amongst some of the staff here. Any more than two is really arduous, as it's a really hands-on task, feeding every two hours.'

'There are seven, though, aren't there? An odd number . . . '

'Yes, there is one lone ranger. We haven't found anyone to hand-rear him yet. This little ginger one here,' she said, pointing at one of the tiny fluff-balls in the basket, squashed up against his brothers and sisters.

'Poor thing,' I said. 'Do you need experience? To hand-rear, I mean?'

'No, well, not really. I mean, we could explain it well enough. Why? Were you thinking you might be able to help? It's hard work, no denying it, but we could show you everything you'll need to do. If you did want to . . . '

'Well, I'd have to check with Phil, my fiancé, but I have to say, it is tempting. I'd hate to see one left stranded.'

'The thing is, these first days are absolutely crucial. That's why we get them being hand-reared as soon as possible. You work here, and you've rehomed cats from Battersea before, haven't you, so I don't see why not. I'll check out all the paperwork and so on, but it should be fine.'

I rang Phil straight away.

'Is it all right if I bring a kitten home tonight, just for a bit? He's only a day old and needs someone to feed him,'

I said, underplaying a little what might be involved. 'It won't be for long.'

'Here we go again,' he laughed. 'Another cat!'

We had actually said we wouldn't get another animal while we had Johnson because he was so old it wouldn't be fair on him.

'But this little one is only tiny – he only sleeps and eats. He really can't do anything to annoy Johnson,' I told Phil.

'OK, then that's fine. It might be fun to have one at the other end of the spectrum,' said Phil.

Once it was all agreed that I could take him home, the vet nurse explained to me what I had to do. The staff in the clinic were very experienced, as there had been a bit of a spate of animals needing to be hand-reared at Battersea recently, but they had a shortage of people who could do it. So once I had said I'd take him they were really helpful and gave me loads of information.

'Hand-rearing is touch and go,' she said. 'They are so, so young. It's really not guaranteed they are going to survive. You have to be aware that the chances are actually quite slim that they'll make it. So you should just try your best, but don't be hard on yourself if he doesn't survive. OK?'

I tried to be as dispassionate as possible, and just do what I had been advised, but I felt a great weight of responsibility for this kitten from the moment that I agreed to take his little life into my hands – literally!

Once he was awake, I picked him up, and he wriggled a bit in my hand. The vet nurse gave me a tiny bottle with an equally tiny teat, and as I held him in my arms, he wriggled again, over towards it, and immediately started drinking without opening his eyes.

'He's a little wriggler, isn't he, this one?' I said, and the name Wriggler just stuck after that.

'You have to feed him every two hours. Just take boiled water with a scoop of kitten milk formula, which we can give you, then cool it down to lukewarm. You can test it on your hand or wrist, like you do for babies.'

Once they had explained it all to me, they gave me this pink animal carrier to put Wriggler in. It was a bit like a really bad eighties sports bag, but it did the job. There was also a heat pad, because it was really important to keep him warm now that he had no mum or brothers and sisters to cuddle up to. I also had loads of knitted blankets, which Battersea supporters had sent us, so I made the bag into a really cosy little nest for him to sleep in on the trip back.

At the end of what had been quite an eventful day, I said goodbye to the staff who were taking the other kittens and we all wished each other luck as we went our separate ways.

I take the train in to Battersea every day from my house in Caterham, so I had to get the kitten home on a packed-out commuter train. All the way to the train station I just kept thinking, 'I really hope he makes it back OK.' I was very conscious of not walking into crowds of passengers who might knock the bag so I negotiated my way on to the train carefully. I didn't look at him much on the way home, as I didn't want to open up the bag, but anyway he was just a motionless ginger thing. He didn't make any noise at all, and in fact it seemed like all he would really do was sleep, drink, wee and poo at that stage.

'He's like a little mouse, isn't he?' said Phil, when I opened up the bag back home. He was as amazed as I had been by just how small he was. We also showed him to Johnson, who just sniffed him a bit and walked off.

Then we settled down to the process of hand-rearing this tiny creature.

When I had volunteered to take Wriggler home I'd known it would be hard, but nothing had prepared me for what was to come over the next few weeks. From that moment on it was like being a full-time mum, for the first time. I had this little life in my hands, and I was totally responsible for it.

That night I put him in the pink bag next to our bed, and set my alarm to go off every two hours. It's important to be on time with the feed. I had to get up, heat the milk and cool it down again, then feed him from the tiny bottle as I had been shown. Despite setting the alarm, I didn't really sleep a wink, partly because I was so excited about this little kitten and partly through fear that I might not hear the alarm and miss the feed. I was also paranoid that he might die, and kept waking up to check he was still breathing.

Those first hours were crucial, and I really wanted to do a good job.

I had done some reading on the internet that evening about how to hand-rear, which explained how to hold the bottle.

Later that night, or rather in the early hours of the fol-lowing morning, I sat on the edge of the bed in the dim light of my bedside lamp with Wriggler resting on my shoulder. The rest of the world outside was silent.

'I really want this little guy to survive,' I said to Phil quietly, as Wriggler nestled up and drank some more milk.

'Well, if anyone can do it, then you can,' he said, smiling.

That was all very sweet, but there was a less glamorous side to hand-rearing a tiny kitten, as I soon discovered.

In the wild, the mother would lick the kitten's bottom to stimulate it to go to the toilet. Now clearly I wasn't going to do that! The vet nurse had told me to take some cotton wool with warm water, before and after every feed, and gently massage Wriggler's bottom, in order to encourage him to wee and poo. I was relieved when Wriggler did a wee. But that first night, when he didn't poo, I panicked and sent the head vet nurse a frantically worried text.

'Don't worry!' she replied. 'They don't poo after every feed.'

But I was worried about everything; I so wanted to get it right.

By 7 a.m. I hadn't had a wink of sleep, and I only just managed to get down some breakfast and a coffee before I had to leave for work.

I was so relieved that Wriggler had made it through that first night, and was still his little wriggly self as we packed up his pink bag and heat pad for the trip back to Battersea.

I got on with my job as best I could that day, but I also had to really clock-watch to make sure I fed Wriggler every two hours. Everyone in the office wanted to see him; there was a real buzz about.

When I got the chance, at lunchtime, I took him back to the clinic and all of us who were hand-rearing the kittens compared notes about our first nights. Another of the vet nurses had a girl kitten called Mistletoe and a boy kitten called Pudding. Then another staff member had two male kittens, called Bell and Jingle, and Amy had the other two females, Sookie and PeeWee.

'Did you do the cotton wool thing?' I asked.

'Yes! Not quite what I'd been expecting to do of an evening, but it worked!' said James.

'But aren't they just so sweet?' I said. 'I was totally unprepared for how delicate and dependent they are.'

Over the next few days, I carried Wriggler back and forth to work in the pink carrier and put him next to my bed at night. During the evening we would sit with him on my lap on the sofa, watching TV, and he would fall asleep in my arms, like a baby on his back. I thought it was nice for him to have the warmth of my body, so I handled him as much as I could in order that he wouldn't feel lonely without his brothers and sisters.

'He looks quite human,' said Phil, 'not really like a cat. And that bottle's nearly as big as him!'

'I know. The website I've been looking at explained how important it is to handle them and keep them warm. It said ... hang on a mo ... "Kittens' bodies should be relaxed whilst asleep and feel pleasantly warm to the human touch. You should notice gentle body jerks as they rest."'

And sure enough, he would start twitching sleepily as

I held him in my arms. It was just so cute. Even Johnson began to take an interest and would get up on the sofa to watch him with a motionless, curious look on his face.

Those first two weeks I had to feed Wriggler literally every two hours – night and day – and I have never been so sleep-deprived in my life. Some nights I didn't get any sleep at all, I was so worried about being late with a feed. Luckily Phil was really helpful and so we took it in turns. And it was actually quite exciting to have this little creature in our lives all of a sudden.

After about a week and a half, I got some tragic news.

'The female tortoiseshells have stopped eating,' said one of the vet nurses. She was really worried. They just weren't growing. The staff in clinic did all they could to save them, but it looked like they just weren't going to make it.

Sadly, nearly two weeks after we had found them, one of the kittens had to be put to sleep, and another two passed away naturally not long afterwards.

It was absolutely awful. I knew just how attached the hand-rearers were to their kittens, especially Amy who had two girl kittens that she lost within a day of each other. We all consoled her, and the other vet nurse who had lost one of hers. Having got so attached to Wriggler in such a short time, I knew how they felt, and it must have cut deeply.

I was worried for a while after that, panicking that something might happen to Wriggler too. But the boys seemed to be doing OK.

'Perhaps the mum knew the girls weren't going to

make it, and that's why she abandoned the litter?' I said, as we sat round watching the remaining four brothers all curled up together, without their little sisters. We'll never know, of course, but nature can be inexplicably cruel sometimes.

Kittens are meant to open their eyes around seven to ten days after they are born, but when his little sisters passed away, at nearly two weeks, poor Wriggler still hadn't ever set eyes on them. The other boys had all taken their first tentative peeks at the world around a week old, or just after, and they were soon romping about with their eyes fully open, taking it all in. But although Wriggler was really quite big, much bigger and more active physically than all his siblings, in fact, he still had his eyes firmly shut.

'What's wrong with you?' I said to him. 'Afraid of what you might see out here in the real world?'

After two weeks, little by little, his eyelids eventually began to open. And I was so relieved when, one morning, he was staring back at me with his big blues eyes. After two weeks the feeding times were extended too, thankfully. So instead of milk every two hours, it was now every three hours, and eventually every four. I gradually started to get in a bit more sleep each night.

As the kittens developed, moving about and taking their tentative first steps, I would sit and compare notes at lunchtimes with the others.

'Wriggler started crawling last night,' I said excitedly, showing them all my dozens of photos of the fluffy ginger ball as he dragged himself along the living room carpet for the first time.

I was a bit worried, though, because Wriggler was on his own as a kitten. I began to wonder if he might be at risk of developing behavioural issues.

'He might get "Only Kitten Syndrome",' I said to Phil one night, during a feed. 'Or think he's a human!'

The website I had found about hand-rearing became my bible, and I looked at the section on socialization. 'Socialization is extremely important for well-adjusted kittens,' it said. 'You should introduce the kittens to other animals as soon as possible.'

So I started to take Wriggler in to the clinic to be with his little brothers during the day while I was at work. There were the other two gingers and the little black one and they loved to cuddle up, lick and climb all over each other, and play in their little basket.

'I think it will help him get used to being a kitten, without his mum,' I said to James, who was hand-rearing two of the boys, Jingle and Bell.

Wriggler seemed to grow really fast at that stage, and people would ask me what I was feeding him; compared to his brothers he was like a massive giant. But I guess kittens all do things at different times, like babies. And he may have been big but he was the quiet one of the litter. He couldn't really miaow, and while his brothers were all quite squeaky, even now he just opens his mouth and nothing comes out. I suppose he's just not a noisy kitten.

Once his eyes were open and he was getting more mobile, running about at home, I trained him to use the litter tray. I was pleased that he took to it really quickly, even covering it up instinctively, without needing to see his mother doing it – I wasn't going to demonstrate that part! As he had so much contact with humans, and was passed around so much at work, he had also become a well-socialized cat quite quickly.

One of the most stressful experiences for me of hand-rearing was weaning him on to solid food. He just loved cuddling up with his bottle, and I had no trouble at all getting him to drink milk. He gobbled that down. But for some reason he took a really long time to take to solids. No matter what I did it was no good, he just wouldn't do it.

'Oh, come on, Wriggler!' I would say in desperation, as he turned it down meal after meal and reverted back to the bottle.

'I'm afraid he'll never learn to eat solids at all, and I'll be bottle-feeding him for ever,' I said to Phil. 'I'm a failure as a mum!'

'Don't be daft,' he said. 'You're a great kitten mum!'

And, after two weeks, Wriggler finally started nibbling his solids, thank goodness, and we've never looked back.

Under normal circumstances I would never have got a crazy kitten while we had our fragile old cat Johnson, but since we took Wriggler on from day one I think it has been all right, because our old cat had a chance to get used to his younger companion gradually. Wriggler didn't really do anything for the first few weeks. He just slept a lot. We also made sure to give Johnson lots of attention so he didn't feel unloved. In fact, he probably got more fussing than usual. And there's nothing I love more now than to watch the two of them curled up together in front of the fire.

I've had cats all my life, but have never had one as fond of being around people as Wriggler. Sometimes it's like having a child – he follows us wherever we go around the house. Or perhaps he's more like a dog than a cat, because he's more dependent on us than cats tend to be. We have a unique bond with Wriggler from hand-rearing him. He's just so attached to us, and he's not fazed by anything. Because he hasn't had his mum to tell him off, he can be a bit nippy sometimes. I even hiss at him on occasion, like his mum would in the wild, to put him straight if he's too cheeky, or I make a high-pitched noise to tell him off. He's learning!

Most of all, Wriggler is just really entertaining all the time. If he hears me going up the stairs he pegs it past me like a missile to get there first, and he loves getting into bed with me. I wake up with him lying right across my face sometimes. I'm sure he thinks it's his bed not mine! And he tears around the house, chasing everything from wine bottle corks to shoelaces. I suppose, being a kitten, everything is fresh and exciting in his world. He looks at something and asks immediately, 'Can I play with that? Yes. Great!'

Wriggler continues to grow and to thrive with every day that passes. He's so bold now, and wants to be friends with everyone. He loves being with people, and I even take him on little kitten playdates, to my friend Kate's house, so he can play with her cat!

Wriggler met my Nan recently, too. She lives on her own in a managed flat, a kind of sheltered housing development, and I suppose she gets quite lonely sometimes. So I took him round to visit her one day, and, as I put Wriggler on her lap, her face lit up and she was immediately smiling and laughing. She really enjoyed meeting him and stroking him, and he was so good with her. As soon as I saw what a nice effect it had on her, I thought 'My goodness, perhaps he could do this for other people.'

I've since discovered an organization that does just that: as a volunteer you take your animals round to nursing homes, hospices and so on, so that people can socialize and play with them. I've got a while yet, as you have to have owned your animal for at least six months, and they have to be nine months old. Once I'm able to, I'm going to send his details and sign him up as a therapy cat, so he can hang out with elderly people and sit on their laps. It's not for every cat, certainly, but I think he'd love it and be good at it. Because Wriggler's been hand-reared, he's used to being passed around, and he's really affectionate.

Now that he's had all his vaccinations, Wriggler loves going outside on his harness, just for ten minutes at a time. I'm still a bit nervous about letting him out. I think something's going to happen to him in the big wide world. Perhaps I'll get him fitted with a GPS! That's a bit extreme, probably, but we'll definitely have him microchipped and I'll wait until he's a bit older before I let him out alone.

Two of his brothers, Jingle and Bell, were rehomed together to a lovely household, and one of the vet nurses kept her kitten, Pudding. We're all still sad about their poor little sisters passing away so young. But there was nothing we could do. And thank goodness their mother chose Battersea as the place to leave her litter, or Wriggler almost certainly wouldn't have lived to become the happy, cheeky little kitten he is today.

Ice: An English Bull Terrier Abroad

Most of our dogs and cats are rehomed in Britain, but people across the world look at the animals on our website and, as long as a pet passport and all the legal requirements can be arranged, a Battersea cat or dog can find itself living in a new country, with a new, perhaps even exotic, life. One Manx cat was recently flown all the way to Scotland for a very eager rehomer; and another dog even found itself having to learn a whole new language, as Ulla Munch-Petersen recounts . . .

Winters in Denmark are cold. We get several months of thick, fluffy snow that coats the whole country. It's great for children, who build enormous snowmen and go sledging in the parks. And it looks beautiful too, giving Copenhagen, where I live, a timeless feel. But no matter how much snow there has been I have always found time to walk around the city, every morning and night, with my two dogs, Thea and Oliver.

Thea was a pure white English Bull Terrier. I got her when she was seven to keep my older dog, Oliver, company. He was a Bassett Hound; I'd got him as a long, wriggly little puppy, and I doted on him. Thea was the kindest, gentlest dog I have ever known and she loved Oliver. She came to me as the victim of a divorce. A friend of mine couldn't keep the dog because her new flat wouldn't allow it. So I took her on, so that Thea didn't have to be put to sleep.

We had a lovely life, the three of us, walking and touring round Denmark's beautiful countryside. But when he was fifteen, Oliver began to slow down. He seemed tired. He'd had a great life, but eventually I realized he had just had enough.

In 2011, towards the end of the winter, the vet came to my house and we decided it was his time.

'He's the oldest Bassett Hound in Denmark, you know,' said the vet, as she lay him on the bed and stroked his tired head.

'Really!'

'Yes. At fifteen, he's probably the oldest Bassett Hound in Scandinavia, actually.'

Some time afterwards I checked it with the owner of the Long Body kennel where Oliver was born, and it was true!

'Well I never,' I said. 'He had a good life, anyway.'

It was so sad to see him drift off to eternal sleep that day. I'd had that dog since he was a big-eyed pup. It really was terrible. No matter how hard it was, though, I had to be there with him in his last moments. I owed him that much. Once it was all over, and his eyes gently closed, they cremated his body at the local animal hospital and I took the ashes away in a cardboard box.

My friend Karin and I took Oliver's ashes to The King's Garden, a huge park complex in Copenhagen, with a big castle, that was once a seventeenth-century king's private grounds. I used to walk with the dogs in the park a lot and it was one of Oliver's favourite places. Karin and I, and a few of our friends, walked solemnly into the park with the box and found a nice little corner to lay Oliver to rest. It was surrounded by giant white flowers and trees and felt very peaceful.

I crushed the box with his ashes in it, a kind of private ceremony, and he drifted off in the wind, across the flowers and the grass.

'Goodbye, Oliver,' I said, and we all bowed our heads.

When I got home, Thea looked lonely sitting in her bed. It was heartbreaking, because I couldn't tell her where Oliver had gone, but I could see she was missing him.

A month later, Thea began to get ill too. Now the ripe old age of thirteen herself, she seemed weak and despondent and I knew something was up.

When I found myself at the vet, this time with Thea in the car, it was like a bad dream I couldn't wake up from. She was shaking and quiet and looked very sick. The vet gave me some medicine and said he thought whatever it was would go away, so I drove home with her. But the next morning she was trembling even more violently and she couldn't use her legs. I rushed her back to the vet hospital.

'Brain tumour,' he said, after some tests. 'There's nothing we can do, I'm afraid. I think we will have to put her to sleep,' he told me sadly. 'I thought she might recover a bit, but it's too far gone.'

'I'll miss you, little one,' I whispered into her ear when the time came and stroked her long white nose. She looked back at me with her sad, black eyes.

With two old dogs, I suppose I had known it was

coming some day, but for them both to go within a month of each other, that was hard.

I carried Thea's ashes into The King's Garden and scattered them next to Oliver, in the garden with the enormous flowers in it. 'Now you're together,' I said.

I left them behind in peace and tried to get on with my life without my family of dogs.

I love to travel, and in my spare time, when I'm not working for a Danish shipping company, I take photographs for Doctors Without Borders, the United Nations and the Red Cross. When I'd told my mother I wanted to be a photographer, she said to me, 'Don't do that – you will never have any bread in your mouth.' So I decided to do media communications at university, and keep photography as a hobby. It worked out great, actually, because I got a good job, and I have also seen some amazing things on my travels. I've taken photos in the Middle East, amongst other places, and also in Bosnia during the war.

When I got my two dogs I couldn't travel as much, of course, but now they were both gone I started to think I might get back into it again.

'I'm not getting another dog,' I told my friend Karin, a few days after I had said goodbye to Thea. We were strolling through the city.

'Good idea, now you can get out and see the world again,' she said. 'Also it has upset you so much, losing them. Not sure you should go through that again.'

'You're right,' I said firmly. 'I'm not getting any more dogs. It's just too painful.'

I started to make plans, and got in touch with a few old photography contacts.

Then, just a month after Thea passed away, relaxing after a long week at work, I was absentmindedly flicking through the *Financial Times* – working for a shipping company I have to keep up to date with global finance. I started reading an article in the magazine supplement called 'How to Spend It'. There was a story about a dancer from the Royal Ballet in London, talking about how she was going to spend the weekend. I wasn't even reading it properly, just skimming it. She talked about going for brunch, and so on and so on, but then she mentioned that her brother-in-law had just rehomed a dog from Battersea Dogs & Cats Home, so they had to find a place where a dog could come with them into the cafe.

When I read the name Battersea Dogs & Cats Home I was intrigued. I had never heard of it before. What on earth was it?

At work on Monday, just for fun, I Googled it. Wow, I thought, when I opened up the website, and saw all those dogs. I started looking through, just out of curiosity. We do have dogs and cats homes in Denmark, but Battersea seemed different. More personal and friendly.

First I typed in 'Basset Hound', like Oliver, but they didn't have any. Then I tried for an English Bull Terrier, like Thea. And, after just a few minutes, there she was: Ice.

There was a picture of a white English Bull Terrier who looked very much like Thea. She had the 'egg-shaped' head, pointy nose, and little deep-set, triangular eyes, just like Thea. But instead of being totally white, she had one black ear.

'Hello,' I said, 'who are you, then? What's your story?'

There was a box with a little bit of information about

the dog. It said she was ten years old. That's a real pity for such an old dog to be in a home, I thought. But I quickly shut down the web page and got on with my work.

After a few days I was tempted to take another look, just to see if Ice was still there. I really hoped she had been rehomed, actually, so she could have some freedom, but she was still up on the site. And she was still there a week later, too.

I told my friend Karin about it. 'Oh, Ulla, not another dog!' she sighed. 'What about your travel plans?'

'I know. I was only looking,' I said sheepishly.

'And you were so sad about Thea and Oliver. Do you really want to put yourself through it again? With an older dog as well?'

I kept quiet after that. But I couldn't stop thinking about Ice.

On the Battersea website you can buy presents for the dogs, so a few days later I thought, well, if I'm not rehoming you, at least I can send you something to make your life a little nicer. So I sent Ice a little treat and note in the post: 'Dear Ice, here is a little something sweet for you, to brighten up your day.'

Now they must think I'm really crazy, I thought. But the thought of her wouldn't leave me alone, so after a few days I called Battersea up and said I was interested in finding out more about the dog. I got talking to a woman in the rehoming department called Tracey, who told me Ice had been handed in to Battersea in November 2010.

'Her previous owner had long-term ill health and didn't feel able to take care of her any more,' she explained. 'She'd had her since she was a puppy, so it was a big transition for

Ice to find herself in kennels. She's ten years old. But she's settled in well, considering.'

'Is she OK with children?' I asked. 'I live in Copenhagen, in a place with lots of children in the houses around me.'

'She's been here for a while now, and although we can't, make any guarantees, she gets on well with everyone here.'

'What about other dogs?' I asked. 'We have a lot of dogs near us too.'

Tracey reassured me. 'She's in good condition and she's a good dog all round. She spends time in offices and in the kitchen with our staff.'

'How long has she been with you, exactly?' I asked.

'Seven months.'

That's such a pity for such an old dog, if she's good and healthy, I thought to myself.

'But I must tell you, before we go any further, that as a general rule we do not rehome dogs to travel immediately on planes, because it can be stressful for a dog who has just been in kennels. How had you planned to get her over to you?'

'Well, I had thought to get the plane . . .'

'No, no, I'm afraid Ice wouldn't dare travel on a plane just yet.'

'What should I do then?'

'You can't fly with her. She'd just be too nervous and stressed.'

A friend of mine later told me that the hold on the plane where they put the dogs is very cold, totally dark and there's a lot of noise, which Ice would have found terrifying after being in kennels.

'I could fly over and meet her first, and then, if everything's OK, I could drive over to collect her in my car, take the car ferry and drive her back.'

'That should be OK. I just need to check with DEFRA what we need to take a dog from the UK to Denmark, in the way of vaccinations and so on. If you could also check details from a Danish point of view, that would be great. When we rehome,' Tracey went on, 'we usually go to check the dog's new home first. But if you decide you want Ice, of course we can't do that. So in your case we would have to get your vet to send us a reference.'

'Oh, that should be easy,' I said. 'I've had the same vet for twenty years! He knows me quite well. So can I come and see her, then?'

'Of course! You're welcome to,' said Tracey.

And right away I started looking at flights to London. I had already decided that Ice must come to Denmark and live out her days with me here. If she dies after one month, I thought, at least she's felt some freedom in a green area. It's better than being in kennels for the rest of her life. Even if she only has a few weeks, she will have felt freedom again.

When I told Karin and my friends I was going all the way to London to look at a ten-year-old dog, of course they thought I was mad. But in the end they saw what I saw, which was a lovely old dog in need of a good home.

'Well, I suppose if you've got the time and the means to look after the dog, and it needs a home, then you should go for it,' said Karin. 'You are mad, though,' she added with a smile.

Once I arrived in London, I took a cab to Battersea

Old Windsor and I was immediately impressed by how beautiful it was there. It was proper English countryside, with the Thames flowing right past the Home; people rowing in boats, and lovely tall trees everywhere. It was very green and very welcoming.

'Come to the office and we'll chat through everything there,' said Tracey, who met me at reception.

I followed her through various corridors to the office, and every now and again I saw a dog being walked on a lead. It was a real joy to see them out and about instead of locked up behind bars.

'We try to get the dogs out as much as we can,' said Tracey. 'Ice loves to be with us in the office or even in the kitchen, and she's happy as long as she's got a big squidgy bed to sit in.'

Once we got into the big office, Tracey sat one side of a big desk and I sat on the other.

'So it turns out that to get her to Denmark, if that's what happens, you will need her to have a rabies vaccination, tick and worm treatment, plus microchipping and a pet passport. Would that be OK with you?'

'Yes, of course, whatever it takes.'

'We have also taken Ice out in the car a few times to see how she travels. She seems fine, fortunately, and as long as she has her cosy duvet, she seems to sleep quite quietly.'

'Well, that's great!' I said. I was impressed by how much care they had already taken on the project.

'Tell me a little bit more about yourself, then,' said Tracey.

I told her about my job, and my flat, and that I needed

a dog who was happy on her own during the day, though I would take her for long walks morning and night.

'Do you live on the ground floor?' she asked. 'Ice isn't very good on the stairs, I'm afraid.'

'Luckily I do, and my flat is in the beautiful historic neighbourhood of Brumleby in Copenhagen. It's a collection of former medical housing association dwellings built in the 1850s,' I told her. 'One of the first social housing schemes. It's very green, with communal gardens, and no cars are allowed. So it's great for dogs. Very sociable. And I also have my own small garden area out the back.'

'That sounds great,' she said, writing it all down in her notebook.

What I liked about that interview was that she didn't give me special treatment because I had come all the way from Denmark. It was all very professional and I sensed it would have been just the same if I'd come from round the corner. I was very pleased to see that.

'What do you know about Ice's past?' I asked again. We had been talking for nearly an hour and I hadn't yet seen Ice.

'We know very little, actually. It's often the case. The lady who had her before became very ill. She was desperate, didn't want to lose the dog at all. But she just couldn't keep her. I think she ended up in a hospice . . . I don't know any more than that. But Ice was well cared for. She's not really a nervous dog, although we did have to move her here from our main London site, because that's near a train line and that did stress her out a bit. But she's been fine here.'

I was impressed again that they would take the time

and care to move the dog all the way to the countryside so it could be happy.

'And she's been here for seven months?' I asked.

'Yes. It's her age. Sometimes it can put people off, unfortunately. People want puppies a lot of the time. Young dogs, you know.'

I told Tracey all about Thea and Oliver, and made it clear that I was an experienced dog owner. And I showed her some photographs I had taken of the area where I live. All in all, Tracey was very kind, very professional and not emotional about anything. And that's the way to do it, as far as I'm concerned.

After an hour, she finally said, 'OK, now you can see the dog.'

She left the room, and while she was gone, I sat and waited nervously. What if Ice didn't like me, or what if I fell in love with her but something went wrong?

When the dog finally poked her nose around the door, and stepped into the room, I was taken aback by just how much she looked like Thea. Apart from her one black ear.

'Hey there, Ice,' I said quietly, not wanting to startle her. She wagged her tail and came a bit closer to me.

'Do you want to go for a walk with her?' asked Tracey.

'Oh, yes,' I said. I was trying to seem calm and collected, but in truth, I couldn't wait to get her outside and running about.

Tracey trusted me to take her around on my own, so I walked around the designated paths for a bit. We passed another dog, and she reared up a bit and pulled on the lead. So I clicked my tongue, encouraged her back and she obeyed.

After about ten minutes I found an agility paddock so I took her in there to run about. It had fences around it and I locked the gate so she couldn't escape. We must have stayed there for about an hour, and she absolutely loved it. There was a big tunnel – I went to the end and she ran through it to meet me.

'You're a happy dog, aren't you?' I said, as she ran about madly and jumped in the air and did a little spin. She was just so happy to be out and playing with someone in the fresh air. I threw a frisbee for her, which she ran and brought back to me, really interacting with me, which was great.

Once she was all puffed out from playing, I had a look at her teeth. It's a good way to tell the condition of the dog. I was surprised that, for a ten-year-old dog, her teeth were really nice, and I knew she was very strong and healthy with a lot of energy.

I took her back to the office to meet Tracey again, and Ice settled into a little bed in the corner of the room. She rested her head on her paws and looked over at me with one eye open.

'So, what did you think?' asked Tracey.

'She was fantastic,' I said. 'She's strong but I can handle that, I'm used to Bull Terriers so I can handle her. She's got very nice teeth too.'

'Yes, we thought that.'

I looked over at Ice, who may have known we were talking about her. She was lying in her basket, looking up at me all sleepily.

'She loves to "sandwich" herself into her duvet, so you can hardly see her sometimes!' Tracey commented.

I didn't want to get too emotional because I thought that if it didn't work out for some reason I would be so unhappy. But all of a sudden Ice jumped up from her bed, came over and sat right by me. She turned round a few times and then lay there right next to me for the rest of the interview.

'Good girl,' I said quietly. I stayed calm on the outside, but I was so happy. My heart felt so big it could have burst right there and then. After another while, Tracey looked at her notes and said, 'Well, if you want her, then it's fine with us.'

'I want her,' I said without hesitation.

It was hard to go home and leave Ice there, but there was some more paperwork to send from the vet's, and the vaccinations and everything for Battersea to sort out. We also had to arrange the pet passport for her. So I took some photos of Ice while I was there to use for that. The whole thing went very smoothly.

I realized that I ought to check whether you can actually take a dog on the ferry, so I rang the local company, which, as it turned out, was partly run by the company I worked for. They said it was fine. The crossing takes eighteen hours and you put the dog on the car deck.

After two weeks it was all sorted and I had my tickets booked, then one Sunday afternoon my mobile rang.

'Ulla? It's Battersea,' said the voice. It wasn't Tracey or anyone I recognized. 'We are so sorry, it's not often we make a mistake,' said the woman very gravely.

Oh my God, I thought, they've rehomed her to an English person after all, because it's easier for them. Or worse, she's dead! As the woman on the phone continued apologizing, I was just thinking, quick, put me out of my misery and tell me!

'I'm so sorry. It's really not often we make a mistake like this,' she continued. 'I know we told you she was ten. Well, we tested the microchip with all her information on it. And now we've found out she's only eight. Once again, I am so sorry.'

'Is that all?' I said, breathing a huge sigh of relief. 'That's not a problem. That's fantastic!'

It now meant I might have an extra two years or more with Ice. It also explained why she had such good teeth, and why she was so robust. Bull Terriers as a breed are very strong, in fact they're sometimes called the 'gladiators of the canine race' because they're so muscly.

It was a pretty long journey to collect Ice, nearly 800 miles each way. First I would have to drive from Copenhagen to the ferry port in Denmark, and then the boat trip to Harwich in England, which would take eighteen hours, plus getting to Battersea itself. Battersea spent the next few weeks sorting out Ice's medical requirements, in order for her to be ready to travel to Denmark. One day, shortly before I was due to travel, Tracey called me.

'We're all aware it's a long journey for you. All that driving,' she said, 'and we were thinking . . . since the hardest part will be the drive from Harwich to Old Windsor and back, we could bring Ice to the Harwich ferry port and meet you there?'

'Wow. That would be fantastic!' I said. 'That would really take the load off.'

So, when the day came, I packed up my car and set off on the long journey. The boat trip was pretty calm, and I stood on deck, tingling with excitement about meeting Ice again and bringing her home. It was a lovely clear summer day in England, and there at the harbour, when I got off the boat, were Tracey and her boss, the Old Windsor centre manager.

'Hello!' they called out. The two of them were standing there, waving at me, and Ice was sitting on a carpet next to their car. She was very quiet, not stressed out at all. I'm not sure whether she recognized me or not – who knows, maybe? But she seemed happy.

'How was your journey?' asked Tracey. 'Not too rough, I hope.'

'No, it was fine. I had a good book with me,' I said. I knew they were a little worried about Ice spending so long on the ferry so I reassured them. 'There will be other animals on there I've been told. So Ice will be in good company!'

Tracey pulled the paperwork from her bag and we sat on a bench. There was a little cafe nearby, so we got some cups of tea and watched the boats drifting in and out of the harbour. Gulls flew overhead squawking or pecking at bits of bread and chip packets on the side. We sat in silence for a moment and soaked up the clean sea air.

'It's nice to get out of the office for the day,' said Tracey, breathing it all in. 'And Ice was fine in the car, in the end.'

'Oh, I just remembered, I brought a duvet for her especially,' I told Tracey. 'So she'll be super comfy.'

Eventually it was time for them to leave, so we signed all the papers.

'Come on then, you. We're going home,' I said to Ice, and amazingly she jumped up.

Tracey was sad to see her go. They had been very close; after all she had been with Battersea for 213 days in total, and she was a very popular dog. I took her over to my station wagon and opened the boot.

'Come here, Ice,' I said and clicked my tongue. She came over right away and put her legs up on the boot, so I hoisted her up. She looked up, turned round a few times, then lay down.

'What about goodbye?' said Tracey.

No goodbye, she seemed to say, let's go! She wasn't even looking up. She was just ready. In a moment, Ice had snuggled down into her duvet for the trip home.

Once they had left, we still had a couple of hours before the ferry departed so I drove to the main entrance and got out of the car to take Ice for a walk in the local neighbourhood. After all, she had a long journey ahead. We went to a little park, where she almost immediately saw a great big German Shepherd. I didn't know how she was going to react, but she reared up a bit, and this dog was off its lead so I started panicking a bit.

'Hey, do you think you could put your dog on a lead, while I pass?' I called out. 'I've got a new dog here. Not sure how she's going to cope with other dogs yet.'

'Oh, take it easy, lady,' said the man as his great big German Shepherd came lolloping over, sniffing about.

I wasn't worried about him causing trouble, so much as I worried about Ice hurting him. She's got a strong jaw and I couldn't bear her to get in a fight or something so soon. In the end, though, she was fine. I suppose I was just being a little nervous and cautious on my first day.

'Good dog,' I said, and patted her on the back as she trotted beside me quite happily back to the car.

When we got on to the car deck of the ferry, there were seven other cars with dogs in them, so we had quite a pack. The security guard showed us where they could go to the loo and where we could let them out, a total of four times throughout the long crossing.

'Oh, that's a lovely white dog!' said a woman from England who was moving to Denmark and taking her own Jack Russell Terrier with her. 'I do love their little long faces, those English Bull Terriers,' she said and stroked Ice's black nose.

'Yes. I've just got her!' I said. 'From Battersea. Though I live in Copenhagen.'

'Gosh, that's a long way to go,' she said. 'We've just moved to Denmark, in the south, from Norfolk. My husband's job's there,' she said. 'But it's been very easy to bring little Suzie over with us. Really easy with the dog passport actually.'

When she heard her name, the long-haired Terrier leapt up in the air and spun a circle.

Some of the other dogs were barking and scampering about on their leads, but they were fine really, considering the odd situation they were in. When they had eaten and watered, we put them all back in the cars and prepared to leave port.

I texted Tracey: 'Ice is on board and all is fine.' Then I went to find my cabin. It was evening and I had quite a few hours before I could check on her again, so I tried to occupy myself with reading. I kept thinking about her down there, hoping she was OK. I walked about on deck for a bit and the wind swept up around me, the air all salty and fresh. When I arrived back at my cabin again, one of the security guards was knocking on my door.

'Oh, Miss Munch-Peterson?' he said. 'There you are.'

'Yes?' I said. I had a sudden awful thought that something had happened to Ice. 'Is everything OK?'

'Have you got a white dog on the car deck?' he asked.

'Yes!' I said, now getting really worried.

'Well, I think she's set your car alarm off.'

'Oh my God. I'm so sorry!'

'It's all right. Just come with me and we can go and sort it out. Don't want to wake the whole ship now, do we?'

As I followed him down the different levels of the ship, down to the car deck, I heard it. Just a faint buzzing at first, then louder and louder, until we got to the door to the car deck. Then you could hear the wailing of the car alarm, which seemed to be bouncing around the whole ship.

And there was Ice, in the front seat, with her paws up on the dashboard, so happy to see us. She must have jumped up and her movement in the car set it off.

'I must have forgotten to turn it off!' I said. I managed to stop the noise eventually, but it was a new car and I wasn't entirely sure how to work the alarm yet.

'We don't really need it in Brumleby, where I live, because it's so safe. And I hardly drive anywhere in Copenhagen anyway, as it's mainly bicycles there,' I said to the security guard.

'Well, you're lucky! I could never leave my car without an alarm where I live,' he said.

In the end, I'm embarrassed to say, I never quite cracked that alarm system. Just a few hours later, I got another knock on the door. Is that your dog? Yes. The alarm's gone off again. So back down to the car deck we went, and there was Ice in the front seat, tail wagging, paws on the dashboard, alarm blaring all around her.

I felt awful, but neither I nor the security guard could figure out how to turn it off properly. In the end I had to go down twice more before the night was out. We became very famous on that journey, but everyone was lovely, and so sweet about the fact that I was bringing this rescue dog all the way from England to Denmark on my own.

Despite the thing with the car alarm, Ice was really great on the journey, no trouble at all. When we arrived in Denmark in the morning, I was relieved to see that she hadn't bitten or chewed anything in the car either.

I knew Tracey had been a little apprehensive about the long journey for Ice, so I had been texting her throughout to let her know how we were doing. I sent her one last text to say we'd reached dry land safely.

The drive from the ferry port to my home is another few hours, and I was pretty tired by now, as well as pleased to have Ice in her new home country. I got a message from my neighbour, Janna, saying, 'Let us know when you get nearby.' When I arrived I almost ignored it, I was so tired, but in the end I thought, all right, I'll let them know I'm back and then get some sleep. But I'm glad I did, because when we got home and walked up to the front door I could hear voices, and people giggling and whispering round the corner.

'Ulla's coming!'

'Quick!'

'Get ready. She's here!'

I went to see what on earth was going on, and there, across the grass of our communal garden, was an enormous table laid out with all sorts of delicious food, cakes and lovely treats. The local children had even decorated it with balloons and Danish flags, and there was of course lots of ice cream, in honour of Ice!

It was so sweet of them, I could have cried, what with being so exhausted from the journey as well. But it was lovely to see everyone, and we welcomed Ice into her new home with a little party.

I was unsure how Ice would react to all these people, and there were a lot of dogs nearby too, so I sat at the table with Ice on her lead as we tucked into the food. Two of the children in the neighbourhood, Tobias and his little sister, Frida, were particularly taken with Ice, and they came over to chat to her and stroke her as we ate.

There was one thing I had forgotten to ask Tracey about. In a word – cats.

Ice saw it before me. This great big ginger moggie, up a nearby tree, stalking a bird. Before I could do anything, though, Ice had dived under the table, as fast as a rocket. And since I was holding her lead, I had no choice but to be pulled under with her. The whole table went flying, and all the cakes and treats with it. There was chaos and pandemonium for a moment, as people rushed over from all directions to catch falling cups and restore jellies.

It was probably a good thing I hadn't asked Tracey about Ice and cats, because I got my answer right there. She hates them! And there's practically a cat up every tree in Brumleby. But since you have to have your dog on a lead here anyway, it's not so much of a problem. And, although she's strong, I can keep hold of her – just about!

Once the celebrations were over, and the table restored to its original position, I took Ice to see her new home. When we got into my flat, she looked around and sniffed in every corner. I suppose she could smell Thea and Oliver. Then she got so excited she just started jumping around.

'This is my new home!' she seemed to say. 'It's fantastic!'

I was so pleased. I had thought she might be a bit nervous, but far from it. She was in her element.

That evening, before our very first walk, I took a lovely photo of Ice peeking out of her new front door and sent it to Tracey in a text: 'Home at last.'

Ice soon settled into her new bed, and found out where her food was, and from the first moment it felt as though I'd had her here all her life. I had actually taken a few days off work, to be with her and get her used to her new home. But she was just fine.

I started to teach Ice a little Danish as soon as I could, and got her to search for a biscuit I had hidden in the living room. I said the Danish word for search, which is *søge*, a few times. 'Good dog. *Søge, søge.*' And she found it almost straight away. The other Danish phrase she learnt that day was the very important term we use for dogs here, *dygtig pige*, which means good girl. I use that a lot: '*Dygtig pige*,

Ice! Good girl, Ice.' I like to use the English words she's familiar with too, because she's used to that. So I suppose she'll be bilingual soon!

I had fallen for Ice at first because she reminded me so much of my beloved Thea. But they couldn't be more different. Ice is her own dog, very independent and wilful. Thea was calm and quiet and soft. And she was lovely, even to other dogs. Ice is very strong willed, much more powerful than Thea, and much more wild.

It took her quite a while to get used to all the dogs in the area. At first she would rear up in her harness, and I spent months training her to accept them around her. She's come on a long way now, and she even has a best friend, called Charlie, who is a Cairn Terrier. They play together all the time and she socializes with all the dogs in the area now.

Every day, morning and evening, we go to a park where dogs can go off the lead so she can have a good run about, and she's happy on her own during the day, sleeping. That's what she's used to now, and she's so happy to see me when I get home she starts running and jumping and spinning in the air.

'It's not Buckingham Palace, Ice,' I say. 'It's only my house!' But she loves it.

We go for long walks, and spend weekends together touring in the south of Sjaelland in a place named Moen, where they have beautiful beaches and forests. At first she didn't like water, but it's good for her feet so I encouraged her and today she loves it. It was very important for me that I could take Ice with me wherever I went, because she's alone when I go to work. So most of the time if I'm here, she's with me. We go round town or to visit people. In fact, she has so many friends in our area now that when we go on our evening walk, I spend a lot of time going up steps to people's doors and back down again with Ice as she tries to go and visit them all.

There's no doubt that Ice wears the trousers in our house. She's too old for me to try to teach her all sorts of complicated things. It's not important to me. So if she doesn't want to sit, or to go out, then we don't, and that's that. She digs her heels in. But she's fine when we're out and about and always very well behaved.

When it came to playing with the local children, Tobias and Frida, I was a bit worried at first. Being a Bull Terrier, she's so strong in her jaw, and I thought I had to be really careful with her around them. But she's been absolutely fine. They go into this little tent, all together, Tobias, Frida and Ice. It's such a small tent I don't know how they can all fit in there! They also have a paddling pool in the summer, and she even likes splashing about in that.

The very first time she saw the thick Danish snow was quite a moment. Ice playing in the ice! She ran out of the house and jumped all around; she absolutely loved it. At one point she completely disappeared – the snow was so thick, and she's so white. All I could see were her little black nose and one black ear sticking out. One year Tobias built a snowman and Ice ran over straight away, all excited, and plucked the carrot neatly from its nose. Dinner!

When I first thought about rehoming Ice, I thought I'd be happy to have her for just a few weeks. After a few months, I thought I'd be happy to have her for half a year. Now I've had her two years, and she's still a very strong, playful and loving dog. I stay in touch with Tracey and Battersea as much as I can, and send updates and photos of Ice. They have even rehomed a second dog to Denmark, so they just need a third to make it a Danish hat-trick! But Ice will always be the first long-distance winner from Battersea.

Jester: A Staffie Love Story

After rehoming an animal from Battersea Dogs & Cats Home, very occasionally a new owner finds they can't keep their new pet after all. And when this is the case, we're always happy to help and try to find the animal another loving home. Sometimes our help isn't required, however, and dogs or cats can go on to suitable new owners without needing to have another stay at the Home. We were delighted when we heard of a case of a vet, Jo Lewis, who had a chance meeting with Battersea's very own canine Cupid . . .

'Who's this, then?' I asked, showing the next person on my list into the consulting room. The man had a lovely, slim brindle Staffie with him.

'This is Jester,' he said, following me through, 'and I'm Andrew.'

It was a pretty standard day for me as a vet. I had just seen a woman with a poorly cat, and after a lot more morning consultations I would be starting routine operations in the afternoon.

'Let's have a look at you then, Jester,' I said.

I listened to his heart, took his temperature and gave him a once-over to make sure there wasn't anything obviously wrong.

'He's very gentle, isn't he?' I said, as Jester stood there calmly while I carried out all the examinations. 'Have you had him long? I don't remember seeing you before.'

'Actually I've only just got him, although he's about eleven or twelve now. It's a bit of a long story, but he was found wandering around London as a puppy and ended up at Battersea Dogs & Cats Home.'

As Andrew started to tell me the story, I noticed he had a really nice voice, and I found it very easy to listen to him.

'Anyway, Jester's owners, friends of mine, have had him all his life, really, but they're about to have a baby. Well, to cut a long story short, he curled his lip at them. Just once, on the sofa, but he'd never done anything like that before. They panicked and thought they couldn't have a dog like that around small children. But he's not at all aggressive, as far as I can tell. He's actually a bit scared of other dogs, and of cats, believe it or not! Anyway, my friends were absolutely distraught, and desperate to find him a new home. But they really struggled – because of his age, probably. In the end, as a last resort, they got so desperate they considered having him put down. But the vet wouldn't do it. So I said, well, I'll take him. I'd dog-sat for them a few times, and I couldn't bear the thought of him being put to sleep.'

'That's so great. That you took him on, I mean. It must have been awful for the other owners. But he seems perfectly happy and healthy now.'

'I thought I should get his vaccinations updated. You know, just in case.'

I agreed it was a good idea and gave Jester his annual boosters. Again he was very compliant and good-natured; I couldn't understand why anyone would have wanted to give him up.

'What do you do? Work-wise?' I asked. 'I mean, it must be a lot taking on a new dog, just like that.'

'I'm in the police. So it has been a bit tough, with my long shifts. But I couldn't bear to see him go to just any-one on a whim, or worse. Anyway, he sleeps most of the day. And we're getting along just fine. Aren't we, Jester?'

I may not have shown it at the time, keeping my profes-sional face on, but I thought it was pretty amazing the way this guy had taken on someone else's dog and had the dedication to take him to the vet and get his vaccinations done. He wasn't just thinking he could cut costs and hope for the best, like some people might.

'Sorry! I've done all the talking here,' he said. 'What about you? Is that an Australian accent?'

'Yes. But I'm English actually. Moved to Australia as a child and grew up there, in Perth. But then, when I became a vet, after a couple of years I decided to work in Eng-land. There just seemed to be more opportunities here. More animal-lovers. I don't know, in Australia it just didn't feel like as many people had the same passion for animals as they do over here.'

As I spoke, I realized it was time to finish off with Jester. I had a whole caseload of other people to see before lunch, and much as I would have loved to, I couldn't stand around chatting all day.

'Well. All done. And thanks for bringing him in. I hope to see you both again. Not for, you know, illness, or any-thing. But if you need anything, let me know.'

'Yes. You've been so helpful. Thanks! I'll let you know how it goes.'

And with that, Andrew and Jester walked out of the consulting room, and I got on with the rest of my day.

Over lunch, I casually mentioned their visit to a colleague, Sarah, one of the nurses. It was nothing hugely out of the ordinary, but I did say what a really nice guy I thought Andrew was, to have taken on an old dog like that. I'm not the sort of person to ask someone out, but it crossed my mind that it would be nice to find someone like Andrew one day, someone as generous and caring . . . and as good-looking.

Life at the practice was challenging and busy, but also very fun and rewarding. It may have been quite a small surgery, but I had a lot of responsibility and was often the only vet there.

I would fly through the door in the morning with a pretty good idea of the patients who would be in. I'd check on the animals that had been kept in overnight for whatever reason, and then start consultations. Each appointment slot was usually fifteen minutes, and cases could be anything from straightforward things like vaccinations and removing stitches to an ER episode with a victim of poisoning or a car accident, or complicated medical and surgery cases. My patients come in all shapes and sizes, from tiny gerbils to feet-long snakes. There is always a waiting room full of people; some with kittens or puppies for their first vaccinations, some long-standing clients about to say goodbye to their beloved pets. Sometimes, a consultation can even go from being a routine check-up to euthanasia in one visit, if people haven't realized how sick their animals are. And that can be just heartbreaking. One of the harder parts of my job is staying in control of my own emotions while being aware of what other people are feeling too.

On top of a fully-booked morning of appointments, I'd often have to deal with any patients that had been transferred back into my care after their overnight stay at the after-hours centre. And that was just the morning's work! In the afternoon I would have operations to perform and blood test results to analyse from the day before. Plus having to phone owners to discuss which treatments would be best for their pets. On top of all that, of course, unlike human doctors in the UK, there are discussions about money to be had, which is always difficult. There's no NHS for pets!

It was on a regular, busy day like this that my colleague, a lovely vet called Jayne, came in looking really concerned and apologetic.

'I'm so sorry, Jo!' she said, sheepishly. 'I've had to book in some last-minute surgery for you. Looks like a tricky job. Dog with a cancerous lump on his leg. I've had a look and I don't think there's anything else we can do but remove the lump. It's got to a size where the skin has stretched and split – it just won't heal and we need to stop the bleeding. It's a bit of a blood bath. It really has to be done straight away and you're the only one available. I'm so sorry!'

'Don't worry,' I said. 'I'm sure it'll be fine.'

I dealt with all my morning consultations and then went in to look at the dog with the bleeding leg. And there on the table was Jester the Staffie.

'Oh, you are in a state. You poor thing,' I said. His leg

was completely covered with blood and he looked very sorry for himself.

I gently anaesthetised him, so that he was completely unconscious, and began to take a look at how I could cut away the tumour. As I looked at the lump I realized it was in a really tricky location, as Jayne had said.

'There's not a lot of skin. Not sure yet how I'm going to close the gap,' I said to Sarah, the nurse who was assisting me.

Although I had of course studied it thoroughly at a theoretical level, I hadn't ever done one of these particular operations, where you have to create a special skin flap over the cut-away flesh to seal the wound up again. This was a perfect situation to put theory into practise. Sarah was standing by with the instruments, but first I had an idea.

'Hang on a moment. I need to sketch this out.'

I went up to the whiteboard we had in the surgery and started carefully drawing diagrams of where best to cut to do the operation and replace the skin properly. As I did so, I thought to myself, 'This is this old dog's one chance – he's not going to have more than one anaesthetic.'

'Right, that should do it,' I said to Sarah, satisfied with my plan.

'Well, rather you than me,' she said, and handed me the clippers to start cutting away Jester's beautiful brindle fur.

I knew nothing could go drastically wrong, but I did feel very nervous because once I cut in I knew I couldn't change my mind. There's no point being shy and not taking enough tissue away from around the tumour, though, because if there's any of the growth left behind the cancer can come back. So you have to take more than the naked eye can see. I knew I could do it – it was just a matter of drawing some confidence from somewhere. I nipped the fur away from Jester's leg, took the permanent marker and dotted exactly round the lump where I was going to cut. Then I cleaned the area and made the first incision.

'It's bleeding quite a lot,' I said. 'I think the tumour is based around the lining of the blood vessels.'

Sarah was monitoring the anaesthetic and handing me the instruments. I stemmed the bleeding, and once the operation was underway I was confident it was going well.

'Did you see the bloke who brought him in?' I asked Sarah, after a while.

'Yes. He had pale trousers on. Quite well-to-do, I thought,' she replied.

'He's a policeman!' I laughed. 'So you got that one wrong. I thought he was quite nice, actually.'

It may seem odd that we chatted a bit during surgery, but in fact it's much easier to stay calm and relaxed that way. As you monitor all the equipment measuring the animal's heart and blood pressure, having a bit of light banter actually helps you to stay focused and not get too tense.

An hour later it was all done. The tumour was completely removed and the wound sewn up.

'Seems to have gone very well,' I said as I finished the dressing.

'So all those diagrams paid off, then. You didn't by any chance have an agenda for doing this one extra carefully, did you?' asked Sarah archly. 'You know, a certain pale-trousered policeman?'

'Don't be ridiculous!' I said. 'Of course not.'

'Well, he looks a million times better!' said Andrew when he came into the surgery to collect Jester. The dog's wound was all dressed and clean, he'd woken up from the anaesthetic and was wagging his tail happily. 'I suppose this must have been run of the mill for you. I mean, you must have seen some weird and wonderful animals in Australia.'

'Well, yes. I mean no, this was quite a tricky operation. Although, I have seen some pretty weird animals here in the UK, actually! In Australia, we have plenty of exotic species in the wild, but pets are not that extraordinary – your usual dogs and cats and things. I don't know anyone with a pet snake there, and there are no hamsters in Oz. But here people come in with all sorts. The funny thing is you don't know, until you click on the notes, what sort of patient it's going to be. It's just a name on the list, like Derek Roberts, or whatever. And then it turns out to be a great big lizard.'

'Or a stick insect,' laughed Andrew. 'I only ask because I saw some amazing animals when I was in Africa. Gazelles, zebras, lions, that kind of thing. I was out there for a few years as a tour guide. Just wondered if you'd had to deal with anything like that.'

'Nothing as exotic as a lion,' I said. 'But I have been asked to do a post mortem on a tarantula! How lovely to go to Africa, though. All that space.'

We stopped speaking for a moment, and in that comfortable silence, I realized that I found it very easy to talk to Andrew. I would never normally speak so freely to a client.

Jester firmly put his paw up on my arm and reminded me that he was there too.

'Anyway. You're all done,' I said. 'Aren't you, little sausage? He was so well behaved. Never once complained. If you could make an appointment to come back in two to three days for a dressing change, that would be great. We'll wait for the final biopsy results to come back but I'm hopeful that we have managed to get it all out.'

'Good stuff. Come on then, you,' said Andrew to Jester, getting up to go. 'It'll probably be a shock for him going home, after all the attention he's been getting here.'

When they left I felt that slight pang again. Andrew was so natural and caring with Jester. I wasn't really looking for a boyfriend, but I thought again that if I ever did find the one, I hoped it would be someone like that. It wasn't long, though, before work brought me back to reality in the form of a small boy, carrying a green cardboard box. He was being pushed into the room by his rather stern-looking mother.

'Tell her what you did. I can't get the full facts out of him, maybe you can,' she said, looking exasperated.

'I only wanted to wash him. But he went all funny. And blue. He will be all right, though, won't he?' asked the boy, biting his lip.

'Let's have a look,' I said. Inside the box was a shivering little hamster, its fur all stuck to its skin and covered in frothy white bubbles.

'I knew he was up to something when he went all quiet up there,' said the mother. 'But I had no idea he was washing the thing. Shampoo all over the bath!'

'Perhaps human shampoo isn't the best way to wash your hamster?' I suggested, when I had got the full story. 'Make him a hot water bottle and put him somewhere warm and quiet for the day and I'm sure he'll be fine. But definitely no more baths for Bertie!'

I saw Andrew and Jester again only briefly, from afar, when they came back to have Jester's dressing changed. I was working on something else that day, and I didn't get to talk to him properly. But I did notice that he was accompanied by a woman. They soon disappeared with Jester into the consulting room. Sarah the nurse caught up with me in reception that afternoon.

'That bloke with Jester, you know, the dog with the tumour. He – well, they – left you these. In reception,' she said and handed me a parcel.

'Oh, that was nice,' I said. 'Chocolates. How lovely of them.'

I wanted to thank Andrew personally for the gesture, so I called the mobile phone number in Jester's notes. When a woman answered I felt nervous all of a sudden. Why was I ringing?

'Sorry. Is, Andrew there? It's Jo from the vets.'

'Oh, hi! Yes, he's driving. Sorry. Did you get the chocolates? We just wanted to say thank you so much, for looking after Jester the way you did.'

The sounds of the car speeding along in the background and the unknown woman answering the telephone suddenly made me realize that, outside of our chats in the surgery with his dog, I really knew nothing about Andrew; he had a whole life of his own, about which I knew nothing whatsoever.

'Yes, I just wanted to say thank you,' I told her. 'It was such a lovely gesture. Anyway. I won't keep you. Hope Jester's on the mend. And . . . thanks again.'

And with that, I firmly put all thoughts of Andrew and Jester out of my mind.

I've always been a dog lover. In fact, one of the reasons I moved to England was that my own dog, a Retriever, had died and my parents had decided we weren't getting another one. I'd always had a dog growing up and thought I couldn't possibly live without one. So, I thought, I'll leave home and get my own dog! I suppose it's a bit drastic to move all the way from Australia to England just to get a dog, but that's what I did. That was when Arthur came into my life. My own little flat-coated Retriever puppy. He was a bundle of brown joy at just eight weeks old. He came to work with me every day and his company saw me through my first years in England. After a long, stressful or tiring day there was nothing better than a night in on the sofa together, with a glass of wine for me and some trashy TV. Arthur would always be such a great comfort and he was my best friend.

I loved my job at the small veterinary practice and I had made some wonderful friends over the past couple of years, but when the opportunity came up to move to a bigger surgery, I jumped at the chance of a new challenge. I would have more responsibilities and more operations to carry out.

Over the next six months I worked really hard for this new and busier practice, and carried out some very tricky surgery. It was great to have all this new responsibility, and to get such great experience, but after a while I missed the intimacy of my old job. Eventually I decided that, having tried it, a big practice wasn't for me after all, and I got a new job at a laboratory. I was responsible for interpreting results from all the samples sent in by vets from around the country. I would talk to the vets and help them make decisions based on the test results. It was very different from an average day working in a vetinary practice, but it was certainly very interesting and I could even work from home at times.

About six months into this new job, an envelope landed on my desk. I noticed that the address on the front had originally been to my original old practice, but it had been forwarded on to my second job, and then a second time on to the lab. So it had really done the rounds before I got it.

I pulled out a card with a picture of a guinea pig on the front with mad sticking up hair. The note inside said:

Dear Jo,

I hope you remember me. I certainly remember you. You saved my leg. It has healed very well since. I can send you a digital picture if you like. Or, even better, we could go for a walk together, and I'll show you just how well it has healed, and buy you a drink, of course.

Love from Jester.

Underneath that there was every conceivable method of contact: email, address, Facebook details and two phone numbers.

Even though a year had passed, I remembered immediately who Jester was. But I wasn't quite sure what it meant, and because all the people who would have known about Andrew and Jester were at my old job, I didn't have anyone around to show it to.

I felt absolutely radiant and tingling all over with excitement, but I tried to keep myself in check. 'Don't be ridiculous, it's probably just a thank you card,' I told myself. 'But then why has he left all those details? Is he asking me on a date? Or is he just being thoughtful?'

I had never really entertained the idea that anything would happen between me and Andrew. It hadn't occurred to me that someone like him would be interested in me. Especially when the last time I had seen him he was with a woman. But when I got that card, I knew exactly who it was straight away, so I had obviously well and truly logged him in my head. And I knew one thing: I was going to accept that dog walk.

I emailed back saying I was definitely up for seeing Jester's leg, and thanks for contacting me. After an email back from Andrew we arranged to meet up. It was a date ... wasn't it?

When the afternoon of the walk came, I didn't know what to do with myself. Andrew was due to arrive in ten minutes but I was ready to go too early. I sat at the window with a glass of water. My own dog, Arthur, was on some medication and was really unwell at the time, so I made sure he was OK and settled. 'Shame you can't come today,' I said, and he put his head in his big paws and looked at me sadly. Then I sat on the sofa and tried to read a magazine. When the doorbell eventually rang I jumped, even though I had been expecting it. I hadn't seen Andrew for a year. Would we even get on?

'Hello, Jester!' I said, and the dog leapt up and started licking me. Andrew looked exactly the same; lovely smile and really friendly eyes. And Jester looked healthier than ever.

'Looks like he remembers you, then.'

'Well, I certainly remember him! Don't I, little sausage?'

I said goodbye to Arthur and we headed out in Andrew's car to some ancient woodland near to where he lived.

'Been here for literally hundreds of years, some of these trees. Part of Henry VIII's land, I think. We love it up here.'

'It's really nice. It does actually feel ancient, doesn't it?' I breathed in the clean air as we walked. 'You know, I couldn't believe it when I got your . . . Jester's card. After so long. I was so pleased that you'd remembered me. And that it made it all the way to the lab where I work now.'

'I'm just glad it did get there. I didn't even know you'd moved. Sorry about the hamster.'

'Sorry?'

'The picture of the hamster. On the card. I don't know why, I just thought it was funny. Its hair all sticking up.'

'That was a guinea pig.'

'It was a hamster!'

'No, I'm the vet. And that was definitely a guinea pig.'

'What's the difference, anyway?'

'Hamsters are small and from Asia. Guinea pigs are much bigger and South American and they don't go on a wheel. They're just completely different animals. Anyway, it was a lovely card. Thank you!'

'Jester said it was a hamster.'

'Jester, you silly thing,' I laughed. 'Let's have a look at this leg, then. How good a job did I do?'

'It's completely healed. Have a look.'

Jester was his usual obliging self as I got down on my knees to check it out.

'Seems really fine, doesn't it?' said Andrew.

'Yes. Glad all those diagrams paid off.'

'Diagrams?'

'Oh, yeah. I didn't tell you then, but that was the first time I'd ever done an operation quite like that. I spent ages drawing it out! The nurse thought I was completely bonkers.'

As we spoke, it was as if no time had passed at all. It felt so natural and comfortable.

Jester seemed to know the landscape in those woods really well and he spent the whole time running off, up and down the dips and craters, chasing sticks and the odd blackbird, though he never caught one. Occasionally he would disappear completely into a great pile of leaves and then emerge expectant, waiting for Andrew to throw the next stick.

'Tell me about your time in Australia,' Andrew said. 'Must have been really hard to leave. All that sunshine and clean air.'

'It was, in a way. It was nice to grow up there. I've got five brothers and sisters, so it was hard to leave them. But it was just something I had to do. You know? I did stay with my aunt and uncle temporarily, for three months, to see if I liked it here, then I started applying for jobs. I got offered about four or five! Apparently my university, and Australian vets in general, have a good reputation. So I had the pick of the crop. My aunt and uncle helped me get a car and find somewhere to live. And now I've got my own place. It's really nice. Freedom.'

'I think it's amazing. Coming all that way on your own.'

'But what about you? Tell me about Africa. How long were you there?'

'Five years, all in. I helped run a tour company for overland travel. Guided tours of the adventurous kind. We started in Europe then drove all the way to Africa in great big four-wheel drive trucks. It wasn't a sit-back-and-wait-to-be-served kind of trip . . . everyone in the tour group had a role to play. It could be tough but it was absolutely amazing. Life-changing. But I had to come back to reality some time. So I joined the police and the rest, as they say . . . '

'What have you got there?' I said, catching sight of Jester, who was galloping right towards us with an enormous log in his mouth.

'I can't throw that. You can hardly even pick it up,' said Andrew.

Jester's mouth was stretched to the limit as he dragged a hulking bit of wood along beside him.

'He'll be bringing back a whole tree next!' I laughed.

'Perhaps it's time to head off anyway. Do you fancy a quick drink? I know a nice little pub, where dogs are allowed. Real fireplace.'

'I need to get back soonish. To let Arthur out and check on him. He's not well. But one drink won't hurt.'

We had our one drink, and when Andrew dropped me off afterwards, for some reason I held out my hand for him to shake it. But he went to do the one kiss on the cheek thing, and I then wasn't sure if we were doing both cheeks so our faces collided. I blushed.

'Don't you hate it when that happens?' he laughed. 'Anyway. We should meet again. Bring Arthur next time! We'll see if the dogs get along.'

'Why not?' I said, inwardly grinning from ear to ear.

I was still tingling with excitement when I got home and cuddled up to Arthur. He was still looking weak from his illness, so I tucked him into his blanket and gave him a little kiss on the head.

'A nice walk with Jester will soon sort you out,' I said and then padded about the kitchen, singing to myself, and fixing up some dinner.

Then I had a sudden horrible thought. I hadn't asked Andrew about the girl he had brought to the surgery. The one who had answered the phone when I rang about the chocolates and had said, 'We wanted to say thank you for helping Jester.' I had almost forgotten about that. I couldn't believe he was with her now, after contacting me. But then, if it was just a thank you . . . Something in my bones made me pause before really getting my hopes up.

Since I had been in England I had been so busy, throwing myself into my work with long hours and neglecting to take the time to get out and meet new people. I'd always had high standards when it came to men, which made it all the more amazing that I felt so comfortable with this bloke I hardly knew.

On our second walk together, Jester met Arthur. I was

so nervous, it was like when people who have kids decide it's time for them to meet their new partner's children. 'Are they going to get on? This is going to be the clincher!' I thought. I wondered if they would fight, because Arthur's a lot bigger than Jester. But they were like brothers from the word go. They checked each other out, sniffed each other and were obviously interested, but there was no element of apprehension or aggression from either side.

The other question on my mind was soon answered too.

Andrew explained that the relationship with the lady I had spoken to on the phone, after he'd left the chocolates, had ended amicably some months ago.

'Really! Oh, I'm sorry. That it didn't work out, I mean,' I said. But in my head I was thinking: 'Yes!'

'It's fine. I really wanted to thank you myself for being so caring with Jester. I mean, the other vets were great, but you treated Jester like he was your own. And you were really pretty. Which helped, of course!'

'Thank you,' I said, blushing. It was so embarrassing to be praised like that. I had no idea how to respond.

'And the way you always called him "sausage". Well, that just got me in the end.'

I looked at Andrew. He was looking right back at me with a kind of serious expression on his face I had never seen before. We hadn't kissed yet. Everything had felt so natural and gradual so far. Next to all those ancient oak trees, in amongst the bluebells, with Jester scampering off to fetch more sticks, our lips met just for a moment, and our walk was finally a date.

Over the next few weeks we were basically inseparable.

If we weren't emailing we were on the phone, or on our walks together with the dogs. Once we were officially dating, all the little details – 'When did you first notice . . . ?', and so on – about when we had first met came out. I said I'd thought he was great when he brought Jester in, how caring he had been. I joked with him that in his case it was probably just that classic situation of someone falling in love with their nurse. But he was adamant he could see who I really was.

Arthur and Jester were getting along great and came everywhere with us. They even slept alongside each other. Arthur was never jealous either, which I had been concerned about, and it was the same with Jester. It was perfect.

Within six months we were on our way to Australia to meet my parents.

I knew immediately that both my parents thought Andrew was great and absolutely right for me. We told them how we had first met, and about the letter, and it felt great to be back home, breathing in the clean Australian air.

'So are you going to show me where you grew up then?' asked Andrew, as we walked down to the beach in Perth. I took him to all the old places I had hung out. My special places. And it felt nice to have him see this other part of my life. Mum brought out all the family photo albums too, at one point, which was a bit embarrassing, to say the least.

We didn't go on a typical adventure all over Australia, as my parents were selling their house, so I needed to tie up some loose ends. But it was a good opportunity for Andrew to meet my family and for us to relax a bit. We even did things that I'd never done when I was living there, like camping in a national park overnight, waking up to the sound of cockatoos in the trees and kangaroos at the foot of our tent.

When we got back to England it seemed natural that we should live together. So I moved into Andrew's house and we soon got a routine going. We're different but complementary in our interests. Andrew works long hours, but is quite sporty and plays squash, football, badminton and enjoys all forms of exercise. I'm very work-orientated too, but I also love music. I went to a specialist music school in Australia, and I've just started learning the violin. And, of course, we both love nothing more than clearing our minds and going for a dog walk, surrounded by nature. With the forest just there on our doorstep, if one of us has had a bad day at work, it makes a big difference just getting out into the fresh air.

With our new life together and our two dogs getting along so well we felt like the luckiest couple on earth.

'Come on, Jester. In you get,' I said, as we loaded up the car one Sunday afternoon.

'He's not moving. What's wrong with him?' Andrew said. 'He's whimpering so much.'

'I think it's his arthritis playing up,' I said. 'I'll give him something extra for the pain and we'll have to rest him for the week.'

Jester had had arthritis down his back for a while, but until that point we had managed to deal with it using every pain relief medication on offer. By the following morning, however, he hadn't responded and was whining and whimpering with an intensity I had never heard before. It was now very clear to me that he had a much more serious problem than just arthritis and had likely slipped a disc in his back.

I knew it would take risky and complicated surgery to give any dog a chance at a good future, even if he got all the pain relief under the sun. Jester had reached a ripe old age, and putting him through the trauma of such a procedure just didn't seem fair on him.

'I know it's hard,' I said to Andrew, 'but I think it's time for him. His whole body is old and tired, not just his back. I really think we've given him a chance and done all that we can. I know how sad it will be to lose him.'

'I can't bear seeing him in so much pain,' he said. 'I'll do whatever you think is right. You're the expert. I'll trust your judgement.'

Although he was young at heart, Jester was sixteen by then. He'd had a long, adventurous and, I hope, very happy life. I've seen my fair share of dogs being put down, but deciding it was Jester's time to leave us was heart-breaking. In the end, we took him to the practice where I had first worked when we had met.

Even though it was part of my job, I still wasn't prepared for losing our dog. I get attached to animals very quickly, so I felt like Jester was my dog too by then. And as we both stood next to him, the memories of how we had first met in this surgery came flooding back. Being back there, the three of us in the consulting room again, felt symbolic of our journey together coming full circle. I had a sudden and immense sense of gratitude towards Jester, and I felt so sad that he would never know just how special he was to me, to us.

One of my old colleagues kindly put Jester to sleep for us. It was very gentle, just a little injection in the front leg. Most dogs have had the sensation of a needle prick at some point for vaccinations, so they don't even seem to feel it, but we put some local anaesthetic on his leg just to be sure. Then, within five peaceful seconds, he was gone.

Andrew remained calm, but I could see how upset he was. We carried Jester in a blanket to the car and hugged together in the car park for a moment, before bringing him back home. Although we were so sad, it was a relief that his little body was now no longer hunched up in pain.

When we got home my brother-in-law had very kindly already dug a hole for us in the garden, so we didn't have to do it ourselves. We buried him under a tree we had bought that had wonderful burgundy leaves and beautiful blossoms. As the sun set, we cooked some food on a little barbecue next to the grave and sat for hours in quiet contemplation. We didn't want to leave him on his own too soon. In the end we lit a candle by his side, then went to bed.

The days and weeks after that were the hardest, because we were used to the little things Jester did, like coming down the stairs with a certain rhythm. He was quite a noisy little Staffie, always making excited whimpering noises. Arthur doesn't make the same noise. What we missed most was Jester just being there.

Andrew and I had always talked about being together for ever. After we had been together for a few years, I had hinted enough times that marriage was important to me. In a way, I felt this was partly because of Jester and how special he had been in bringing us together. I wanted to mark our bond in a really special way and marriage seemed right. I think Andrew just saw it as ticking a box for society at first, and neither of us are that sort of person. I told him that I didn't want to get married because society wanted us to. I wanted to do it for me. For us.

In the autumn of 2011 Andrew announced that he was arranging a surprise trip for my birthday, and one late November evening I was whisked off to London St Pancras for a train journey to a secret destination. After wandering the Christmas markets of Cologne, *glühwein* in hand, we boarded our own private cabin on the sleeper train and wound our way through the moonlit Rhine Valley to Salzburg, our final destination.

'This is lovely!' I said. 'It's always been a schoolgirl dream of mine to come here – all the music and history!'

'I know,' he said, smiling.

We arrived at our apartment, which was the most beautiful and historic building I had ever seen.

'It's six hundred years old, apparently, according to the housekeeper, Igor,' Andrew told me as we walked to our room.

'It's amazing!' I said, taking it all in.

We left our stuff in the room and were on our way out for my birthday meal when we were met by Igor on the stairs. I was on the landing, just locking up the apartment, when suddenly I heard a distant melody playing.

'The people in the other room must have their music on nice and loud,' I said.

Then, as I listened more, I realized it was one of my favourite songs. I looked up the hallway towards this spooky old door, and noticed the flickering light of a candle through the doorway. I knew Andrew must be up to something, but I had no idea what! He wasn't giving anything away. I opened the old door and we followed the candles lining the rickety wooden staircase up into an empty attic.

When we got there we saw a door, which led out on to the roof. The view was spectacular; you could see all the lights of Salzburg and a 360-degree night sky. Everything was a bit rickety, though – it was 600 years old, after all! I even had to shimmy along a wooden beam to get to the centre of the roof. But any health and safety concerns went completely out of the window once I realized what Andrew planned to do up there. Out of the blue, under the dazzling night sky, he precariously got down on one knee.

'Will you marry me?' he asked.

'Oh my God! Of course I will,' I said, and it was so romantic it was all I could do to keep from bursting into tears. I even proclaimed myself the happiest woman in the world!

'You planned all this!' I said. And he told me he had known for ages that this was the place he would propose. I found out afterwards that he had even been sweet enough to ask my dad's permission.

So Andrew saw what I meant after all, that it was such an important thing in our lives to have met through Jester. It was nice to have a really positive reason to get all our family and friends together to share in this with us. When we organized the wedding, Andrew got into the planning just as much as I did in the end; picking out the suits and flowers, his face would just light up.

When the big day came, Friday 26 April, Jester featured in our wedding with a memorial tribute. He's the reason we got together, so he had to be there in some way. I wanted people who didn't know us so well to understand how special he was in getting us together, and that Battersea Dogs & Cats Home, who took him in as a puppy, have a special place in our hearts. We don't need a lot of things, so we asked people to donate money as a wedding gift to Battersea.

Funds from the drinks at the bar went towards the charity collection too. We called it Jester's Bar. After all, he was the one who asked me for a drink in the first place, not Andrew, so it made perfect sense to have a bar named after him.

Now that we're married, and back in our home, I look out of the window at Jester's tree in full bloom, and know he's always with us.